W9-CNX-814

What they are saying about *Fishing With Dad*:

"Bravo to . . . fifty authors for providing such wonderful writings in celebration of angling! I would have thought it impossible to gather this lineup of writers in one collection. This one's a keeper! *Fishing With Dad* is a must-have for everyone who loves to fish and everyone who loves to read!"

—Randy Lemcke, Vice President, Plano Molding,
& Chairman of the Board, American Sportfishing Association

"This collection of articles written by the 'Who's Who of Fishing' is a must-read for everyone that loves the water and the joy of fishing."

—Eddie Smith, CEO, Grady-White Boats, Inc.

"Both royalty and the common man have enjoyed angling for hundreds of years. The beauty of the surroundings, the serenity of water, the anticipation of the strike, and the anxiety of the fight have offered common ground to mankind of numerous civilizations covering the entire globe. This unique publication presents a common language whether one enjoys the fly rod or the baitcast rod. Sit back, read, and smile."

—Paul Fuller, ASA/Eastern Fishing & Outdoor Exposition, LLC

"As a father of two kids who love to fish, these stories bring back memories of days on the water with my father. *Fishing With Dad* is a book that reminds me to make the same lasting memories for my children. *Fishing With Dad* is a beautiful collection of stories that highlights our sport by some of the most prolific writers of our time. It should be read by every angler in America."

—Gregg Wollner, Executive Vice President,
General Manager, Normark Corporation (Rapala)

"At Fred Hall & Associates we don't manufacture anything, we don't warehouse anything, we don't sell anything. All we do is promote sportfishing. For 63 years we have spent 365 days a year promoting sportfishing and the family values inherent in the sport. *Fishing With Dad* is a valuable work that matches our philosophy and will help promote fishing in a positive way."

—Bart Hall, Managing Partner, Fred Hall/ASA Consumer Shows

"Fishing With Dad gathers in one amazing book what generations of fishing friends, fishing families, and fishing writers have long known: catching fish is only a small part of the allure of fishing. Fishing is about connections with the natural world, time with friends and family, and opportunity for personal reflection. *Fishing With Dad* is about hope for our future."

—Eric C. Schwaab, Resource Director,
Association of Fish & Wildlife Agencies

"*Fishing With Dad* is a wonderful collection of stories expressing how fishing can touch the lives of many people in many ways. Once you read this book, you will understand the wonderful experience available from sharing the fishing experience with those who have never been."

—Rob Southwick, Southwick Associates

"WOW, *Fishing With Dad* expresses why fishing is the absolute greatest sport in the world!"

—Jason Meninger, Adventure Advertising, LLC

"This book, like the effort it is named for, represents one of the most worth-while efforts the industry has ever undertaken."

—Ronell Smith, Editor, *Fishing Tackle Retailer*

"This anthology is the perfect way for avid anglers and readers to support the FishAmerica Foundation, dedicated to keeping our fish and waters healthy."

—Johanna Laderman, Director, FishAmerica Foundation

Fishing With Dad

Edited by JOHN BRYAN
Foreword by JIMMY CARTER
Introduction by HOWELL RAINES

Skyhorse Publishing

Copyright © 2012 by Skyhorse Publishing, Inc.

All Rights Reserved. No part of this book may be reproduced in any manner without the express written consent of the publisher, except in the case of brief excerpts in critical reviews or articles. All inquiries should be addressed to Skyhorse Publishing, 307 West 36th Street, 11th Floor, New York, NY 10018.

Skyhorse Publishing books may be purchased in bulk at special discounts for sales promotion, corporate gifts, fund-raising, or educational purposes. Special editions can also be created to specifications. For details, contact the Special Sales Department, Skyhorse Publishing, 307 West 36th Street, 11th Floor, New York, NY 10018 or info@skyhorsepublishing.com.

Skyhorse® and Skyhorse Publishing® are registered trademarks of Skyhorse Publishing, Inc.®, a Delaware corporation.

Visit our website at www.skyhorsepublishing.com.

10 9 8 7 6 5 4 3 2 1

Library of Congress Cataloging-in-Publication-Data
    Fishing with Dad / edited by John Bryan ; introduction by Howell Raines; foreword by Jimmy Carter.
        p.   cm.
    ISBN-13: 978-1-61608-676-3 (hardcover : alk. paper)
    ISBN-10: 1-61608-676-9 (hardcover : alk. paper)
    1. Fishing—Anecdotes.   I. Bryan, John, 1949–

    SH441.T32   2007
    799.1—dc22

                                                          2006100972

Printed in the United States of America

A Letter to the Reader

The idea was to see if fifty living writers would donate their time, their expenses, and their writings to help the future of fishing—to help generate some money and visibility for the fishing industry's conservation and education foundations: the FishAmerica Foundation and the Future Fisherman Foundation. The answer was yes and the result is this book, *Fishing With Dad*.

All of us who have been involved with *Fishing With Dad* are heartened that 100 percent of the proceeds and royalties that would normally go to the book's writers and editors are being donated to the FishAmerica Foundation as it helps keep our fish and waters healthy in all fifty states, and to the Future Fisherman Foundation as it annually provides educational programs for hundreds of thousands of new anglers.

These two foundations operate under the auspices of the American Sportfishing Association, and during my three years (2003–2006) on the ASA staff I continually saw the good work of these foundations and the integrity of their staff members and volunteers.

The FishAmerica Foundation and Future Fisherman Foundation are worthy of attention and support: *www.fishamerica.org* and *www.futurefisherman.org*.

Good fishing and good reading!

—John Bryan

Acknowledgments

Much appreciation to: the writers in this book—all busy folk—who donated their time, consultation, energies, and writings without compensation or reimbursement; literary agent Dan Green who donated important consultation regarding the book's publication; outdoors editor Jay Cassell who provided interest and consultation; Gene Bay who provided hospitality during a luncheon for the writers; Mary Ellen Mercer who handled a variety of details concerning permissions, content, and communications; the Recreational Boating and Fishing Foundation for encouragement to use the title and images from their own "Take Me Fishing" mass media campaign; the American Sportfishing Association which enabled a staff member to attend to this project; Skyhorse Publishing's Tony Lyons who has embraced this project with a full-steam-ahead enthusiasm; and Nick Lyons whose name and friendship have carried the day.

Contents

CONTENTS

CONTENTS

Foreword

One of my favorite places to fish is Pennsylvania's Spruce Creek—a stream that rises from deep springs and meanders through meadows cradled between mountain ridges. Its trout swim through gentle waterfalls and riffles, dark pools under overhanging hemlocks, and occasionally take flies thrown by Rosalynn and me.

Years ago angling evolved into a pastime that Rosalynn and I share and that has introduced us to a wide circle of friends whom we otherwise never would have known. And it was of course inevitable that we would introduce our children and grandchildren to the sport—the best way to answer their plea, "Let's go fishing."

We have fished in diverse waters: from Alaska to Georgia, England to Finland, Venezuela to Argentina, and New Zealand to Russia. While fishing, we have come to know and learn from people who live completely different kinds of lives, and to reveal in unguarded moments the personal characteristics that are usually concealed from others.

As Herbert Hoover posited in the foreword to his 1963 fishing book, fishing offers " . . . a mockery of profits and egos, a quieting of hate . . ." How wonderful it is that the fifty writers for *this* book have voluntarily gathered here to celebrate angling and to generate resources to help fishing's future.

If you are one of us, you'll be compelled to read this book. If you haven't yet embraced the fly rod, I invite you to sample these waters. And hopefully you'll soon be saying, "Take Me Fishing."

—Jimmy Carter

Introduction

John Bryan has put together a collection so rich and expansive that it seems futile to comment on individual contributors. Suffice it to say that I am lucky enough to know personally a good many of the writers who are my contemporaries and to have fished with several of them. In a sense, though, all these authors have taken us fishing countless times on the waters of memory and imagination, and they can be beckoned to do so again any time we ask. That is to say, through their words, they have become friends of a special sort, angling companions who invite us to contemplate the difference between fish stories and fishing stories. A "fish story" may turn out to be a lie, but as this volume demonstrates, fishing stories occupy a special niche in the literature of the English language. Part of their magic resides in the telling, which must be masterful, and part of the magic lies in a quest which millions of human beings throughout history have found magical in and of itself.

As these stories indicate, there is no single explanation for why we want to make contact with these mysterious scaly creatures, so unself-conscious in their beauty, so magnificently focused on the simple act of being in a watery world we can never know as intimately as we'd like. Catching a fish and, better still, releasing it back into its interrupted life are complex emotional experiences. Storytelling that aspires to be called "literary" strives to convey those experiences in ways that are original, surprising, and moving. We may differ in our estimate of which of these stories reach that high standard. But take it as guaranteed that every page is a reminder, brothers and sisters of the angle, of how lucky we are to know the incantory power of hearing or speaking three words: Take me fishing.

—Howell Raines

The Evolution of a Flyfisher

JOAN SALVATO WULFF

I came into fishing as an innocent: my predatory skills, if I had any, were undeveloped. Loving woods and waters I caught calico bass and perch in the nearby Oldham Pond but, in trout streams, not knowing how to "read" water, nor the comfort, food, and safety needs of trout, I saw only the interesting patterns on the water's surface as if they were art.

If trout were rising I could be effective, but if they were not I became painfully aware of this lack of fishing instinct, especially in the company of anglers whom I think of as "natural born predators." In addition to understanding the hydraulics of the stream, to a man they had exceptional vision, as it related to water, seeing trout under the surface when I could not. A boyfriend, the late Johnny Dieckman, was the first of these and later in life Lee Wulff and Ed Van Put are the two who jump into my mind as always surprising me with their ability to catch fish.

With nothing to start with, I had to substitute my ability to fly cast to unlock the secrets of the stream, covering the water and learning inch by inch.

From this beginning, over the ensuing 70 years, I've been lucky enough to fish for most of the fresh and saltwater species that can be enticed to take a fly. Fishing, and especially fly fishing, has been the constant thread in my life. It's been a wonderful journey and, in the last several years, I have come to realize how differently I see the sport from when I began. It's an evolution I believe I share with others who have a passion for fly fishing.

The early stages of fishing are familiar to most anglers: the focus is on 1) the number. How many did you get? 2) The biggest fish. How big? Show me a photo. And then 3) the most difficult: the wise old brown trout instead of the eternally innocent brookies; permit instead of bonefish. Feeling as if you've learned something.

These three stages play to our competitive nature; measuring ourselves against others whenever there is something to count. And they may stay with us forever in terms of particular species: most, biggest, most difficult. I, for instance, in the latter category, still feel the "need" to catch a 15–20 permit.

After Stage 3 the scope broadens; we enter the stages that are about more than catching fish.

It was Lee who raised my consciousness to Stage 4: giving something back to the resource; looking at the sport from the point of view of the fish. It's about preserving their gene pools as well as their habitat. Lee's wisdom, as early as 1939, that "a good game fish is too valuable to be caught only once" has been the concept that has let growing numbers of anglers enjoy the sport with, perhaps, the same number of fish.

The national conservation organizations are there to lead the way: the Federation of Fly Fishers, Trout Unlimited, the Atlantic Salmon Federation, the International Game Fish Association. I am a member of all of them and find that each group's efforts are distinct and necessary to keep our sport healthy.

In addition to making the sport more meaningful, there is another benefit to "belonging": gatherings of fishing experts willing to share their expertise at conclaves, symposiums, and club programs. It's a win/win situation for anglers of all levels. As involvement grows, your coterie of acquaintances expands and I can easily say that the best people I have ever met have been in this stage of my evolution.

If the first 3 stages are the "youth" of our fishing lives, "giving back" could be considered to be our "middle years," because there *is* more!

The golden years: Stage 5. *Just being there.* When people ask me to name my favorite place to fish, I can only say "wherever I am." And my answer to the question, "which is your favorite fish?" is "whatever I'm fishing for."

Evasive answers? Perhaps. It's just that, as my experience has broadened and I've learned the character of different waters and species of fish, I have come to love and admire them all. It's like partaking of good food. Think of how many different dishes you really love and appreciate each time you have them. Different, but equally wonderful. Remember, I'm talking about a lifetime.

In these years, *catching* fish has become less important; I can be fishless and still have had a good day. I can now fish "through" a companion and be as happy about their catch as they are because I know the challenges, and feelings of joy and satisfaction, that commemorate success.

These years are also a time when I can handicap myself if the fishing is too easy. Lee introduced the idea: "If you catch 3 fish on the same fly, change the fly. See what else they will take." "Reduce your tippet strength." "Use a smaller hook." Lee was an inspiration through the "pureness" of his approach. He always gave the advantage to the fish, through his simple tackle. He used no drag; just a click to keep the reel from overrunning, even with Atlantic salmon and tarpon. And with this tackle, he established a standard: one minute per pound to land the fish. The fish then had to swim away without the need to be revived. Lee's skills in playing fish were legendary.

I love this stage; the pressure is off! Challenge yourself! The competition is now with the fish—not other anglers.

I have one more stage to include in these golden years: #6. Replace yourself. This is about bringing young people into our sport. Unless we do this, our sport will be diminished; first in numbers of anglers and then, with fewer anglers working to preserve the habitat, in quality. Grandkids are the obvious and I am particularly blessed in this regard. I introduced Alex and Andrew to fly fishing when each became 5½ years old with two hands on the rod and a roll cast. They have both caught trout, and Alex has caught Atlantic salmon, on Royal Wulffs. Because I don't tie flies, I gave them fly tying lessons with a professional when they were 7. When I am long gone, they will be fly fishing together.

My cup runneth over.

Old age is approaching but I don't want to limit my enjoyment of the sport by defining it. In these past two years I have caught the largest tarpon of my life (approximately 125 lbs) and enjoyed sailfishing in Guatemala. This summer I was able to fish for steelhead on the Dean river in British Columbia, after hoping to for 40 plus years.

My most memorable fish are those I didn't land: a monster Atlantic salmon on Norway's Alta river, which played *me* for a few minutes, and another huge salmon on New Brunswick's Restigouche. The latter was on my last, "last cast."

It was nearly dark and, having covered the water from 20 feet on out, the cast was the longest I could make. The fish struck and dashed upriver, partly out of the water, which is how we knew he was a big one. Then he turned and raced downriver, into my backing. The guide thought the river was too high to follow the fish in the dark and headed back to shore, in spite of my protests. I found myself unhappily positioned 90° from where the salmon was heading. The end was predictable: the fish never stopped—and nearly emptied my reel before the hook pulled out.

However, the reason I continue to think of this particular fish is not because I lost it, but because of the *wonder* of it all: how *magical* it was to reach out into that enormous river with a tiny artificial offering, when it was dark enough to keep me from seeing the fly land, and actually connect to a wild creature of such a size.

And magical it is. Starting as an innocent, this very ordinary woman has had an extraordinary life through the magic of fly fishing. And I plan to continue. So it's not over till it's over, and this very ordinary woman, having had an extraordinary life through the magic of sport fishing, plans to continue.

Joan Wulff has written three books: *Fly Casting Techniques*, *Fly Fishing: Expert Advice from a Woman's Perspective*, and *Fly Casting Accuracy*. She and her late husband, Lee, started the Wulff School of Fly Fishing in 1979. Her fly casting columns ran for twenty-two years in *Fly Rod & Reel* magazine. "Fly fishing has been the single most important theme in my rather long life," she writes. "It has taken me to beautiful places far from civilization and cement; has allowed me to feel the heartbeat and energy of a wild creature; and has given me my best friends."

Environmentalists vs. Native Trout

Sometimes the good guys are part of the problem . . .

TED WILLIAMS

Having been an environmental activist for most of my life and having worked for and with national environmental organizations for 30 years, it grieves me to report that the biggest and, in many cases, only impediment to recovery of vanishing native trout is the environmental community.

That's not to say that most environmental outfits actively oppose trout restoration projects. And that's not to say that the few who do wouldn't back off if they'd stop talking long enough to listen to biologists.

Enviros tend not to see, handle or understand fish and to distrust the motives of agencies dedicated to their recovery. Thus, in announcing a lawsuit to halt use of TFM, a remarkably safe and selective chemical used since the 1950s to kill sea lampreys, a splendid organization like the Vermont Public Interest Research Group can advance the argument that Atlantic salmon—native predators every bit as ecologically important to Lake Champlain and its basin as wolves to greater Yellowstone—are being restored "strictly for sport fishing."

Without two naturally derived piscicides—rotenone (from derris root) and antimycin (from bacteria)—most native fish restoration simply cannot happen. Rotenone has been used to kill fish for centuries on two continents; modern fish managers have used it for the last 70 years. In all that time there has never been a documented human injury. There's no record of antimycin, introduced for fish control in the mid-1970s, harming anyone either. Both rotenone and antimycin are easily neutralized with potassium permanganate, and both break down fast in the environment. In fact, one of antimycin's few drawbacks is that it sometimes breaks down too fast; under some conditions its half-life is less than an hour. Antimycin's great advantage is that the recommended dosage is usually between 8 and 12 parts per billion, so you can strap a bottle on a pack horse and treat a whole chain of high-country lakes. And, unlike rotenone, fish can't smell it and therefore don't take evasive action.

But enviros tend to fear all pesticides. Moreover, they frequently reject as spin all data that proves a pesticide safe even as they spin data themselves to depict it as dangerous. For example, the environmental community parrots the fiction that rotenone, applied to fish habitat at 0.5 to 4 parts per million, has been "linked to Parkinson's disease." It conjured this from an unrelated study in which Emory University researchers induced Parkinson-disease-like symptoms (not Parkinson's disease) in lab rats by mainlining concentrated rotenone into their brains.

Although rotenone and, to a much lesser extent, antimycin kill a very few non-target gill breathers such as insect larvae, these organisms bounce back within weeks; and, with their alien fish predators removed, they are far more prolific.

One of the most effective environmental outfits I know is the Center for Biological Diversity. I work closely with it in my environmental reporting, and I have helped raise thousands of dollars for it through my work on a major charitable foundation. As its name implies, it exists solely to protect "biological diversity." Except that the threatened Paiute cutthroat, probably the rarest trout in the world, doesn't count with the center.

Citing wives' tales and spewing pseudo science, the center has derailed Paiute recovery by suing the US Forest Service and thereby frightening away the California Department of Fish and Game, which has jurisdiction over native fauna and doesn't need the Forest Service anyway. About 11 stream-miles of California's Silver King Creek watershed in the Carson-Iceberg Wilderness of the Toiyabe-Humboldt National Forest comprise the entire native range of the Paiute cutthroat. In 1912, before bucket biologists made mongrels of all the fish in all their natural habitat, another bucket biologist—tending sheep in the area—inadvertently saved the Paiute by transporting a few trout to a fishless stretch above impassable Llewellyn Falls.

Had the Forest Service proceeded in the fall of 2003 as planned, it would have accomplished a first in salmonid management—restoring a native to 100 percent of its historical range. Then the Fish and Wildlife Service would have removed the Paiute from the Endangered Species List, another first. But could delisting have been an unwelcome development for the litigious center, reducing its arsenal of legal weapons? Yes, according to one professional trout advocate who worked hard for the project, and whose colleagues helped evacuate some of the mongrels to a different watershed in order to placate local sportsmen: "When an organism loses its Endangered Species Act protection it's no longer any use to groups like the Center for Biological Diversity."

"If you're attempting to fix an expensive watch, you don't reach first for the sledgehammer; neither should the state necessarily be poisoning streams in a wilderness area without looking at other options," proclaims the center. Had it read the literature, it would have understood that there are no other options. The stream's too big for effective electro-shocking. And, while antimycin (classified by EPA under "no threat to human health") would be great, it's no longer registered in California because the only manufacturers (Nick and Mary Romeo, working out of their home) can't finance the endless lab tests required by the state's new pesticide code.

"This watershed," continued the center, "is historic habitat for the mountain yellow-legged frog, a species in serious decline." Had it read the literature, it would have understood that yellow-legged frogs don't occur in the proposed treatment area.

As part of a legal settlement with the center, the Forest Service is currently engaged in more National Environmental Policy Act review, re-studying everything the state has already studied and everything the scientific community already knows about rotenone and fish reclamation. The agency had hoped to resume work in 2004, but pressure from an ill-informed public has shut down the project again.

The Pacific Rivers Council, with which I also work closely and for which I also have helped raise thousands of dollars, does all sorts of fabulous work, too. Yet it swallowed the BS about rotenone hook, line, boat and motor. It filed a scathing critique of the project's first environmental assessment; and it issued an "action alert" in which it recycled the misinformation about the yellow-legged frog and made the astonishing claim that "neither the Silver King Creek nor Tamarack Lake drainages historically supported the threatened Paiute cutthroat" when these were the only habitats that had supported it.

7

The National Audubon Society is making progress. For example, its magazine recently condemned "chemophobes" and defended piscicides in a piece entitled "Trout are Wildlife, Too." But the society is routinely embarrassed by its affiliates. Seven years ago the California Department of Fish and Game rotenoned alien pike in 4,000-acre Lake Davis in order to protect endangered steelhead trout and Chinook salmon of the Sacramento and San Joaquin river systems. But, instead of helping fight a real threat to biodiversity, local Audubon members and other enviros attacked an imaginary threat to water quality. They mounted vicious protests, held all-night candlelight vigils, chained themselves to buoys, cursed, wept, marched around the lake with placards that said things like "Burn in Hell, Fish & Game!" For crowd control the state deployed 270 uniformed officers, including a SWAT team. Currently, on the National Audubon Society's Web site, Harry Reeves, editor of the Plumas Audubon Chapter's newsletter, goes on and on about the alleged evils of rotenone and laments: "Bald eagles, white pelicans, and other birds and mammals scavenged poisoned carcasses that lined the shores." They did indeed, and not one was sickened because rotenone-killed fish don't harm wildlife.

Also weighing in on the Web site is one Ann McCampbell of Santa Fe, New Mexico—the nation's busiest piscicide protestor, who rarely misses a chance to spread bogeyman stories about rotenone and antimycin and who professes to be so allergic to all chemicals that she can participate in public hearings only by phone—a tedious, time-consuming process that tests the patience of everyone involved. The rotenone used in Lake Davis, writes McCampbell, who also claims to be a medical doctor, "made residents sick." It did not.

Concern for people and scavengers is admirable even when based on hogwash. But now that pike are back in Lake Davis (possibly because of sabotage) and now that Fish and Game is too frightened to eliminate them, I wish the environmental community would express as much (or even some) concern for the endangered salmon and steelhead, which surely will be ushered into oblivion unless rotenone is used again.

To save Montana's state fish, the westslope cutthroat trout, the Montana Department of Fish, Wildlife, and Parks proposes to kill introgressed Yellowstone cutts dribbling alien genes into the South Fork of the Flathead River. To do this it must apply antimycin and rotenone to 11 high-elevation ponds in the Bob

Marshall Wilderness. The westslope cutt, named for Lewis and Clark, is as much an icon of American wilderness as the grizzly. So you'd think that any group advocating wilderness would rally to the defense of this magnificent, vanishing creature.

But Wilderness Watch is doing its best to kill the project, making absurd and untruthful pronouncements such as "Poison has no place in wilderness stewardship." (Piscicides are essential to wilderness stewardship.) And: "Both poisons have adverse effects on aquatic biota." (They do not.) Wilderness Watch expresses outrage that managers would have to make some noise with motorboats and helicopters. And while it correctly observes that the ponds were originally fishless, and might even make a case that they should remain so, it claims that the westslopes (to be stocked as eyed eggs) have been diminished by domestication and therefore threaten the natives. Considering the gross genetic pollution now underway and the group's ongoing attempt to block removal of the mongrels, I can't imagine a more hypocritical and disingenuous argument.

In New Mexico's Gila National Forest, Wilderness Watch has been agitating against the use of antimycin in the ongoing recovery of the endangered Gila trout. It's all about sport, according to Wilderness Watch: "The purpose is to remove stocked trout and replace them with the listed Gila trout, in an effort to boost the population to a level that will allow delisting and resumed sport fishing of the species." Other untruths include: "It is not known whether antimycin is a carcinogen." (It is known that it's not.) And: "It is highly likely that the poison will adversely impact the endangered Chiricahua leopard frog that inhabits the area." 1) The Chiricahua leopard frog is threatened, not endangered; 2) Antimycin is very easy on juvenile amphibians, has no effect on adults, and the Forest Service evacuates tadpoles from target streams anyway. And: 3) "The poison antimycin will kill . . . all the native macroinvertebrates and amphibians in the streams." (Most likely it will kill none of the amphibians, and it will kill very few macroinvertebrates. Researchers from the University of Wyoming's Department of Zoology and Physiology, reporting on their stream studies, write: "Antimycin alone seemed to have little to no effect on invertebrates, with drift rates not substantially different than control sites during the antimycin addition.")

Wilderness Watch is also trying to derail restoration of New Mexico's state fish—the Rio Grande cutthroat, endangered in fact if not by fiat. It upbraids the state's Water Quality Commission for ignoring the rantings of Ann McCampbell who, for example, testifies that the antimycin label carries "a skull and crossbones . . . warning that it is fatal in humans if swallowed." (I'd agree that the public shouldn't drink it from the bottle.) Here, too, the alleged motive is frivolity and greed: For no purpose other than to amuse anglers and generate license revenue, the US Forest Service, the New Mexico Department of Game and Fish and the US Fish and Wildlife Service are conspiring to "dump poison in 30 miles of Animas Creek and 21 miles of the Gila River to kill introduced non-native trout and then re-stock the streams with native Rio Grande Cutthroat trout. . . . The Rio Grande Cutthroat is not an endangered species, but is a popular sport species among fishermen. . . . It is both sad and ironic that it was Aldo Leopold who convinced the Forest Service to protect the Gila as our nation's first wilderness in the 1930's—now, it is in danger of being converted to a fish farm for recreationists."

I see a different irony: It was Aldo Leopold who wrote the following in his essay *Wilderness for Wildlife*: "If education really educates, there will, in time, be more and more citizens who understand that relics of the old West add meaning and value to the new."

Acid rain is not the main threat to brook trout in New York State's Adirondacks. In fact, compared with alien fish introductions, it's unimportant. Perch, sunfish, bass, pike, bullheads, etc. got flung around so long ago that there's not even a record of what used to be trout water; and these aliens—particularly bass—are still being flung around. Thus defiled, ponds and lakes in this country simply cannot sustain wild brook trout.

But since the early 1970s the New York Department of Environmental Conservation (DEC) has been guided by the State Land Master Plan. This farsighted document prescribes various managements for various land classifications. For each wilderness area it requires the department to formulate a plan and, for that plan, to inventory all plants, fish and animals. While it forbids permanent structures in wilderness, it provides a few exceptions essential to wilderness management—such as fish-barrier dams. It forbids helicopters and other motorized vehicles in wilderness except in "extraordinary conditions"—such as rescuing people from disaster or brook trout from alien fish. It establishes that the single most important thing managers must do for wilderness is to preserve and restore native flora and fauna.

Following the mandates of the State Land Master Plan, DEC fish managers have identified what they call "heritage trout"—pure strains of brook trout that evolved in the Adirondacks and that, apparently, have never been contaminated by hatchery genes. Mostly, DEC has been working with three of these strains, named for the lakes from which they were collected in the nick of time— Windfall (where they've since been lost to alien fish), Little Tupper (where they're in the process of being lost to alien fish), and Horn Lake (where they've been lost to acid rain). In the last 15 years managers have restored heritage trout to about 50 remote ponds. Domestic brook trout live about three years, but heritage trout live six or seven; so they grow lots bigger. Four-pounders are now common. "When I was in the office our single most requested piece of literature was the reclaimed pond list," says Larry Strait, DEC's regional fish manager who retired in 2001. "That was no accident."

The Adirondack Council, another environmental group that does great work and for which I have raised lots of money, exists, in its words, to "sustain the natural and human communities of the region." Log onto its Web site, and you'll get hollered at by a loon. Loons are a symbol of wilderness, but the wild brook trout loons depend on aren't—at least not to the council, which doesn't see or hear them. Nor do wild brook trout count as part of the "natural community" the council is pledged to defend. The council rails against helicopter and motorboat use by DEC trout managers and says it wants them "to follow the same wilderness rules as the public." It says it finds the practice of reclaiming ponds with rotenone "offensive" and wants it banned.

When I interviewed communications director, John Sheehan, he repeated all the standard wives' tales. For example: "There appears to be a relationship between rotenone use and Parkinson's disease." And: "Rotenone essentially kills everything that breathes with gills." It was clear that the council hadn't bothered to learn the first thing about fish restoration or wild brook trout. "The trout they're putting back generally exist in another place or several other places or are the same acid-resistant strain of Little Tupper trout that they've been stocking," Sheehan declared.

But Little Tupper trout are natives, not the supposedly acid-resistant Canadian-domestic hybrids DEC used to play around with. Heritage trout recovery is all about sport, he explained: "The problem we've had is that rotenone is generally used to create sporting opportunities, not as a means of preserving specific species necessarily. Generally we're not thrilled about killing off entire ponds and replacing them with monocultures." Yet Adirondack brook trout evolved in monocultures; in fact, they can't survive without them.

Armed with all this misinformation, the council urged DEC to adopt a rule that forbids managers to fly or drive into wilderness except in "off-peak seasons"—i.e., before Memorial Day and after Labor Day. DEC—increasingly staffed by young enviros who don't see, handle or understand fish and who fear all pesticides—complied in November 2003.

The only time you can check to see if ponds are thermally suited for brook trout is when they're stratified, and they're stratified only in summer. You can't reclaim ponds when everything is iced up. And because brook trout are fall spawners and rotenone doesn't kill trout eggs, you can't eliminate domestic and introgressed fish much after Labor Day. So the new rule effectively ends heritage trout recovery in wilderness.

"The department has made it impossible for resource managers to engage in meaningful debate," says Strait. "Trout Unlimited [pushing heroically and lonesomely for virtually every native trout restoration project across America] was denied the opportunity for a public hearing, and their comments were given short shrift. The Adirondack Council has rejected science. That's a shame because they could be great allies if they'd look at what we were able to accomplish over the last 15 years."

In Montana's upper Missouri River system, where westslope cutthroats have been extirpated from all but two percent of their historic range, the state Department of Fish, Wildlife and Parks is using a total of 20 gallons of antimycin and 10 gallons of rotenone to make a westslope sanctuary from 77 miles of upper Cherry Creek, now infested with brook trout and introgressed rainbows and Yellowstone cutts. [See "Angler of the Year: Ted Turner," *Fly Rod & Reel*, January/February 2002.] You've heard the old saw that just one concerned environmentalist can "make a difference." Well, it's true but not always good. For four years the Cherry Creek project, arguably the most ambitious riverine piscicide treatment ever attempted in North America, was placed on hold purely because of a lay person's fantasies about antimycin, rotenone and even the potassium permanganate with which they are neutralized at downstream stations. William

Fairhurst of Three Forks, Montana, sued in state court on grounds that the department was "polluting" a public water supply. The utterly meritless action was finally dismissed, but while it was underway, and for much of the time Fairhurst was threatening a federal suit, the department's legal advisors made managers sit on their hands.

The first phase—treatment of 105-acre Cherry Lake and about 11 miles of stream with 10 parts per billion antimycin—was completed with superb results in August 2003. "We had sentinel fish posted in net bags throughout each treatment site every day; and we got 100 percent mortality," reports project leader Pat Clancey. "After a second treatment next year, we'll seed this stretch with westslope eggs, and we'll stock catchable adults in Cherry Lake just for the recreational fishery."

But Fairhurst isn't finished. Now he's filed his federal suit on grounds that "the Federal Insecticide, Fungicide and Rodenticide Act requires the Environmental Protection Agency to prevent unreasonably adverse effects on the environment."

During the alleged pollution of upper Cherry Creek in the summer of 2003 Clancey and his team observed the most sensitive invertebrate in the watershed, a species of caddis, happily scavenging poisoned trout.

Ted Williams has been writing full-time on environmental issues, with special attention to fish and wildlife conservation, since 1970. In addition to freelancing for national magazines, he contributes regular feature-length conservation columns to *Audubon* and *Fly Rod & Reel* where he serves as Editor-at-Large and Conservation Editor respectively.

What Comes of Reading Old Fishing Stories

G.M. WICKSTROM

My Dear Harry Briscoe,* I was happily absorbed in the routines of my retirement, when came your e-mail wanting to know about me and John Taintor Foote. You assumed that I surely had read this estimable American writer of the years between the great wars. What did I think of his fishing stories? When, shamefaced, I had to confess that for me Foote was but a barely recognized name from out there somewhere, you sounded clearly distressed and a bit scornful.** To rub it in, you found an out-of-print volume of Foote's fishing stories, thrown out by a Houston library, and sent it to me for my edification, improvement, and possible delight.

So, in order to reinstate myself in your esteem, I've now read the stories; though what I really had in mind doing just then was planning how I was going to load my fly reels with lines for the coming season. It can get so complicated that I have to print out a schedule of lines-on-reels to carry with me like my license in order not to use a size five when it's a six I want. But I digress—please don't scold.

Assuming that someone else, someday, might end up reading this, I must remind them, not you, dear old friend, that the title story of the volume is "A Wedding Gift," written in 1923, in those "roaring twenties," just about when my parents were thinking about . . . I leave you to guess.

---

*Harry Briscoe is the Houston-based petroleum geologist, angling entrepreneur, and owner of Hexagraph fly rods.

**Foote also wrote plays for stage and screen. He died in Hollywood in 1950.

This story is the best and most famous of the lot and spins a yarn that with only a stroke of formal adjustment could be turned into a one-act play, a *comedy of manners*, and so legally within my authorized field of analysis. Perhaps I should turn it into a one-act and go around to Trout Unlimited chapters performing it. What do you think? Anyway . . .

It's a polished story, brilliantly devised, and goes like this: Our narrator bumps into the story's "hero-of-sorts" at noon in New York's Grand Central Station—just as I bumped into you with those new hexagonal rods of yours at that fly fishing show in Denver, when you were still in cahoots with the old master, Walton Powell.

Anyhow, our hero George Baldwin Potter (that moniker ought to alert us that we are in trouble) is in a nervous state when our narrator tries to calm him with a hurried lunch before the arrival of the 1:45 train that, we learn, is bringing his estranged and lovely young wife, the "darling" Isabelle, for what may be their reconciliation. This is, in fact, a story about "darlingness."

With the minutes ticking off to when the train must arrive, George Baldwin, bit by interrupted bit, insists on telling the tale of his disastrous honeymoon. It's a confessional of a sort. Only trouble is that George can't keep to the subject and repeatedly drifts off into one digression after another—all about his real passion, fly fishing.

Waiting to meet one's wife reminds me: I wish I had a dollar for every time I've looked around for my wife out on the stream and, not seeing her, have begun to worry and have my fishing ruined as a result. Lost focus, you know. You'd think she'd be a bit more thoughtful when I'm considerate enough to want to keep her within sight and hearing. So I'm in sympathy with George on that score.

We have to remember that George is of that feckless and privileged, upper (quite upper), well-off-and well-situated northeastern establishment class, and, as one might expect, a proud product of Yale. (Where else could he have gone—well, perhaps to Harvard. . . . Still, Princeton has that wonderful fly fishing collection nested in that cozy little room on the lower level of the university library. It's enough to make any sensible angler want to matriculate at Princeton.)

You must also understand about George that his angling skills—he's a dry-fly purist—are by the lights of that long-gone day in the history of American fly fishing not to be doubted. He's the real thing; though, to us now, rather child-like in his grasp on daily life and its realities.

Oh, but the story! George has made this excellent marriage with the refined, cultivated, protected, "darling girl" and literally tricks her into a fishing honeymoon at a camp deep in the Maine back-woods with "the best squaretail fishing on earth." She thinks, however, that they're off to fashionable Narragansett and has packed three trunks full of fashionable clothing for every occasion there. When she realizes how she's been duped, that they are off to the woods instead, she's furious and repeatedly dissolves into tears.

But off they go anyway: by train to Bucks Landing and from there the big push by tug boat, canoe, portage, and hard hiking in to their posh camp-lodge. But first they must overnight at an inn at the Landing. It's there that George discovers to his horror how Isabelle has packed for the trip with myriad gowns and frocks and explains that she couldn't find room for the fishing tackle that George had given her and was depending on her to bring along. It's a horrible night of tears and rage and poor George's doting consternation. As the saying is, "He just doesn't get it."

The next day's journey on to camp is no better. But arrive they do at last, much too late for dinner. Maybe fishing the next day will improve matters.

George wants us to understand that he fishes only quickly moving streams, spurning lakes and ponds. However, he will deign to go out on the lake at the lodge this once in order that his darling bride might perhaps catch a trout. . . . Just this once . . . , and once out there she thrashes around until she hooks a six-incher by default and in doing so loses George's beloved Spinoza fly rod overboard into deep water. It's like the end of the world, but George claims he remained ever calm and loving. . . .

Only the timely borrowing of another's Spinoza enables him to carry on with his fishing honeymoon. You must understand that he could not possibly be expected to fish his drys with any rod but a genuine Spinoza. It would be simply impossible, he assures us.

If you are sitting there remembering, dear Harry, that I too had a fishing honeymoon, back in '48, three grand weeks, eighteen days on the water, in

Yellowstone and on the Madison, please don't make an odious comparison between me and George. It just won't hold water. Read on!

So—things go from bad to worse. For George, it is simply and terribly unfair that Isabelle is so stubborn and will not enjoy that which gives him so much pleasure, being out there with all those heavy brook trout within range of a Spinoza. Why couldn't she be happy for him? What, in heaven's name, do women want!!

What Isabelle wants, in addition to pretty wild flowers, is to get the hell out of there— Oh, that word "hell." George used it on her when she messed up his landing a really fine fish, which insupportable verbal affront convinced her that she must take drastic measures. And so in the deep of that night, as George slept and dreamed his dreams of dry fly selection, she conspired with their guide, Indian Joe, (weren't they all named "Injun Joe"?) to hike, portage, and otherwise paddle her back to Buck's Landing from where she can beat it home to Papa. Which she does.

Leaving George only to wonder at the empty impression of her darlingness left on the bed beside him. Women! Indeed, what is it they want! Don't ask George.

That's the story with which George, in the Grand Central Station café, regaled our narrator, so alarming him that the last thing he wanted was to accompany George to the platform to buffer this first meeting since their honeymoon disaster of this pitiful young husband and wife.

As the story ends, the narrator takes to his heels, leaving our "hero-of-sorts" quite in the lurch to face the fearful music of a lovely lady wronged.

It just occurs to me to wonder, Harry, are you thinking that I somehow wronged Betty with that fishing honeymoon of ours? What new bride, I ask you, wouldn't have given most anything in the world to catch, as she did, grayling hand over fist in Cascade Lake and next day almost as many sixteen-inch rainbows in Grebe?

★ ★ ★

Reading these John Taintor Foote stories has plunged me back into my old habit of trying to analyze what I read—in a word, playing the critic. Your damned Foote stories, Harry, have now become an obsession. I need to figure out how and why they both please and at the same time really put me off.

I think it has to do with the American class system. That may be at the root of the matter, good old supposedly classless America. Classless? Not for me. I've always known I'm *trash* from the wrong side of the tracks. I know my place. And what's more I've written about it before in that essay "Angling and the Class Struggle" in my last book. Admitted snob that I am, I am, nevertheless, innocent of "George Baldwin Potterhood," and proud of it.

And I ought to be out there on Boulder Creek working some rainbows and browns of my acquaintance, not haggling over some eighty-four-year-old fishing story. I ought to be out there making a serious effort to do the Polish trick with nymphs. The method reads like clubbing fish with those super-heavy nymphs. And for that matter, when I was in Poland I saw nothing that looked like trout water. Of course I got only to the edge of the Carpathian Mountains south of Krakow. Doubtless there are trout up in those mountain streams, and maybe the Polish nymphing system works on them . . .

But my thesis, Harry! My thesis is that the writing about American fly fishing changes direction radically and rather suddenly as it flows from the ridge of the historical divide of the Second World War and specifically The GI Bill of Rights. After that, fishing writing could never be the same again.

How's that for a thesis, Harry!

Come to think of it, I'll bet you've all along been remembering my confession that almost immediately after Betty's and my honeymoon, on our first fishing trip back home, when I got to acting in what she thought was an inappropriate manner, she struck me a terrible blow to my right temple with a heavy iron cup—and it was only because I wanted another cup of coffee and some decent fishing. That was high up on the ridge where the Continent itself divides. But what that has to do with George Potter, you ask? Wait and see! But I assure you right now that Betty was not then and is not now an "Isabelle."

Did you know, Harry, that three times I've had to protect that woman from assault: once long ago from two thugs who tromped through the water she was fishing, another time from slobs fishing off forked sticks with marshmallows and beer, when they thought she was wading too far out in a pond we were fishing. (I have to admit that Betty, her not-so-darling self, gave them a blistering lecture on angling decorum and rights.) Most recently a federal agent in Rocky Mountain National Park savaged her when she had trouble finding her license in her complicated gear. A fine way to treat a nice septuagenarian white-haired lady!

"Get on with it," you say! You have a nerve complaining. . . .

Yes, I think it was World War II that drove the George Baldwin Potters from the streams of angling literature. That immense war with its twelve million men and women under arms, mixing them up from all over the country in a shared emergency! It changed the country forever.

The war was The Great Leveler and did much to mature our democracy. My experience in the war was that if there were any Georges in the ranks they damn well kept quiet about it and were quickly weaned from any ideas of privilege they may have brought with them from home.

In an interesting way, there was no longer a rigorously delineated East and West to the country. Even more interesting was that if either prevailed over the other, it was the New West making its claim to most thoroughly identify the country. An angling metaphor for this change might be the way the dominance of the Catskill dry fly, George's beloved Hendricksons and Cahills, gave way to the big, spectacular attractor flies of Western usage.

Adding insult to injury to George's social and economic privilege was the emergence of the new academic faculties after the war. The GI Bill of Rights sent thousands and thousands of nobodies like me to college and thousands of them on into teaching. The new, liberal, de-classed professoriate was at the country's intellectual helm. And thus was created overnight, after 1945, a new American sensibility that a fellow like George had either to embrace or slink away from into relative oblivion.

Harvard and Yale, both, when the congress entertained legislation for the GI Bill of Rights, resisted tooth and nail. They feared that it would mean the end of their suzerainty over higher education. Those venerable bastions of privilege and class knew well, or thought they did, that American education could not endure the vulgarization of the nation's intellectual life that such legislation would surely entail. The Ivy League feared being awash with the great unwashed. Fortunately they lost out, and people like me went to college and

ended up teaching the young our renegade ideas about politics, art, and religion—sex, science, and life itself.★★★

Latter day Yaleys, I admit, still can win their day: they even become presidents with disturbing frequency. But they become presidents, not altogether, by
the ancient right of Yale, but sometimes even in spite of it. One can just imagine
the gnashing of teeth in the university halls and clubs at this break-down of
traditional privilege that was once thought to be from everlasting to everlasting.
The new *trout bums* are sweeping down, like barbarians, out of the remote
steppes of our culture.

Foote's son Timothy, from whose collection of the stories I'm working, and
that you sent me, Harry (Lyons Press, 1992), is aware that change has taken
place in the late-modern American social and economic sensibility, a change
that leaves his father's stories and their characters well back in another time. He
correctly identifies them with the high comedy of so many of those wonderful
films of the 1930s. I've written about one of them, *Libeled Lady*, starring
William Powell and Myrna Loy, a comedy with fly fishing at its center. The cultural resemblances between Foote's "wedding" story and that MGM film are
unmistakable.

Timothy Foote goes on to think of the stories as *comedies of character*, rather
than, as I do, as of *manners—comedies of manners*. And, since true *comedies of manners* are now nearly impossible to write and maybe even understand—because
there is no longer any consensus on what manners, in fact, are—we are often at
a loss with the form. Sucking at a plastic water bottle, everywhere and in public,
has become the defining emblem of the new social person.

In the matter of character, Bernard Shaw once remarked that the secret of
Lady Macbeth's character is that she has no character. She's but a *function* on the
stage. About our George, I can think of but two quite thin dimensions of character for him, if, indeed, he has any at all. One is his affected and dogmatic
angling, the other, his obtuse and severely limited response, his disastrous naiveté,
in matters of the darling female sex.

★★★In England the new provincial "red-brick" universities appeared on a similar cultural scene
to take from the ancient Oxford and Cambridge their accustomed privilege and control over
the national intellectual life.

These sorts of "characters," the George Baldwin Potters of fly fishing, have disappeared and have been replaced by *multiples of Lefty Kreh*. The George Potters of *sex* have been replaced by John Updike's suburban, perennially on-the-make, Pennsylvania car salesman Harry "Rabbit" Angstrom. Neither comes from Yale nor a fine prep school. They no longer come from fine homes in Connecticut, and commute down to Grand Central and the city on Metro North, and from there down town to the "street" or to impressive offices in mid-town. There are no apartments on the Upper East Side, no lunches within a pleasant walk of a fishing tackle shop like prestigious old Mills and Son on Park Place. Today's angling characters can only trundle off to the local, ubiquitous Orvis store, identical all over the country, even on Fifth Avenue. There they dream their all too similar dreams.

Harry, I wish you had been there with me in the old days when I visited the venerable Mills establishment. I was looking for fine, narrow, stiff dry fly hackle and failed to get it. My suspicions are that the clerks knew a nobody when they saw one and were reluctant to show me the really good stuff they had stashed in the back room. Nevertheless, it was exciting to climb those four steps from the sidewalk into the musty, worn and random interior of the shop. I think the atmosphere was deliberately allowed to run down in order to give the better-class custom that might come in at the lunch hour some sense of another way, a more rustic, rugged way of life, and so provide them with a fantasy of themselves as real outdoors men. Yes, I'm glad I was there even if I felt out of place. I think those guys could smell trash.

Finally then ("At last!" I can hear you say), it's rather disconcerting to read the Foote story, cut off as we are from those times by the immense social upheavals and transformations of World War II, in good part worked by war veterans-become-college-professors with a new, more egalitarian vision of American life. With them we crossed a divide of cultural consciousness where an Isabelle can never be quite the "darling" she was in her story, nor a George, even for a moment, think of his angling and love-life in that silly way again. Isabelle has given way to real women, like my Betty and your Jane. George is long gone. You and I moved in on him and moved him out.

Anyway, thanks, Harry, I'm much better off now that I'm able to say that I have indeed read the fishing stories of John Taintor Foote.

G.M. Wickstrom is a professor of drama, retired to Boulder, Colorado. He is the author of *Notes from an Old Fly Book*, *Late in an Angler's Life*, and "The Great Debate: A Fantasia for Anglers"—an imaginary debate between F.M. Halford and G.E.M. Skues. He also publishes the serials *The Bouldercreek Angler* and *The Bouldercreek Actor*. Wickstrom may well be the oldest writer on fishing in America. He avoids the how and where of angling in favor of the what and why. "Writing on fishing," he comments, "can be a subterfuge for writing about almost anything: politics, art, religion, sex, the works."

The Lucy Coffin

W.D. WETHERELL

My father, so long a distinguished member of the Philadelphia bar, was totally incapable of making up a story. His clients were expected to tell him in simple words what had happened, and then he would try to shape the plain words, the unadorned facts, into an argument a jury would find compelling. Imagination, exaggeration, hyperbole—he actively disapproved of all three. This was bad luck for me, since I was born with an oversupply of each, something he blamed on heredity, a great-uncle who wrote advertisements for Florida real estate back in the Twenties, and, before me, was the closest thing to a writer the family had.

So the one story Dad told me I listened to very closely. It was a fish story of course. Fly fishing was Dad's one vulnerability, the only thing we could tease him about, or theme his birthday presents around, or, on great occasions, actually share with him out on the water.

He was good at it, he fished all over the world, and his eyes came alive on a river in a way they didn't even in the courtroom. He never had the usual fisherman's virtue of patience . . . he despised patience, considered it the most mediocre of virtues . . . but what he had instead was endurance, getting out on the water before anyone else in camp and coming back far later. And he looked the part, too, once he started putting some years on. Wrinkles made him more handsome, not less. People always imagined him with a pipe in his mouth, squinting toward the sunset, though the truth is he never smoked.

That this passion was fueled in part by a rather dry, stiff, passionless marriage should perhaps come as no surprise. There were lots of dry, stiff, passionless marriages in the Philadelphia of those years. My parents didn't divorce, they had old-fashioned notions about what was owed their children, and I don't remember any particular arguments. Mother went her way, Dad went his, at least until her last years, when there was a softening, a drawing together, that surprised no one more than them.

I'm not sure when I first heard Dad's one and only story—there doesn't seem to be a place in memory where I didn't know it. He was just old enough to have served in the last days of the war, and it wasn't until almost a year after it ended that he was discharged. He went back to law school and graduated quickly—which means the story begins in the late spring of 1948.

He decided that before starting his practice he would treat himself to one grand fishing expedition. He would take a train to Vermont, then spend the summer hiking and hitchhiking through the hills, fishing every single stream and pond he came upon, boarding at farmhouses where he could find them, or camping rough in the woods. For three months, he would care about nothing except fishing, think about nothing except fishing, press the summer so deep in his memory it would never shake loose.

And that's pretty much the way it turned out. He traveled north along the Connecticut River, and when he came to a tributary, he would fish upstream toward the west, then strike out cross-country and follow the next tributary downstream to its junction with the big river—a back and forth, weaving kind of progression that meant there was very little water he missed. The days of the log drives were over, but there were plenty of old-time rivermen left who were more than happy to tell him where the big trout were hiding—and they weren't often wrong.

Back in the Depression, tramps and hobos had been distrusted, even feared here, but once the farm wives realized Dad was just fishing, a veteran, he was often given a room free of charge. In the morning, there would be chores he could help out with, and afternoons he would spend chasing the browns and rainbows that lived in the deep pools, or fishing for wild brook trout in the beaver ponds where most of these rivers had their starts, wading in the muck if he had to, sometimes taking all day to build a raft.

Thanks to his zigzag pattern, his getting stuck on rivers he loved best, it took him June and a good part of July to advance northwards sixty miles. There was still a lot of Vermont left to go before he hit Canada, but suddenly, between one tributary and the next, the landscape dramatically changed. The Connecticut veered away into New Hampshire, and the rivers flowed north towards Quebec and the St. Lawrence. The forest, instead of being dominated by maple and pine, was now mostly spruce, with boreal swamps and undulating sheets of pewter-colored rock. The farms were few and far between and mostly failed—this was a land of empty farmhouses where ghostly curtains blew out through shattered glass.

The first part of the story, the background, my father told quickly, with a lawyer's fine sense for how much he could ask of a jury's patience. But he would always hesitate here, take his glasses off and put them back on again, look out the nearest window, smile ruefully, then turn back again, his voice pitched now to a lower key.

"And then something odd happened, something I hadn't counted on. You have to understand that I was pretty cocky in those days. I thought, when it came to fly fishing, I was the hottest thing to ever hit Vermont. But once I got into the deep woods, the lonely country, things changed. I couldn't catch a fish, no matter how hard I tried. Not a trout, not a sucker, not even a chub. They all had locks on their jaws and for the life of me I couldn't find the key."

It was late August now, hot, with low water in all the streams. He slept in the woods most nights, though when it rained he found shelter in abandoned logging camps set in pockets against the ridges. On one nameless stream, fishing through a tunnel of alders, his leather wallet of flies, his best flies, dropped into the water and floated away, so he was down now to his rejects and spares.

"For the first time all summer, I began feeling sorry for myself. A thunderstorm hit me that night, so I was a pretty sorry sight once morning came. The only thing keeping me from heading to the train station and home was that the terrain was growing gentle again, with those beautiful open hillsides similar to what I had seen further south. I'll fish one more river, I decided. Just one more and then I'm done."

He was walking along, drying out in the sunshine, when he came upon an iron bridge with unusually elaborate scrollwork, and past it, a tree with a crudely-painted sign. *Hand Tied Flies!* It read. In that lonely countryside, it startled him; it could have said *Hand Cut Diamonds* and he wouldn't have been more surprised. There was an arrow pointing uphill along a road so rough a mule would have turned around in disgust. Figuring he had nothing to lose, he started up it—and that's when he had his second surprise.

On the top of the hill, set under a grove of ancient maple, was a small white farmhouse with an attached red barn. It wasn't derelict or abandoned like so many of the highest places but well-cared for, neat, even prim. Holsteins had trampled the yard up, but there was a garden surrounded by a picket fence, and it wasn't a vegetable garden either, but a flower garden, with tall showy gladiolas that were obviously meant to be cut and brought inside.

There was no one around, at least not at first, but when my father circled behind the barn he came upon a tool shed where a husky young man sat on a wicker chair listening to the Red Sox game on the radio. On the workbench beside him were piles of chicken feathers and Christmas tinsel and small black hooks. It was as if, my father said, the man knew he was coming and wanted to get right down to business.

"I saw your sign," my father said.

The young man looked Dad over. "Fly fisherman?"

"I try to be."

"Then you'll want six of these."

He handed over a Prince Albert tobacco tin. Inside were half a dozen of the rattiest looking, most outlandish flies Dad had ever seen. There looked to be muskrat fur in it, and duck quill, and a huge shank of rooster hackle—and Dad's first temptation was to laugh out loud.

"How much?" he asked carefully, not wanting to offend him.

"A dollar for the six."

"Does it have a name?"

"No. Well, sure. The Lucy Coffin. There, I just named it. You try that, fish it up on top slathered in fly dope, and if you use anything else you ain't as smart as you look."

Those of you who know fish stories can sense where this is headed. Dad stuffed those flies in his pocket, then forgot all about them. The last river he fished in Vermont was the Willoughby. As with all the other places he fished in

August, he couldn't find a way to get the trout to rise—until, desperate, he remembered the Lucy Coffin. Tying one on, he threw it out there with a why-not kind of cast—and promptly rose a three-pound brown that fought him stubbornly for a good half hour. Six more fish followed, each almost as big, and when he finally gave up because of darkness, trout were still jumping toward it out of the black. For the last week of his trip, he fished nothing else—and everywhere it immediately resulted in the same kind of triumphs.

That was Dad's story, his one and only. Even as a kid, I wondered about it, not so much whether it was true or not . . . since Dad didn't make anything up, I knew it was true . . . but at the sweetness that would come into his tone, especially during the last part about that lonely, forgotten farm. It seemed more wistfulness than the summer really warranted, though obviously, being alone like that, at a time when a place was at its most beautiful and forgotten, had left an enduring impression.

I'd like to say, as a kid, I never tired of hearing him tell this story, but the truth is, I did get tired, particularly when I reached my teens. A magic fly? A fly that worked miracles? Sure, Dad. Right. Anything you say.

And then, from a storyteller's point of view, he made a smart move. The summer I was sixteen, driving me back from a camp counselor job I had in Maine, he detoured over to show me Vermont. We fly fished several of the streams he discovered in 1948; Dad, unlike most men who are experts at something, was more than willing to let me go off and learn on my own, playing dumber than he really was, knowing I would either fall in love with it on my own or it wouldn't take.

We only had four days. On the third, I suddenly woke up to the fact we were now doing more driving than fishing, going off on dirt roads that led away from the rivers uphill. All these detours seemed of the same pattern. "We're low on flies," Dad would announce, then suddenly swerve the wheel to the right. We would drive to the top of the hill where the road gave out into ruts, Dad would get out, look over the abandoned field going back to brush, maybe take a few steps toward what remained of a farmhouse . . . a cellar hole, a blackened chimney . . . then come back to the car shaking his head.

"Well, it was around here somewhere. Things have changed, all this forest. I was on foot, never bothered with maps. Half the streams I didn't even know what their names were. Being lost was part of the adventure."

I tried to be helpful. "Maybe it was over by that river we fished yesterday? I saw a lot of old farms."

My father considered this, then shook his head. "Well, maybe, but I don't think so, Paul. I searched there pretty thoroughly last time."

"Last time?"

He smiled, shyly. "Oh, I had a business trip to Boston a couple years back. Came over here for a few days, looked around. It wasn't fishing season. Mud season, so I couldn't get very far." He raised himself up on tiptoes, put his hands around his eyes like binoculars. "See that open meadow over there? Let's see if we can find a road, then, if it's not there, we'll do some fishing."

He was quiet driving home. It was by far the best four days together we ever had, it got me started fly fishing, but I was confused at how silent he seemed, how disappointed. If we hadn't found his fly shop, that was okay by me. The Lucy Coffin? Hell, we caught plenty of trout without it—which is what I wanted to tell him, but he had his lawyer's face on now, his *losing* lawyer's face, and I knew that was something I couldn't dent.

When my mother died three years ago, Dad took it harder than any of us would have expected. As I said, during her last years their dependence on each other kept growing as their friends and colleagues one by one disappeared. Passion Dad had missed out on in life, but at least he found a quiet warmth, and losing that, at his age, hurt him deeply.

When I first broached the idea of a fishing trip, Dad was hesitant. He still fished, but mostly in ponds now, trolling streamers from a rowboat. I made it sound like I was the one who badly needed to get away . . . I had just finished a book; I was worn out, in need of a change . . . and, though he could see right through my stratagems, Dad wasn't immune to what June was doing to the air, even in suburban Philadelphia.

But he still hesitated; there was a meeting at his retirement community he was supposed to chair, and I had to come out with the argument I'd been saving as my clincher.

"We'll go and see if we can find the old place where you bought the Lucy Coffin. Maybe even find the same man."

"Dead," Dad grunted.

"How do you know that? You said he was about your own age, didn't you? He could still be tying flies. And even if he's gone, we'll make a real effort to locate where that farm was, that shouldn't be impossible."

"It's vanished. I couldn't find it last time."

"You had me in tow."

"Well no. The time after that, I searched pretty hard."

"You went back again?"

"Four or five times now."

"Four or five times?"

I'd been on the lookout for signs of dotage, but still this surprised me—he said it in a sly, secretive way, like he'd admitted sneaking off to Las Vegas. I didn't know the story had such a hold on him still. For me, it was nostalgic, going back up there, and I suppose I expected it was merely that for him, a story that sleeps wherever stories sleep in men his age, not something that actively burned.

He was waiting for me in the parking lot when I got there Thursday morning—the leathery, craggy-looking version of Dad, a rod tube sticking out from his ancient duffel bag, his waders slung around his shoulders like a bandolier.

Our drive north was on the quiet side—except for grandkids, none of the subjects we came up with seemed to take hold. Always before we could fall back on politics, me kidding him about being a Republican, him teasing me about being a Democrat, but that kind of teasing isn't possible anymore. Only once did he broach anything even remotely serious. We were up in Massachusetts, we had just gone through a long stretch of malls, and he waved his hand around, as if indicating, not just what we could see out the window, but the deeper, more essential part we could only sense.

"Countries are like old men, Paul. They get ugly when they get old . . ." and the truth of that, the doubled truth, kept things pretty quiet until we hit Vermont.

It was much better after that. The long evening shadows cut across the interstate, there were caddis flies dancing like flames around the top of the highest birches, and when we got out of the car at our motel the smell of late-blooming lilac made us look at each other and smile. Next morning, up early, we drove into the mountains, and the farther we drove the younger and fresher the land seemed. I got Dad to tell his story again, not the end he always rushed toward, but the earlier part, those June weeks when he had wandered around the foothills with no motive in live other than catching rainbows, brookies and browns.

We fished some of the same streams. Dad took forever stringing up his rod and pulling on his waders, but once in the river he did fine, not shuffling along like an old man in slippers, but high-stepping like a stork. We both caught trout. They weren't the natives he remembered, they were probably two weeks off the stock truck, but the rivers rushed the same way they always rushed, the willows danced the same dance in the wind, and there were afternoon hatches of mayflies we did very well with, fishing deep into dark. If anything, Dad seemed to have more energy and pep at the end of the day than he had when we began.

"Rhubarb pie," he said, taking a deep sniff of evening air. "I can still smell it. All these farm wives baked great rhubarb pies."

We spent the next day on a little tributary that wasn't on the map. I had to peel the alders back so Dad could enter the best pool, but when he did he caught three wild brookies, the last, for that water, a real monster, pushing fifteen inches. We admired it for the few seconds he took to let it slip back from his hand to the water. "One to quit on," I said, not really thinking about my words. "Yes, one to quit on," Dad said softly, thinking about them hard.

That night we found an old tourist home, the kind you wouldn't think existed anymore. *Titus Takes Tourists* read the sign out front—and Titus turned out to be even older than my father, with a thick mountain accent I could barely understand. But Dad could understand—he and Titus sat up talking half the night. "Twenty bucks!" his wife said, when it was time to leave. She acted embarrassed to ask so much, so, at least in this respect, we were back in 1948 at last.

But it was time to go home now. I had a book signing scheduled in Washington and Dad still wanted to chair his meeting. I had big ideas about driving it all in one day, so we left early, when the fog still lay clotted on the river. We crossed on an old iron bridge, and instead of a regular paved roadbed, there were thick old beams that made it bumpy. Something about the bumps, or the smell of creosote, or the lacy pattern of the metal got Dad thinking.

"Is there a road up here to the right?" he asked, before we were all the way over.

"It doesn't look like much of a road, Dad." I pointed in the vague direction of Philadelphia. "We've got a long drive ahead of us."

"Is there an old barn? Small, like it was made for miniature cows? Two gables, crazy windows?"

He was looking directly at me when he asked this—he was testing himself by not looking out the window.

"What's left of a barn, yes. There, you look yourself. Underneath all that poison ivy."

Dad nodded without looking, as if I were telling him nothing he didn't already know. "Turn right," he said, with a strange tremor in his voice—and then he closed his eyes, as if only by doing so could he find the right way. "There should be a bog in half a mile, then an apple orchard, then a small wooden dam."

Maybe there were those things—the washouts and ruts kept my attention fixed on the driving. A switchback got us onto an easier grade, and the upper part went under a tunnel of purple lilacs that must have been the last to bloom in the entire state. They don't grow wild, someone had once planted them, so maybe we were on the right track after all—and yet no mental effort I was capable of making could make that thick forest disappear, picture this as ever having been open.

The road ended in at a washout that could have swallowed a tank. I parked on its lip. Dad, without saying anything, opened his door and started striding through the trees. Certainty—his whole posture was shaped to it—and though I was a long way from feeling this myself, I started after him.

I caught up pretty fast. There were some spruce, then a band of dying birch, and I remembered that birch were the trees that grew first on abandoned land, and just when I was trying to figure out how many years this could take, I came into a little clearing in the middle of which stood a house.

It was standing, I'll say that much for it. The tin roof seemed pinned by rusty lightning rods to the simple Cape that stood beneath. The siding had long ago been weathered into bone color, hunters had riddled much of it with bullets, and the windows were starred with broken glass. In front was a porch that had once faced the road, but its supports had collapsed and the gingerbread trim, algae-covered and blistered, lay in pieces in the tall grass that licked the sides.

Dad stood staring down at something, and when I came up to him he pointed, bent stiffly, reached out his hand. Below a broken window the planks had been replaced with fresh, clean pine, making it look as if someone had chosen this spot to begin their renovations. Had they started, then, faced with the enormity of the job, given up? Except for that and a deflated soccer ball we found near the pyramid-heaped ruins of the barn, there were no signs of recent life.

Some of the debris had been pulled over to where an enormous apple tree had muscled out its own clearing. Dad reached down to turn through the planks. The third or fourth had purple lettering burned into its side like an old tattoo—he held it up to the light so we could read it—but it seemed an advertisement for seed or fertilizer, and didn't say anything about hand-tied flies.

"Is this it?" I asked.

I stood there staring toward the farmhouse, trying to imagine paint on it, a shiny new roof, curtains, flowers. I don't know what Dad saw. Again, as with the forest, the hand of time was too heavy for me to lift.

Dad's voice, when he started, was pitched very soft, like the voice a gentle man uses when someone is sleeping in the next room. And he touched the apple tree while he talked. That seemed important to him, the simple rough contact.

"What I'll never forget is how she was standing there waiting at the top of the road. Not waiting for me—waiting for anyone, their life was so lonely. I remember thinking how the sign for flies was their way of luring strangers just so they could have a little talk with someone besides themselves. If so, it was a good lure—it caught me easily enough."

A brown and shriveled apple, last year's, clung to the branch. He reached his hand toward it, and the motion alone was enough to make it fall.

"There was just the two of them. Her brother was seventeen—heavy, strong, and so round-shouldered he was nearly humpbacked. He could take care of cows all right, and winter he worked with the loggers. Their father had gone off to a defense plant after Pearl Harbor and that's the last they ever saw of him. Their mother died of cervical cancer a few years later. Lucy had the care of her, there was no one else. The parents or grandparents were either very brave or very stupid to have made a farm so high. The boy's name was Ira and her name was Lucy. Lucy Coffin."

The name, which I expected and didn't expect, seemed to come out of him hard. He coughed, or pretended to, and I followed his eyes back to the road.

He remembered what she looked like that first evening, he said. A young woman his own age standing there with an apron on, staring intently toward the dusk, wiping, with a wonderfully impatient gesture, the curly red hair that fell down across her eyes. She was beautiful, of course, though not in a way he had ever learned to see as beautiful before. He thought first of a tomboy, someone freckled and athletic, but she was past that stage now, and the chores hadn't yet roughened her skin. In the brief interval of grace that lay between he saw a girl so fresh and brave and natural it took his breath away, right from that first moment.

"I ended up staying with them for two weeks—they were absurdly grateful for my company. It was like they lived on an island and I had brought them news of the outside world. It was incredibly hard, the life they led, especially during the war years. It was thirty-five miles to the nearest movie house, and they told me how they would use horses to get down their road, then shovel out their old Ford from the snow, push and shove it to get it going, putting on chains when they got to macadam, then drive all that way just to see a double feature, getting back after midnight so they could tend to the cows. Ira liked fishing, so we hit it off pretty quick. He tied flies, sold a few now and then down in town, but they were cheap, gaudy things, nothing special. He really didn't understand what was happening between Lucy and me. Her bedroom faced the barn, and I remember waking up with her, getting out of bed quietly, pulling on my sweater, walking over to the window and seeing Ira stripped to the waist chopping away at five in the morning, and then at night he still wouldn't be finished, all the work he had."

Neither one of them knew much about anything except work. Once a month there were those expeditions to go see Clark Gable or Bette Davis, but except for these their life had few ornaments. Dad explained how he found an old kite in the barn leftover from when they were little, but neither one remembered how to fly it, and when he tied a tail on, got it up in the air, they thought he was a magician. And a picnic—they had never thought it possible, to go somewhere pretty and eat outside just for fun. At night, the three of them sat by the radio listening to the Red Sox and then Jack Benny. When Ira trudged off exhausted to bed, he and Lucy would walk outside together with a blanket and lie under the stars.

Neither one of them was a hick, he wanted to make sure I understood that. Lucy had an energy and directness nothing could stop, except for the one great bafflement that had her in its grip—how to be brave and deal with what life had brought her without her bravery digging a trap for her, making the loneliness even worse. For all the harshness in her life, she had a wonderful laugh and once started it would run away with her, set him laughing, too—laughing so much they cried. And silence—how many other girls her age knew how to make silence say everything? If he could teach her about kites and picnics, she could teach him about sweetness . . . never before had he suspected life was capable of being so sweet . . . and, in the end, what sadness was, too.

One afternoon they helped Ira finish his chores so they could all go fishing. Ira fished hard, but without much skill, and spent most of the time admiring my father's little Payne fly rod. After their picnic, he and Lucy walked upstream toward a waterfall. She had borrowed Ira's hat for the sun, a battered old porkpie with flies tucked in the band, and before long, that's pretty much all she was wearing, that floppy red hat. He laughed over that, and she laughed, too, bending over a little pool where the water was so thin it acted like a mirror.

My father explained all this while holding onto the apple tree, but now he stepped away, seemed actually to break that invisible cord, and walked slowly back to where I stood in the center of those rotting old planks. He looked old . . . I was startled at how old he suddenly looked . . . and maybe it was the dark evening shadows doing that, or maybe it was the contrast with the young man I followed so intently in his story. Time had stopped while he was telling it, but it was ticking again, and, judging by the way he closed his eyes, Dad felt the rush of those minutes even more than I did.

"I thought about asking her to come away with me—I thought about nothing else that last week. Would she have come? It would have broken her brother's heart. Still, I think if I had pressed her she would have come. Our worlds were so different. When I asked her about her future, she wouldn't tell me about any dreams or plans, but then right toward the end she did. 'I'd like to be in pictures,' she said. Out of all her loneliness, she could come up with nothing else."

My father's voice deepened—it was like he was struggling to recapture his lawyer's tone, get back into that safety zone where words expressed simple, incontrovertible facts.

"Lucy is one day younger than I am. She was born on October sixth and I was born on October seventh, and I teased her about how much younger she was, how much wiser I was. Every single birthday since I've thought about where she might be, what life has brought her. I've always wondered if we kept pace somehow, she in her world, me in mine . . . I got up in the middle of the night, being careful not to wake her. I didn't leave a note for her, but I left one for Ira on the kitchen table, along with that little Payne fly rod. I walked down the road in the moonlight, and never before had I seen anything so beautiful, and yet every step was torture. I can feel this even now, understand that Paul? Arthritis, that young doctor of mine says whenever I go for my checkup. But that's not what a man my age feels in his knees. It's all those times you walked away from someone you should never have walked away from."

I went over and took his arm, since he actually seemed faltering now, and there were those roots and rocks to navigate before we got back to the car.

"So there wasn't a fly?" I said. "No Lucy Coffin?"

"Oh, there was a fly all right." He reached into his pocket, brought out his leather fly book, the one he used for his very best flies. He opened it, held it toward the keyhole of light still visible in the west.

"Ira could tie in a clumsy, self-taught way. He gave me some Black Gnats before I left. Six of them. Years when the memory hurt worst, I would take one out and tie it on. I have one left. Here, open your hand."

I felt something sharp and tickly against my palm; I folded my fist tight to make sure it stayed there, that it didn't drop loose. *Mine now.* I didn't say it, but, like a small child accepting a present, that's what I felt.

"Yours now," my father said, reading my thoughts. He smiled—not a happy smile, not a sad smile either, but one that seemed pressed into the thin, permeable layer that lies in between. I could see him stare toward the first stars, sensed him using the silence to set up a line to go out on, like an old experienced storyteller from way back when, not someone who just had the one.

"I fished Ira's fly pretty hard all those two weeks, and never caught a thing on it, but for once in my life I didn't care."

W.D. Wetherell is a novelist who also writes frequently about fly-fishing, including his books *Vermont River*, *Upland Stream*, and *One River More*. He lives and writes in rural New England.

Midstream Crisis

LAMAR UNDERWOOD

As the year began, I decided to embrace the advice of my friend Sparse Grey Hackle, who told me: "Let the wolf out!" He was dead right. It was the only way to go. No more Mister Nice Guy!

My New Year's resolution was a notice served on all creatures, great and small, that in the open seasons ahead I was going to fill my hand. I was fed up with two-trout days, three-bass weekends and no-deer vacations. I'd had it with calling to bird dogs that wouldn't stand still and turkeys that would [two ridges away!]. I didn't want to see another pheasant getting up 200 yards away down a corn row or another bay full of ducks and geese rafted up and preening their feathers under skies that had flown in from Palm Springs.

Government wags told me that in the previous season some 2.5 million hunters had shot 12 million ducks. The calculator that lives beside my checkbook told me that works out to five or six ducks per hunter. I didn't get any five ducks! Who the hell shot my ducks?

All around, the previous year had not just been bad; it had been a disaster. I zigged when they zagged. The northeasters and I booked into the same places at the same times. I frightened the spots off brown trout while bass slept through my offerings. The deer left the mountain country I hunt, but those from the woods alongside my house found my tulips and peas in the spring, then shredded two young pines during rubtime in the fall. Plenty of geese crossed the pit blinds I hunkered in all season, but they were so high they were a menace to aviation—and they held express tickets.

My dismal performances afield forced me to face what the late John Foster Dulles called "an agonizing reappraisal." Clearly, my tactics were lousy; my timing stank, my equipment belonged in a museum.

I knew better than to seek some all-embracing formula as my game plan. Each subject would have to be tackled separately, tactics and gear made precise. The geese, I felt, would be the simplest problem to deal with. I began squirreling away the bucks to purchase a 10-gauge magnum automatic, with which I intended to wreak havoc on the Eastern Shore. My more immediate problem— and infinitely more complex—was what to do about those trout.

Since the Romans knew nothing about splitcane rods and matching the hatch, they invented a calendar that starts the new year off from the pit of winter. For me and millions of other fishermen the real new year begins on the opening day of trout season. My usual opening-day scenario looked like this:

An already-pudgy figure, bulked further by enough clothes to outfit the Klondike gold rush, stands hip deep in a flow of black water torn into sudsy rips by protruding rocks and bearing of the countryside what the winter snows have been holding in storage: sticks, leaves, tires, a bloated cat, the occasional beer can. Overhead the sky is a glowering mass of putty, against which the bare branches of the trees snap and creak with iron-hard stiffness as blasts of wind arrive from Siberia. For hours our man alternates making casts, peering intently at the jaunty little flies that ride the current like miniature galleons, and fumbling stiff fingers through his flybox in search of new offerings. To find a greater fool, you would have to look inside an icefishing shanty.

The bottom of a trout stream is its food factory, and on this day it will not be violated by anything except the soles of el piscator's waders. Although he will soon abandon his dry flies [how quickly the credo fades: "I'd rather catch one on top than five down deep"], our man will make only tentative probes into the depths. His wet flies, streamers and nymphs will sweep harmlessly over the heads of the stone-hugging trout. Troutless by 3 o'clock, he will seek the solace of the lodge where fire, firewater and kindred snake-bit companions will be waiting with tales of woe and livers in various stages of distress.

Long before opening day dawned last season, I was determined to never again be a part of this demented tableau.

For weeks I hit the books with an intensity seldom mounted in my profes-sional life. Schwiebert, Whitlock, Marinaro, Swisher-Richards, Caucci-Nastasi—the great masters of fly fishing for trout were devoured. Their instruction manifested itself in a barrage of catalogs and small packages of flies arriving daily from every comer of troutdom. My wading vest bulged with trinkets. Latin names of bugs came trippingly off the tongue.

Opening day, I stood thigh-deep at the head of a pool of black water, frigid and swollen with runoff. Coming to the stream, I had received the usual assort-ment of reports that the fish were in a coma. The voice on the car radio had said something about snow. None of these things intimidated me at all. This year I was ready.

To meet this early and elemental trouting condition, I pried open a box of nymphs. These were not ordinary nymphs, but masterpieces of illusion-cater-pillar-like, hairy-leggy-juicy-looking. Each was weighted with enough piano wire to outfit a Steinway. Never mind that they would hit the water with the finesse of a slam-dunk. They would go down, my friend, down, down to the very noses of these frozen wisenheimers. I would fish these creations with a leader hacked to three feet. [Long leaders, I had learned, rise in the pushing and swelling of the current.] The whole outfit would ride down with high-density sinking line topped by a fluorescent strike indicator to tell me when I had a customer.

You don't cast such a rig. What you do is sort of heave the whole mess out and to one side, paying close attention that a hook in the ear is not the imme-diate result of the effort.

I watched the curls of line and leader straighten downstream toward a boulder that slashed the smooth flow. I tried to form a mental image of what the nymph was doing—sinking, tumbling, ticking over rocks. The line straight-ened past the boulder. I paid out three more long pulls from the reel, watching the strike indicator bob on downstream.

Suddenly I thought I saw it dart forward. I came back with rod and line and felt the weight of a trout. As the brown—a lovely 15-incher—darted and splashed on the way to the net, my elation soared. My patience and virtue and hard study were to be rewarded. The masters of the game were indeed wise and learned men.

After that, you can imagine my heart-hammering excitement when the next 30 minutes yielded two more fish, about the same size as the first.

Then the devil sent his disciples to descend upon me, like a plague of locusts. First one, then two, then three other anglers were crowding into my stretch of water. Not one asked what I was using. They simply assumed I had found "The Place."

Never mind, I told myself. You can afford to be generous. I waded from the stream and pointed up toward uninhabited water. In a few minutes I was sloshing, much too fast, through a bouldery run of pocket water when I felt my right foot sliding down an eel-slick ledge. I lurched hard to the left, but that leg would not bear the burden. I went down into the water on my back with a teeth-jarring crash. Totally submerged for a second, I stood up and cursed my luck and the worn felt soles of my waders. I was drenched, achingly cold, and clearly out of action for the rest of the day.

As I waded to the edge of the stream, I discovered another result of my accident with dramatic suddenness. As I made a little sideways move with my left leg to step around a rock, I felt a nauseating wave of pain. I did not want to feel such a shock again, ever, so now I picked my way gingerly along, trying to protect the knee.

Yuk! Yuk! See the man all soaking wet and limping toward his car. Fat-ass must've fallen in. Yuk! Yuk!

A prominent physician whom I trust sentenced the knee to six weeks of healing. Because I could not wade the stream, I could not fish for trout. The great fly hatches of early spring for which I had prepared myself so diligently came and went: the Blue Quills, the Hendericksons, the Grannon caddis, the March Browns.

My mood was foul and depressed. Without my jogging program, with which I had successfully been losing weight, I quickly regained ten pounds. Going to work in New York on the train one day I was struck by a thought as morbid as any I've ever had: The obituary page of *The New York Times* named very few males in their 90s. No, the ages of the boys getting their names in the paper were in the 70s and 80s. At age 45 I had the startling realization that in all likelihood I was more than halfway to the barn. Life begins at 80? Give me a break!

Okay, my somber mood told me, so you've lost some of your good moves and speed. You can't hit a 60-yard mallard or sink a three-foot putt. On the tennis court children who can't get into an R-rated film have you gasping like a beached whale. The guide can show you a tarpon at 60 feet, and you may or may not be able to get the fly to it [probably not, given any kind of wind]. But relax, buster. For the years have given you wisdom. Look at what you did with those opening-day trout!

I was still clinging to this slightly uplifting notion when I finally got back to the river in late May. One of the year's best hatches remained. According to the grapevine, the Sulphurs had arrived in tentative numbers two days earlier, and all signs pointed to their major emergence late that evening.

The hatch of *Ephemerella dorothea*, which goes on with diminishing consistency for about six weeks on good eastern streams, ranks as a favorite because it stirs smart, self-respecting trout into an unusual orgy of gluttony. Unlike some mayfly hatches, which deliver more sizzle than steak, the appearance of the No. 16 yellow-and-dun flies in the last hour before darkness produces fishing so fast and exciting that it is the stuff for cool hands and stout hearts.

My favorite slick-water was flat empty that evening. My recent misfortune was all forgotten as I waded into position and made a few desultory casts while waiting for the hatch to begin. The air was heavy with humidity, and low clouds on the ridges promised that darkness would come early and perhaps a thunderstorm with it.

The time that passed seemed interminable. Nothing came off the darkening water, not even caddis. A kingfisher flew upstream, scolding my presence. I heard a great horned owl up on the mountain and an answering cry from nearby. Then I saw the first delicate yellow mayfly climbing steeply toward the trees. In a few moments there was another, then another, then another, and then I actually saw one in the instant it left the water—and beyond it the swirl of a trout.

My line arched through the growing dusk. I saw my artificial Sulphur begin its jaunty ride down the feeding lane where the trout had swirled. It floated on downstream unharmed. There were other rises all over the pool now—not splashy water-throwing slaps, but subtle bulges and swirls.

I really started worrying when my bogus Sulphur made three more rides through the melee without interesting a trout. What was wrong? The fly? The leader? My thoughts screamed as I watched the hatch and rises go on: You've been out of action so long you don't know what you're doing.

In the middle of this burst of self-condemnation I saw something—flashes of darting trout just beneath the surface. That was it! The trout were not taking the surface duns! They were nymphing, gulping the insects as they rose to the surface and in the film as they emerged into winged shape.

I was prepared for this, but my hands trembled as I opened the flybox and got out a floating nymph. The light was going fast, but I managed to tie on the fly without digging out my night light. In my excitement, however, I dropped my reading halfglasses into the stream. Klutz! Fool! I should have had them on a cord around my neck.

No matter. I had the right ammo now, and the fish were still going strong as I roll-cast the nymph to the top of the pool. Instantly a trout was on, and I felt a flush of ultimate satisfaction.

The fish was a strong pulsating weight as it struggled upstream for a few seconds. Then the line went slack as the trout bolted downstream almost past my legs, a momentary shadow that caused me to gasp: I was into my largest trout ever.

The reel screamed appropriately as the fish bolted downstream. He reached the lip of the falls that terminated the pool and turned to face the current. The steady pressure on the 5X felt unbelievable. I had the feeling of the fish backing up, backing to the edge of the tumbling water. He was going to be washed over the lip! I had to do something! I palmed the flange of the reel, increasing the drag, and thereby succeeded in instantly breaking off the trout as surely as though I'd been trying to.

I reeled in the sickeningly slack line and looked at the 5X tippet. So many trout were still taking the sulphur nymphs all over the pool that the excitement smothered the loss of the big fish. I quickly had another floating nymph out, ready to tie on. I felt my shirt pocket for my reading glasses and remembered where they had gone. I held the fly at arm's length against the gloom of the darkening sky. No way. I could not thread the eye of the hook in that dimness.

No problem. My night light had a magnifying glass that fit over the top of the light. No sweat, just stay cool.

I was deeply aware of the rises continuing all over the pool as I pulled the light out and draped its cord around my neck. I felt deeper into the pocket for the magnifying glass. It wasn't there! I flipped the switch on the light. Nothing! *Click, click. Click, click.* Still nothing! Okay, the batteries are dead. You're on your own. Now just hold the fly very still against what is left of the sky and tie it on.

My panic rose as I tried unsuccessfully to tie on the No. 16 Sulphur. I tied a No. 14. It would not go. In a final burst of madness and inspiration, I dug out a No. 10 Blonde Wulff, the biggest fly in my vest. Maybe it would work on these feeding fish.

Perhaps it would have. I don't know. I never got the Wulff tied on. My vision is 20-20, but at age 45 I could not see close up well enough to tie on a fly and resume fishing a hatch that I had waited for all winter.

I reeled in slowly, felt the end of the leader reach the reel, then broke down my rod. The splashes of feeding trout popped out from the darkness. I could not see the rises now, but they were distinctive above the murmur the current made as it tailed from the pool downstream.

Slowly the disappointment drained away. The easy moves, the good speed. Going, going with the years. Yet it was true: You were wiser, vastly richer in the things you knew. Such as realizing right now that what made fishing so great was that on any given outing, things could happen that you would remember all of your days. Few other times in life could offer that.

That is the easy part of change—the knowing, the feeling. The other side is that you have left something precious behind—something you had used up and would have to go on without.

Flashes of lightning came across the ridgetop, then the roll of advancing thunder. The feeding grew quieter, then died out completely. The bursts of lightning helped me find my way up the hillside to the lane that led back to the car.

I did not know if I had reached the end of something or the beginning.

The wind blew on the high ridges, gusting along the slopes, coming down to the river.

Lamar Underwood is the former editor-in-chief of *Sports Afield* and *Outdoor Life*. He is currently editorial director of the Outdoor Magazines Group of Harris Publications. He has edited several books for Lyons Press, including *The Greatest Fishing Stories Ever Told*, *The Greatest Hunting Stories Ever Told*, and *Into the Backing: Incredible True Stories about the Big Ones That Got Away—And the Ones That Didn't*.

Man's Best Friend: Should You Take Your Dog Fishing?

RHEA TOPPING

Talk about a can of worms! This subject is so controversial that I almost lost a good friend over our differences of opinion. And, folks, that's exactly what it boils down to. There is no right or wrong, no rule which dictates that one must never take one's canine pal along on a fly fishing excursion.

Lee Wulff used to say, "Time is something you can never give back." So, regardless of the application, keep that phrase in mind and decide whether taking Fido along could possibly be detrimental to anyone else's fishing time.

I am what people call a "dog person." In fact, I don't think I have ever met a bad person who loved dogs. I mention this to qualify the fact that, I still feel that dogs don't really belong in most fly fishing scenarios. At least, not when there's even the most remote chance that you might meet another angler and jeopardize their fishing.

I have had two days of fishing ruined by someone else's dogs.

Disaster #1

It was the first afternoon of my first experience fishing for Atlantic salmon. We were on the Miramichi in Eastern Canada, and the fishing had not been spectacular for some time, attributed largely to netting and poaching problems on the river. As it was fairly late, we went to the Home Pool, which was close by, and which had consistently had the best numbers of fish recently. We were a group of eight, mostly strangers, and we used the traditional rotation system.

Suddenly, this lovely lab jumped off the bank into the river, and proceeded to paddle between me and the angler just upstream who, in fact, was the dog's owner. The two of them thought this was great fun. A nice refreshing swim across to the far bank and back, and several "good girls" later, I thought my guide was going to have a stroke. He was apoplectic. He grumbled, "might as well call it a day . . . that dog will have put every fish down in Home Pool. There's NO chance of anyone hooking a salmon tonight!" And he was right.

To this day, the owners aren't aware that their dog had the slightest influence on the fishing that afternoon. Nor do they realize that they may potentially have ruined the already-difficult-enough chance of landing an Atlantic salmon that afternoon for several other anglers. Who really knows? Perhaps we would not have had any hook-ups that afternoon anyway. But here is an incident, stemming from ignorance, not malice—an incident that could have, and should have been avoided.

Disaster #2

The Beaverhead was high, and the recent rain had affected the visibility. Nevertheless, it was a beautiful, sunny fall afternoon in Twin Bridges, Montana. My friend, Annette, had invited us over from Livingston to fish with her. We loaded our gear into her husband's drift boat and trailered it to the put-in just outside of town. As we were backing it into the river, a large black lab, sans collar, came dripping and shaking out of the river onto the loading ramp, with a large tree limb in his mouth. We tried to ignore him, but that was not what he had in mind at all. As we set off down the swollen Beaverhead towards the Big Hole, our new best friend swam alongside, limb in tow. Whatever bank we would maneuver over to, to fish the pockets, Mr. Lab would get there first. We traversed that river a hundred times, and each time, there he was. What a lovely dog, a great swimmer, with tremendous retrieving instincts.

By then, I was enjoying him far more than either my fanatical fishing friend, Carole, or Annette, the self-appointed rower of the day. I thought she was going to bean him with the oar on more than one occasion. Five hours of floating with that lab, and not a single fish—natch. I finally convinced them to let me put him in the boat, as he was not only really tired, but we had traveled so far from the put-in, that there was no way the poor dog could have found his way home—particularly across cattle country, where gun-bearing ranchers are prone to be rather protective of their stock.

I took a series of photos of this retrieving fool during the course of the float trip, and I use them as a very effective example in the Dog vs. Dog Controversy section of my slide show on Fly Fishing Etiquette—it gets the point across.

Of course there are exceptions to every rule, and many, many anglers get great pleasure out of taking their dogs along on fishing trips, and many are perfectly behaved and cause no problems. It is not for me to judge, or even suggest any rule against doing this. But, for those who do, please remember: it's fine as long as it doesn't affect other anglers.

And on the other side of the coin, here's a story about a great fishing dog.

Chester LaFontaine: A Catch and Release Canine

Chester fished with Gary for nearly ten seasons, and appeared in the fly fishing videos, *Successful Fly Fishing Strategies*. Gary swore that Chester was "the Einstein of dogs"; that he was fully bilingual in canine and English, and that he could take Chester absolutely anywhere, including the Little Lehigh in Pennsylvania, and that the dog would be perfectly behaved and not disturb man nor fish. That's quite a reputation to live up to! This is how Gary related the story to me.

On this particular day, Gary and Chester were fishing with a friend on one of the many prolific rivers near Deer Lodge. The friend was some distance downstream of them, and hooked a fairly sizable whitefish. Now, some people feel very strongly that whitefish are a nuisance, a junk fish, and can ruin a good day of trout fishing. The best solution is to eliminate the species. Obviously this guy was of that school, and so, without giving it any thought, the fellow removed the hook, and tossed the unfortunate fish up on the bank. It landed about 30 feet from the river's edge in the tall grass.

Chester, being the perfect dog and never missing a trick, had keenly observed the hook-up, the hook removal, *and* the whitefish-from-the-river-removal. He had never seen any fish harmed in all his angling years. Furthermore, he could see no reason to distinguish a whitefish from any other species. A fish was a fish was a fish.

Out of the water (where he had been helping Gary locate trout), up the bank, Chester to the rescue. He put his nose to the poor fish's side and proceeded to nudge it, inch by inch, slowly down the hill in the direction of the water, from whence it came. This was no easy feat—we're talking tough conditions, folks—bumpy terrain, high grass, stones, and quiet a distance. Had Chester learned this technique at a previous Easter Egg Rolling Party, perhaps?

Slowly, carefully, the old dog literally worked the whitefish back down the embankment and into the water. Unfortunately, the fish immediately turned belly up. Again, this was something Chester had never witnessed. He was used to seeing fish released right side up, and then swim quickly away. He knew there was something terribly wrong. He knew fish weren't supposed to swim off upside down, so being "the perfect angling dog," Chester took his paw and, ever so gently, rolled it over in the water, right side up. Within a few seconds, the fish took one last look at Chester, and beat it downstream as fast as it could swim.

This is a true story—no exaggeration—there were witnesses, and I saw the slide sequence of this event with my own disbelieving eyes.

Rhea Topping is an accomplished fisher, teacher, and writer. She achieved the Federation of Fly Fishers' (FFF) Master Instructor rating in 1997, the second woman to do so, and has certified new instructors throughout the world. Rhea has served as both a Regional and National Director of FFF. She was FFF's 1999 Woman of the Year and received the FFF Lew Jewett Lifetime Award in 2003. She was also associate producer of Joan Wulff's *Dynamics* DVD and Mel Krieger's *Patagonia* and children's DVDs. Her most recent book is *Rod Rage— A Guide to Angling Ethics*. She believes that in order to learn, at any age, it must be fun!

Steelhead Dreams

A personal Odyssey in search of the fish that matters most

E. DONNALL THOMAS JR.

Nothing challenges foul weather gear quite like rain-soaked Alaska brush, which somehow manages to feel wetter than water itself. After floundering through a mile of dripping alders and devil's club, the atmospheric conditions next to my skin feel like a steam bath, but I know better than to complain even to myself. Hot and wet thanks to the exertion, I'll be cold and wet as soon as I stop scrambling over logs and settle down to fish.

Finally the stream announces its presence up ahead as the gurgle of current rises above the sigh of the breeze through the canopy. My first visual contact with the water immediately justifies the effort required to get here. Two days of rain have filled the cup, but not to overflowing. Cool, clear current laps the rocks a few inches higher than it has in weeks. With a high spring tide building downstream, the river looks like an engraved invitation to the fish that have been treading water out in the bay, waiting for a shot of rain to lure them upriver. With luck, this will turn into one of those days . . .

But I know better than to count on it. The allure of wild steelhead owes no small debt to their unpredictability and the notion that at any given time you may be laboring to deliver perfect casts to water that may not hold any fish. As I drop my pack streamside and organize my gear, I remember days like that right here, on one of my favorite hundred yards of steelhead water in all Alaska. Those memories come easily enough; there are plenty of them to choose from.

But then I remember another morning, a year ago practically to the day, when I waded out into the stream here and hooked seven bright fish in quick succession, only to pack up, hike back out and drive home to get Lori because the fishing was so incredible I couldn't stand the thought of not being able to share it. Steelhead affect me that way, and I know no other game fish that can confound through their presence every bit as much as through their absence.

If the stream has extended an invitation to the fish today, it has extended an even more urgent one to me. Of all the outdoor activities I pursue with passion, none offers quite the same combination of hope and serenity as fly-fishing for wild steelhead. Fish or no fish, I can literally lose myself for hours at a time on water like this, in no place quite like Alaska.

So once again, I finish off the knot, gird up my waders and step out into the water to cast . . .

Full disclosure: the paragraphs that follow will not tell you much about how to catch steelhead in Alaska. They will tell you even less about *where*. Instead, they'll focus on the reason *why*, and if you don't feel ready for that discussion, you're probably not ready for the long days of rain, cold fingers and confusion that commonly serve as a prerequisite for the event itself.

To understand why steelhead fishing in Alaska represents a special version of a special outdoor experience, it's necessary to understand its limitations elsewhere. The four decades plus I've spent chasing anadromous fish around the world provide a background appropriate to the discussion.

In 1963, when I was still an adolescent, my family moved from upstate New York to the Pacific Northwest. An enthusiastic angler since I was old enough to hold a rod (around age three according to family archives), I'd spent my early fishing career on tiny East Coast streams where a 12-inch brook trout represented a real trophy. The thought of catching fish measured in pounds rather than inches excited me beyond belief. Accordingly, after our arrival in the Puget Sound area my father and I turned our full attention to fish that looked to us as mysterious and foreboding as Bigfoot himself: steelhead and salmon.

The latter didn't pose much problem—at least with conventional tackle in salt water—but the steelhead were another matter. We lacked mentors, who could have helped a lot, and in retrospect our first naïve efforts to catch steelhead look positively pathetic. Our results reflected our skill level. Given that I was discovering girls around the same time, the number of fruitless hours I logged on the Skykomish and the Skagit stand as a real testimonial to my own stubborn streak.

Then one sunny day after a long hike up the Olympic Peninsula's Queets River, I hooked and landed a 16-pound summer-run hen and everything changed. I had proven that steelhead existed and that I could catch them. That first fish functioned like a secret password to an exclusive club and the fact that I soon began to catch steelhead regularly only added to my obsession.

Somehow I managed to keep my education on track despite the distractions of the outdoors and the general '60s craziness. When it came time for medical school, I told myself I was returning to Seattle because the University of Washington School of Medicine was one of the country's best, which happened to be true. Fact is, I couldn't imagine spending four more years in a place without steelhead.

Although I'd grown up fly-fishing for trout, steelhead had proven such an intimidating quarry at first that I fished for them with conventional tackle like everyone else. The fact that I almost never saw anyone with a fly rod during the countless days I spent on steelhead streams only enforced the notion of a leap too big to take. But as my knowledge of the fish and the water grew from inept to expert level, the need to extend the challenge grew as well. One day I headed to the banks of the Skykomish with a fly rod in my hand and promised myself I would never fish for steelhead again with anything else. I suppose I've broken my share of promises over the years, but not that one.

Even so, I began to grow restless with the state of the fishery. By serendipity, that first fish from the Queets had been a wild native, a pearl inadvertently cast before a swine barely capable of appreciating her. The steelhead I'd learned to master since were predominantly hatchery fish, and it was only a matter of time until the illusion of equivalence began to falter. Like Stepford Wives, hatchery steelhead turn out to be counterfeit, depending on superficial resemblances in order to masquerade as the real thing.

As this realization sank in, I began to abandon familiar, productive water close to home and explore relatively remote drainages on Hood Canal and the Olympic Peninsula. Long, wet hikes took me farther from people and closer to wild steelhead. But as much as I enjoyed those waters, it was hard to fish them without experiencing a certain uneasiness. Seattle was well along in its transformation from the big small town we'd known originally to a tech-fueled megalopolis. Development is the ultimate enemy of wildlife everywhere, and if the native runs on the Sound's east side had fallen relentlessly to its pressure, the rest couldn't be far behind.

Formal education completed at last, I said goodbye to the coast with no small measure of regret and headed for rural Montana, motivated less by professional opportunity than an abundance of fish and game. I still chased steelhead during periodic visits to my parents' house, but I could feel my relationship with the fish slipping away through my fingers into the realm of memory and dream. And there matters stood until I made what was probably an inevitable decision given my temperament and enthusiasm for wild places: I headed north.

In many ways, a move to Alaska is more like a move to a foreign country than to another state. I feel sorry for Alaskans who can't remember the novelty and excitement of their first few years as fulltime residents, and even sorrier for the few who never experienced those emotions in the first place (unless they were lucky enough to have been born there). Life on the Kenai introduced me to a flood of new experiences, none more stimulating than my reintroduction to a group of old friends: anadromous fish. Despite the richness of its own wildlife and habitat, there's no way around the fact that Montana lacks an ocean, and I hadn't truly realized how much I'd missed the sea and its periodic gifts until I found myself back in a maritime environment.

Proximity to the storied Kenai River meant abundant opportunity to fish for salmon. The challenge of figuring out how to catch big Kenai kings on fly tackle—an idea that hadn't occurred to many people at the time—kept me pleasantly occupied for a while. But by the time I'd watched the termination dust whiten the mountains in front of our house for a second season, steelhead had started to swim upstream through the current of my dreams.

The nearest runs lay but an hour's drive to the south, and that fall I began to haunt the Anchor River. Fish proved few and far between, but I kept at it hard enough to find some. I hooked steelhead and they hooked me, and by the time the ice arrived to stay I realized all over again why I'd always regarded them as the greatest game fish in the world.

But the circle didn't really close until a Close Encounter of the Third Kind far away in Alaska's southeastern panhandle, the ecologically complex sliver of temperate rain forest that lies between the peaks of the Coast Mountains and the North Pacific. Bears had lured me to the area. My first evening on Prince of Wales Island, I was hiking down a creek to hunt a beach with my longbow when I reached a pool just above the tide line and found it stuffed with steelhead fresh from the sea. The fish looked bigger than the water that held them. Bears forgotten, I returned early the following morning with my fly rod. The fish had dispersed overnight, but the stream was small enough so that I had no trouble finding them. The morning evolved into one of those days to which numbers, weights and even attempts at lyrical description cannot do justice, and so I will not try. Those events took place over twenty years ago and I've operated under their spell ever since.

Southeast Alaska's fishery offers plenty of the two elements I'd found lacking when fishing for steelhead Outside: wild fish and wild places. Except for a hatchery return on the Klawock River, all the region's steelhead are native fish. Anglers elsewhere sealed their fate the moment they began to accept mass-produced steelhead as stand-ins for the real thing. Accept no substitutes! Alaskans haven't yet and we can only hope they never will.

And the wildness of the place matters every bit as much as the wildness of the fish. One likes to think that rugged terrain, inclement weather and geographic isolation will insulate southeast Alaska from the kind of development that changed the face of steelhead fishing farther south, and perhaps it will. But complacency is never a safe attitude toward wilderness and keeping wild places wild is always more productive than trying to restore them.

Those who know the steelhead of southeast Alaska will never question the value of the effort.

I'm really not trying to be secretive about the streams I enjoy fishing. Go to the Alaska Department of Fish and Game Web site, download the Area Fishing Guides for southeast and you'll have most of them at your fingertips. Granted, over the years I've derived special pleasure from catching steelhead in small streams that don't even make those generally comprehensive lists: a steelhead angler's equivalent of a first ascent. But the identity of most of my favorite waters lies well within the public domain.

Including this one . . . An hour or so has passed without interruption from the fish. It's hard to be precise about time, since I never consult my watch when I'm steelhead fishing. The process creates its own temporal rhythm independent of numbers and second hands: cast, mend, strip, lift. It occurs to me that the effect on the human brain must be akin to chanting a mantra.

No fish . . . what a surprise. Of course I'm being facetious, since experienced steelhead anglers never really expect to catch fish on any given day. This observation represents a self-fulfilling prophecy, since those who really expect to catch fish seldom last long enough to become experienced steelhead anglers. To paraphrase Marie Antoinette, let them eat pink salmon.

Actually, the last paragraph should have begun: "No fish *yet*." That last little monosyllable makes all the difference in the world. The steelhead angler's ability to thrive on anticipation alone practically defines the nature of the beast. In the end, it's really only a matter of time, and what's that anyway? As Peter Lorre's character suggests in *Beat the Devil*: "The Swiss manufacture it, the French squander it, the Americans say it's money and the Hindus claim it doesn't exist."

Whatever the case, I can't think of a better place to let it pass than on a southeast Alaska steelhead stream with a fly rod in my hands.

E. Donnall Thomas Jr. writes about fly fishing and other outdoor topics for numerous magazines including *Gray's Sporting Journal*, *Alaska*, and *Field & Stream*. His angling books include *Whitefish Can't Jump* and *Dream Fish and Road Trips*. He and his angling wife Lori divide their time between homes in Montana and Alaska.

The Secrets of the Littlehorn

WILLIAM G. TAPPLY

The Littlehorn River begins at the outlet of a small cottage-rimmed pond, follows the old Boston & Maine railroad tracks behind gas stations and strip malls and suburban backyards, passes under three highway bridges, and ends several aimless miles later in another pond. In April, when the hatchery trucks make their deposits, the bridges swarm with fishermen who cruise red-and-white bobbers through the pools.

By June, the rocks in the riffles begin to rise above the sluggish currents. Perch and bluegills and an occasional largemouth bass move up and down from the two ponds into the pools. Except for the kids from the condominium complex, who hunt turtles and frogs there, nobody pays any attention to the Littlehorn after Memorial Day.

Except me. The Littlehorn runs less than a mile from my house. For better or for worse, the Littlehorn is my home water. I wish it was better. But at least it's mine, and if it were better, it probably wouldn't be my secret.

You won't find any blue line on a Massachusetts road map to represent the Littlehorn River. It's on the topographic map, but it's got a different name.

The Littlehorn is my name for it. It's got pools and riffles and runs, exactly like Montana's Bighorn. Except it's in Massachusetts. And it's a lot smaller.

There are holes in the Littlehorn where a careless step might send water sloshing over your hip boots. You might need more than a rollcast to reach from one bank to the other where it widens and slows below the third highway bridge. Mostly, though, it's little. Its trout are smaller and scarcer, too, and the hatches are considerably sparser and less dependable than they are on the Bighorn.

But I've caught trout from the Littlehorn in every season of the year. As far as I know, nobody else in the world can say that. But then, nobody else has spent as much time as I have probing its depths, monitoring its temperature and its insects, drifting flies through it, and just sitting on its banks watching it go by. Over the years, I've discovered where the springholes and deep undercuts are, and I know that these are places where some of those hatchery browns go to escape April worms and July droughts. They learn to elude herons and minks, and they learn to eat insects and minnows, and gradually they become wild trout.

I know these things. So I feel I've earned the right to keep the Littlehorn a secret. I share it with nobody. If you were to ask me about the Littlehorn, I'd tell you, "Oh, they dump in some stockers in April. Good place for kids with worms. Otherwise, fageddaboudit."

★ ★ ★

One evening in mid June a few years ago I made an exception to my rule. I was working my leisurely way upstream, floating a small white-winged Wulff through the riffles and against the banks. I was catching nothing, nor did I expect to. For now, the company of the Littlehorn was enough. I expected some Light Cahills to come off toward dusk. I planned it so I'd arrive at the pool below the washed-out milldam at the right time.

When I rounded the bend, I found another angler standing knee-deep in the middle of my pool. She wore baggy man-sized hip boots, a long-billed cap that flopped over her ears, a blond ponytail, and a pink tee shirt. She took turns slapping the water with her fly line and slapping the mosquitoes off her bare arms.

She was in my river, fishing in my pool.

She was about eleven years old.

I sat on a rock to watch her. She cast awkwardly, but she kept at it, apparently unaware of my presence.

Soon the sun sank behind the trees and a few cream-colored mayflies began drifting on the water. Upstream of the girl I saw a swirl. Then another. Exactly where I knew they'd be.

I couldn't stand it. "How're they biting?" I called.

She jerked her head around. "Oh, gee, Mister. You scared me."

"Sorry."

"I never catch anything. It's fun anyway."

I got up and waded in beside her. "Let's see what you're using."

She stripped in a Mickey Finn streamer, big enough to frighten a northern pike, tied to a level thirty-pound tippet.

"Want to catch a trout?" I said.

She grinned. She wore braces. "Some day I will," she said.

"Why not tonight?"

She shrugged. "Why not?"

I told her my name. Hers was Mary Ellen. She insisted on calling me Mister. I cut off her leader and replaced it with a seven-footer tapered to 4X. Then I tied on a Size 14 Light Cahill. "Cast it up there," I told her, pointing with my rodtip to the place where the riffle flattened and widened at the head of the pool. "There are three hungry trout there."

She managed better with the tapered leader. On her third try the Cahill landed lightly, drifted barely a foot, then disappeared in a quick, silvery flash. She turned to look at me. "What was that?"

"A trout," I said. "You've got to set the hook." I showed her what I meant. She watched me, frowning.

They were nine-inch browns, survivors of the spring hatchery deposit. And they were naive and cooperative. Mary Ellen hooked the third one she rose. She derricked it onto the bank and fell upon it with both hands.

I helped her unhook it. "Want to bring it home?" I said.

"Oh, no. Let's put him back."

I helped her unhook and revive her trout. When it flicked its tail and darted back into the pool, she waved and said, "Bye, bye, fish."

That was one time I didn't mind sharing the secrets of the Littlehorn.

★ ★ ★

Last July, a three-day gullywasher raised the water level of the Littlehorn nearly a foot. It was still drizzly the morning of the fourth day when I waded into the head of the pool below the first bridge.

I tied on a smallish muddler and drifted it through the currents. I cast absentmindedly and without expectation, not even moving, just fishing that pool, happy to be there. I caught a small bass, and a little later a hand-sized bluegill. The hum and swish of trucks and cars passing over the bridge behind me was muffled by the damp, heavy air, and as I got into the rhythms of the water, the traffic sounds subsided completely from my consciousness.

It took the big trout half an hour to decide to strike. When he engulfed my muddler, I glimpsed the golden flash of his broad flank beneath the stream's surface. He turned and bulled toward the brush-lined opposite bank, and I knew it was a heavy fish. I raised my rod tip and let the line slide through my fingers. Then he jumped, and I saw that he was bigger, by several dimensions, than any brown trout I'd ever seen in the Littlehorn. He was as big, in fact, as worthy browns I'd taken from the Bighorn.

The sounds of traffic filtered back into my consciousness, and I was suddenly aware that I was standing there, in plain sight in the middle of my secret stream, with a monster trout on the end of my line.

I considered the consequences. Then I snubbed the line around my finger and lowered my rod to give the fish a straight pull. I felt the leader tighten, stretch, then pop.

"Bye, bye, fish," I said.

William G. Tapply wrote the "Reading the Currents" column for *American Angler*. He also wrote frequently for *Gray's Sporting Journal* and *Fly Tyer*. He wrote twenty-eight novels, ten books about fishing and hunting, and hundreds of magazine articles. He was Writer in Residence at Clark University and lived in Hancock, New Hampshire. He passed away in 2009.

The Saga of
the Yellowfin

MARK SOSIN

It wasn't my idea. The late Joe Brooks, a friend, master fly fisherman, and one of the first inductees into the IGFA Hall of Fame, spent time convincing me. "You can do it," he insisted. "You're young and strong with plenty of endurance." Joe felt that the time had come to catch a husky yellowfin tuna on fly and the place to do it was Bermuda. Without waiting for an answer, he simply said he would set up the trip.

Pete Perinchief, who never failed to let you know that he was On Her Majesty's Service and whose family had lived in Bermuda for three or four centuries, handled visiting fishermen. He was skeptical that anyone could catch a yellowfin on fly (which they call Allison tuna in Bermuda), so he brought his good friend Louis Mowbry with him to watch the attempt. Louis was the curator of the Bermuda aquarium and a man with impeccable credentials. My wife, Susan, and another friend of Pete's made up the party.

On July 3, 1969, we set sail for Challenger Bank aboard Captain Boyd Gibbons' Coral Sea. His brother, Terry, served as mate. The procedure is to anchor the boat in the shallower water of the bank and let out enough anchor line so the stem of the boat was near the dropoff to deeper water. The current would carry the chum over the edge and attract a variety of fish including the prized Allison tuna. Hog-mouthed fry was the chum of choice, a small silvery fish that flashed and radiated in the exceptionally clear water.

The tuna did not appear for a considerable amount of time, so everyone busied themselves catching a variety of other species. Suddenly, they were there, big, torpedo-shaped brutes moving swiftly through the slick as they feasted on the free food being drifted back to them.

Pete Perinchief changed his mind. Instead of letting me cast a fly to the tuna, he announced that all of us on board would catch one first on conventional tackle. To say I was disappointed was an understatement, but I remained silent. Pete, Louis, and their friend all caught a tuna, with only one man fishing at a time. It takes time to land an Allison on a 30-pound outfit. My concern was that the small school would leave our chum slick and my chance with the flyrod would be gone.

When the three men had caught their fish, Pete told me I had to catch one on regulation gear first. By the time I battled that tuna into submission, I wasn't so sure I could land one on fly. It was a tough fish and I was a bit winded when I finally brought that critter to boatside.

It's important to understand that state-of-the-art saltwater fly tackle in 1969 was not even close to what we use today. The rod was made from the traditional E-glass and would be considered a less desirable version of the modern 10-weight. Flylines were catalogued by letters in those days instead of numbers. The line was a GAAF which is about what a 10-weight is today. The late Myron Gregory had not yet sold his system of standardizing flylines with a numbering system. My reel was a Seamaster spooled with 275 yards of 30-pound test Dacron backing and the full flyline. The class tippet on the leader tested less than 12-pounds with a short, 30-pound test abrasion tippet that measured less than 12-inches.

A few tuna still fed aggressively in the slick when Pete suggested that now was the time to try one on fly. The flies I had tied for this undertaking were a combination of polar bear hair and mylar, giving them that shiny appearance in the water that would hopefully attract a tuna. I'm a right-handed caster, yet they gave me the left side of the cockpit, so I had to release each cast on the back-cast. The fly landed among the tuna and I started to strip it in short, sharp jerks. The tuna kept swimming around it, eating dead fry instead of the tempting polar bear and mylar fly.

Frustration began to build. I was convinced that a tuna would grab the fly on the first cast and inhale it. It didn't happen. And, it didn't happen on the next dozen casts. I had come all this way to catch a tuna on fly and the ugly face of failure was staring right at me. My father cast and retrieved flies in chum slicks since the early 1940s and he caught fish. I did, too, under those circumstances, but then I never cast to a tuna before,

Finally, in pure desperation, I asked Terry Gibbons to toss a handful of fry right behind the boat. He did and I cast the fly in the middle of it. Instead of retrieving the fly, I let it drift with the chum. To this day, I can still see that tuna eat the fly going away from the boat and I vividly recall the flyline shooting off the deck the instant I set the hook. Until that moment, I had never read or heard of anybody else dead drifting a fly in a chum slick. Today, it is common practice.

The first run was devastating. That tuna kept going and going as the reel handle spun in reverse and backing disappeared at an alarming rate. The fish wasn't going to stop. We were anchored and no one was about to chase the fish with the boat. This was going to be a dead boat battle and I began to realize I was about to lose the tuna because the reel did not hold enough backing. You could see the gold of the reel spool between the remaining coils of Dacron. It was only seconds before it would end as abruptly as it started.

Not knowing what to do, I smacked the rod butt three or four times with my right hand. The fish stopped with a half-dozen turns of backing still on the reel. The tuna reversed direction and swam toward me. Now, I had to crank all the line back on the flyreel with a one-to-one retrieve.

Just when I thought things were under control, the tuna streaked for the horizon again. I could hear Pete Perinchief with his distinctive accent muttering his famed *Good God Miss Agnes* in the background. Once again, it appeared that I would be spooled, so I started hitting the rod butt again and it worked a second time. The fish stopped, turned around, and started swimming toward me.

As the fortunes of war changed and the result of the battle seemed to shift, the others on board began a discussion of how to handle this fish near the boat if I did in fact manage to land it. While I was in the throes of fighting that fish, my wife, an observer all day, heard them talk about grabbing the flyline, pulling the fish toward the boat, and gaffing it. She knew this was wrong and began to plead with them to talk to me first before they did anything. Fly fishing for big fish was new to them. Finally, she said, "You're going to break the fish off if you touch the leader, please don't do anything until you ask Mark."

They listened to her. I explained to Terry Gibbons that he had to free gaff the fish without touching line or leader. Equally important was how he gaffed the fish. "You want the fish swimming in a circle and moving away from the boat at the instant of gaffing," I explained. "Come up from behind the fish so the gaff does not pass in front of the line. That way, if you miss, the fish does not swim under the boat and break off and the leader does not break against the gaff."

Terry Gibbons gaffed that fish perfectly on his first attempt and threw it on the deck. I never physically touched the fish, allowing Pete and Louis to put it on ice and to weigh it back at the dock. The fish weighed 53 pounds 6 ounces on an officially certified scale and was the first tuna ever taken chumming. Obviously, it was a world record. For a long time, Pete Perinchief and Louis Mowbry erroneously concluded that the fish had to be sick for me to be able to land it. They later realized that the fish was perfectly healthy and that what they had witnessed pushed the frontiers of fly fishing that much further toward the horizon.

That catch is still considered by many to be a significant angling achievement.

Mark Sosin is an award-winning writer, photographer, and television producer. For over 20 years, Mark has been the producer and on-camera host of *Mark Sosin's Saltwater Journal*, broadcast to 50 states and several foreign countries on The Outdoor Channel. He has written more than 3,000 articles for major magazines as well as 28 books on outdoor topics. He is included in the IGFA Fishing Hall of Fame, the Freshwater Fishing Hall of Fame, and the International Fishing Hall of Fame.

The Fishing of Caribou Creek

PAUL SCHULLERY

Ihad a few days in Denali National Park. It's not a place known for its fishing, but that kind of reputation can be a good cover for some interesting water, so I asked around. Several locals—a ranger, a bus driver, a guy I just happened to strike up a conversation with—told me that Caribou Creek was the place to go for grayling. Some said this with the confiding, conspiratorial tone of people who like to think they're on the inside track, but none of them seemed to have fished there recently. I suspected that one or two of them never had; they were cheerful dealers in hearsay. So often, fishing tips offered with the greatest air of generosity and sincerity are the most untrustworthy.

Caribou Creek was a tiny tributary of a larger river. This larger river was one of those uniformly gray glacial types that drain off the north side of the Alaska range. Except for the ones that host salmon runs, rivers like this seem generally thought of as the poorest fish habitat, and the ones in this neighborhood were widely described as fishless. The fine silt looked deadly to any animal as dainty as a grayling.

The milky water of these rivers is deceptive, like liquid fog—opaque enough to make the bottom seem deeper than it is, and therefore oddly entertaining to wade. With the hesitating gait of someone whose feet kept landing an inch or two sooner than expected, I crossed the few braided channels of the river until I reached the mouth of the creek, which emptied into the river from an acute upstream angle. Just where the clear water met the silty, a tiny fish darted from my boots, lost to sight before I could tell if it went upstream into the creek or down into the river. This seemed like a good sign.

From where the creek emerged at the base of a nearby foothill ridge to where it joined the river was less than a mile, and I could see no place where it was more than a dozen feet wide. Clear and cold, it wound through the low tundra of the flat valley bottom unnoticed by almost all the car-tourists who stopped to scan the country for moose, caribou, and grizzly bears. Locals regarded it as worth fishing, but standing there looking up its brushy course, it was easy enough to imagine that no one did.

It was a kind of stream I especially love—origin and destiny all encompassed in one sweep of the eyes, with all the hydrological elements and drama of the largest rivers miniaturized and presented diorama-fashion. Each little meander featured a perfect pool, sometimes broken by a bit of log or rock, modestly over-hung with willow and other brush, the water dark with the promise of depth and life. Even the riffles, bordered with overgrowth and the occasional undercut bank, begged for a few casts. The fish would be smaller than advertised, I was sure, but they had to be there. "Perfect" was the only word I could bring to mind, and it recurred every time I rounded another tiny bend and pitched a small Adams up onto the slick of another pool. The fly would land perfectly, and drift back toward me over the deepest flow line of the current—the *thalweg* of the hydrologists—until I lifted it back and laid it out again, perfectly. I have rarely felt so competent.

It wasn't that the creek made me a better fisherman—I don't do anything perfectly on my own—rather it seemed that no other choice was offered. The casts reached just as far as they should, settled right where they needed to, and floated as enticingly as any I had ever seen, just because of the creek's hospitality to my particular fishing abilities. Nature had put this one together so that I could only get it right, again and again. Nothing else was possible.

Nothing else, however, included the catching of fish. After that little one spooked from my steps at the mouth of the creek, I saw none. I didn't have time to chase the stream all the way back up to the hills, but considering the acces-sibility of the whole area it seemed unlikely that one reach would be more pro-ductive than another.

Out of habit, I tried to mind my lack of success, and was surprised that I was unable to get very worked up about it. Though I generally stay on the aes-thetic high road about these things, I've never been completely successful in convincing myself, as some people apparently have, that "When I go fishing it's enough just to be out there; I don't have to catch anything."

I know all about just being out there. I spend lots of time outside without fishing tackle. I also go fishing to be out there, but taking tackle along generates a different sense of direction, and a different need. When I fish, I like to catch something, and if I can't catch something, I like to know that I came close to catching something. As the bumper sticker says, "I fish, therefore they exist." Even if I land no fish, a couple assertive rises or a powerful strike at a deeply fished nymph will carry me a long way and make the day much more satisfying.

But the fishing of Caribou Creek was different. It brought failure itself to an unexpected kind of perfection. So many flawless casts over so many lovely, fishy spots were an almost exhilarating reward even without the participation of the grayling.

I didn't drift entirely off the deep end into existential abstraction. I wondered which of my time-honored excuses would best fit this failure: Was it too bright a day? Had another fishermen had just worked through the same water? Did I use the wrong fly (a personal favorite excuse)? Had a moose or (more appropriately) a caribou preceded me up the creek, sloshing along and scattering all the grayling?

I was so curious about the lack of fish that I did something I would never do on busier streams in the lower forty-eight. On my way back downstream I waded right through the middle of several pools and riffles, just to see if anyone was home. Nobody was, heightening the mystery. The grayling might just as well have gone to Fairbanks for the weekend.

But when I got back to the main river, I was still so taken with the perfection of the little creek and how well it fit my fishing style that I kept on casting, making sublimely pointless but equally smooth casts for fifty yards down the murky river itself, my small nymph swinging easily through several riffles and eddies just like there was the faintest hope a fish would take it.

I hesitate to suggest that my happy failure at Caribou Creek was a sign that I was advancing in some way as an angler—that I was growing into some more mature and self-possessed form of fisherman. But I have noticed since then that the euphoria I so often feel on a stream seems to come on just a little more readily, or with less obvious reason, than it used to.

These are subtle things, not susceptible to empiricism. I'm not a different person, and I suppose I will always resent getting skunked. But lately when it happens, Caribou Creek is likely to come to mind and I have to admit that failure seems to matter less than it used to.

Paul Schullery is the author, co-author, or editor of three dozen books on nature, conservation, history, and outdoor sport. Among his numerous awards are an honorary doctorate of letters from Montana State University and the Wallace Stegner Award from the University of Colorado Center of the American West.

Still Unravished

ART SCHECK

We would have taken the condo even if its deck hadn't overlooked a little clearing next to a brook. Rentals in town were scarce and we needed to find one. But having a trout stream, however small, 150 feet from the back door took some of the sting out of the rent we'd be paying for a narrow three-floor space with decrepit appliances and ratty carpet. I saw myself lounging on the deck in the evening while trout rose in the pool exposed by the clearing, and then strolling down to the water with a seven-foot fly rod, making one cast that hooked the best of the risers, and returning to the deck before the ice in my drink melted.

Almost a month passed before I set foot in the brook. I was rich in trout water in those days. A short drive in any direction took me over fast, cold flows; my office and the offices of my main client were next to pretty good streams. The brook behind the condo hardly qualified as a novelty. Still, it was there, and like all water that looks like it might hold fish, it wanted exploring.

Toting a fiberglass 4-weight rod, I stepped along the downstream edge of the clearing for the first time on a warm September afternoon. To a tourist looking at it from the condo's creaky deck, the brook might seem an unremarkable little stream resembling hundreds of others that have cut crooked grooves in the New England landscape. But as I knelt in the tall grass next to the tailout, I saw that the pool was deeper than its width implied—not knee deep, or even thigh deep, but at least waist deep.

That the little stream held brook trout didn't surprise me, but the first one still brought the "Aha!" of confirmation that feels as good the thousandth time as it did the first. The little char rose in the middle of the pool to eat my size 14 foam ant, squirting water into the air and turning back toward the bottom in a flash of dark color my eyes barely caught. He pulled against the soft tip of the little glass rod with all seven inches of his strength. I enjoyed his wiggling and tugging for a moment, then stripped in some line and slid my left hand down the leader to pinch the fly stuck in the trout's lip.

Fishermen get all mushy and sentimental over wild brook trout, often lapsing into clichés about the North Woods, campfire smoke, wooden canoes, and A Better Time. We can't blame the fish for the clichés. Nor can we deny the truth of the sentiment, however hackneyed it is. In the East, the brook trout is the fish that belongs, the one that was here before us. To hold one is to hold something very old and right and, in our world, rare.

The fish lay in the current for a few seconds, letting me admire his shape and colors. Then he thrashed, the barbless hook came unstuck, and he was gone.

Another brookie, one a tad shorter than a dollar bill, rose to the ant in the rough water at the head of the pool. As he pulled against the pressure in his mouth, the little trout spooked two others that shot through the tailout and disappeared downstream. I stripped the fish close and reached down to twitch the hook free.

Having established the fact of fish, I felt free to explore. I had no reason to head upstream rather than down, since I knew nothing about the water in either direction. But upstream usually seems the right way on new water. Something in a fisherman wants to face into the current, wants to move toward the source. Each step against the flow feels like a step away from all the things that fishing is better than.

Above the home pool, the stream bounces downhill for forty feet through a narrow, deep chute. Standing waves mark the locations of rocks big enough to resist the force of spring floods. Here, just a few yards above the clearing, dense brush grows all the way to the high-water mark. As I picked my way along the left bank, all I could hear was the voice of the water.

For a hundred feet above the chute, the brook runs over bare ledge, as New Englanders call exposed bedrock. Unable to carve a channel, the stream spread out, nibbling at its banks over the decades and centuries until it created a wide, shallow stretch. Trout have no reason to live in such water. I waded quickly, flicking a few casts to shaded spots and a long fracture in the ledge. A fish came up for the ant in the choppy water between the upstream riffle and the bare ledge, but I missed him.

The stream curved to the right and I followed it into a stretch of pocket water. I waded slowly now, leaning into the current and placing each foot carefully on the uneven bottom. One of the larger pockets held a six-inch brookie that snapped at my floating ant three times before finding the hook.

I stopped to rest next to a pair of big rocks that squeeze the current at the head of the pocket water. Thirty feet upstream, a sharp bend to the left presented a nice challenge. On the outside of the bend, floods have dug a hole in the bottom and cut a hollow in the bank. Trees lean over the deep spot, their lowest branches only a yard above the water. The deep, dark water back under the branches swirls slowly in an eddy. Trout will fight for such a spot, and the biggest one wins it.

But the main current runs down the middle of the bend before angling toward the right-hand bank and picking up speed at the head of the pocket water. No matter where I stood, any cast to the shaded eddy would drop the line on faster water. And since I'd need to make a sidearm cast with a narrow loop to drive a fly under the branches, I probably couldn't throw enough slack to get a good drift longer than a few inches. The current would instantly snatch the line and leader downstream, and the fly would just as instantly drag across the slow water of the eddy. Not even a wild brook trout likes a dragging fly.

Casting gurus usually have a brilliant solution for such a problem, typically a stunt involving an eighteen-foot leader and a complicated, anatomically improbable wrist movement that creates several yards of slack line that hits the water in a perfect upstream curve. My solution is to look for a way to cheat.

The low September water had exposed a band of gravel on the shallow side of the bend. If I crept upstream and hugged the brush, I could get above the eddy and swing a wet fly or small streamer into the deep, shaded hole. It seemed a more promising approach than an upstream cast with a dry fly or nymph, so I started creeping.

The tree lying across the brook came into sight as I reached the short gravel beach. It looked like it had been there for a while: time and weather had stripped the bark from the trunk, and spring floods raging against the underside had eaten a curved, six-inch-high hollow in the wood. The tree also looked like it would be there for another lifetime or so.

Few people in the East have ever seen a tree trunk as thick as a man is tall. A friend discovered a stand of old-growth timber, trees with fifteen-foot circumferences, back in the woods beyond the boundary of her land in Vermont. She likes to hike back there during a gentle snowfall and look at the giants. She says it does her good to stand among things so big and ancient and watch the snow fall while the branches move in the wind high above her.

Several generations ago, someone who had cleared the land along the brook for crops or pasture had spared the great tree. Later, whoever owned the land gave up on farming. The giant fell across a broad riffle, perhaps knocked over by a hurricane or nor'easter, and new, thick woods grew up around it.

On the left bank, the huge trunk rests against a boulder about a yard wide. The low September water raced downstream less than eighteen inches below the eroded trunk. Two big rocks stick up out of the water just downstream of the fallen tree, and the gap beneath the trunk was partly blocked by a few big limbs and an assortment of smaller branches jammed against the rocks and the underside of the immense log.

When it was alive, the tree must have been six feet thick, maybe more. I could not see over the trunk until I climbed the boulder next to the left bank. Standing on tiptoe atop the boulder, I looked over the giant log.

And beheld some men's idea of paradise.

Above the fallen tree, the brook runs straight for perhaps two hundred feet over a mixed bottom of cobble and gravel and rocks. Larger stones poke above the surface, each making a cushion in the current where a trout can hold and wait for food. The water keeps its depth all the way to the banks; I judged that most of it would reach my knees or lower thighs. Alders and underbrush grow to the high-water mark, and some of the bushes hang over the banks. The riffle at the upstream end makes a long eddy along the right-hand bank. Above the riffle, the stream curves and vanishes in the thick second-growth woods.

A trout rose against the bank about fifty feet upstream.

I let my vision drift over the stream's bed, not trying to see anything in particular. My eyes found the shadow of a trout, then the fish itself, then another
shadow and fish, and then a good brookie at least a foot long holding in the
middle thirty feet away. I counted seven trout before relaxing my calves to stand
flat-footed on the boulder.

When was the last time someone fished here? I thought.

A few hundred yards upstream, the brook passes beneath a road. Shortly
after we'd moved into the condo, I'd walked to the bridge to look for fish and
access to the water, and had found only the former. The brook is narrow and
very deep under the bridge and for as far downstream as I could see; the banks
next to the bridge are almost vertical. The jungle begins ten feet from the
bridge. Anyone who wanted to get into the water would have to step off the
bridge abutment and hope for the best. I couldn't imagine anyone doing it.

I watched a parade of ants moving along the giant log. *No one has fished this
water for a long, long time*, I thought. *Maybe never.*

I poked my head above the trunk again. The trout hadn't gone anywhere.
By local standards, a couple of them were bragging size. A hundred feet away, a
fish took an insect from the surface.

The opening of a poem floated up in my mind:

Thou still unravished bride of quietness,
Thou foster-child of silence and slow time. . . .

Such thoughts come of too much reading in youth. John Keats probably
never even caught a trout. That's why he had to write about old crockery and
nightingales.

Still, his lines worked for this place. I'd found something unravished back in
the woods between a busy road and a condo development.

But how to get at the trout?

I slid off the rock and looked beneath the huge log. Taking that route would
require getting in the stream on my hands and knees and crawling over a slippery bottom in at least a foot of very fast water. And I couldn't even make the
attempt until I'd managed to remove the tangle of deadwood jammed beneath
the giant trunk. I might have tried it in my twenties. But not in my forties.

I looked left and then right, but I couldn't see how far the trunk ran into
the jungle on either side of the stream. The wall of alders pressing against each

side of the great log leaned in, their mingled branches blocking my view along the fallen tree. Maybe a rabbit—a scrawny one—could get through the brush and undergrowth. But I couldn't, at least without a chainsaw.

The smooth trunk lacked even a hint of a hand- or foothold. I was stymied.

I climbed onto the boulder and looked at the virgin water for another little while. A few caddisflies were popping up, and every now and then a trout would dart to one side or tilt up in the current to eat one. I was tempted to try a cast from the boulder. But even if I kept the line out of the branches hanging over the stream behind me and avoided spooking the fish and somehow made a good presentation from that awkward angle, what would I do if I hooked a trout? Drag it hand-over-hand up the far side of the trunk?

I stood on the boulder until my calves had cramps and my ankles ached.

On my way back downstream, I swung a small Muddler into the eddy on the outside of the bend and caught a fat, foot-long brook trout. As I sloshed homeward, I thought about the fallen tree and the promise it guarded.

Eight days later I was atop the boulder again, standing on tiptoe and watching the trout. This time I spotted a shape that I thought had to be a brown trout because New England brookies rarely grow much over a foot long. Then the fish moved and I saw his colors and my breathing stopped for a few seconds.

In mid-October I went back without fishing vest or fly rod, just to study the lay of the land. Hard rains had raised the water, and the gap beneath the trunk had shrunk to barely a foot. I tried to force my way into the jungle, twisting my body and trying to squeeze between the little trees that grew as close together as bamboo, but gave up after a few minutes and went home to attend to the scratches on my face.

I had plenty of good water in those days, so I wasn't desperate or obsessed. But the angling mind follows its own wandering channel, and mine began to hatch crazy ideas after trout season ended.

A ladder. A short, light ladder. A seven-foot aluminum job should do it. I could use it to ascend the downstream side of the trunk, and then lift it over the tree and descend on the upstream side.

Right. That maneuver ought to spook every fish in the brook—particularly when the ladder slipped on the algae-covered bottom and dumped me into the stream. With my luck, I'd fall and break something on the upstream side of the log.

Steps. Why not add steps to the log? I could make cleats out of a 4-by-4, drilling holes in them at home and then affixing them to the log with the longest spikes that the hardware store sold. As an extra safety measure, I could spike a length of knotted rope to the log so that I'd have something to hold.

I contemplated this solution for quite a while over the winter. The risk of breaking bones or drowning remained, but it seemed reduced to a reasonable level. I had done stupider things to reach fish.

Ah! What if I borrowed or rented a chainsaw, cut my way into the jungle for six or eight feet, and spiked my wooden steps to the log where it rested on safe, solid ground? If I fell while climbing or descending, at least I wouldn't land on rocks or in water; I'd merely be impaled on dozens of narrow stumps.

But fastening cleats to the log would give access to anyone who came along. This I was unwilling to do.

Perhaps a ladder was best. I could cut a short path into the jungle on each side of the big log, and tote a lightweight ladder whenever I wanted to fish my virgin water. I'd just have to make sure that no one saw me sneaking upstream with a fly rod and seven-foot ladder.

I had all winter to think about the trout that lived above the log, and eventually I figured out what to do. Spring brought pleasant weather, just the right amount of water, and good fishing on all the local streams. I didn't visit my fallen tree until an evening in early June. I stood on tiptoe on the boulder half an hour before sunset and waited.

The mayfly spinners came out of the brush and began their aerial mating dance as the light began to fade. They swarmed over the brook, fluttering up and dropping down, males and females finding each other and coupling in midair, until the females, the tips of their abdomens swollen with yellowish orange egg clusters, began to ride the water while the spent males, their brief purpose fulfilled, fell to the stream.

Brook trout, dozens of them, rose in the water above the giant old log to eat the mayflies drifting with the current. I stood on the boulder, my calves trembling with the strain, mayflies landing on my hat and beard, and watched my trout rise and feed, rise and feed, until I could barely see the surface of the water. Even then, I could hear my trout rising and eating in the darkness upstream.

The best thing to do about those fish, I'd decided, was to leave them and their home unravished. I watched them until I'd seen enough and the stream had become just a crooked streak of pale silver lit by the moon, and then blundered back downstream and toward home, lighting my way with a little flashlight.

No doubt I could have figured out a way over or around the tree. I'm a resourceful guy. And maybe—no, probably—I'd have caught some very good brook trout. But now, a thousand miles and a decade away from that brook and its secrets, I'm glad to have left the challenge unmet. It does me good to close my eyes and see those fish rising in the dusk.

Art Scheck has written more than 100 articles and 4 books on angling and fly tying; his books include *Fly-Fish Better* and *Tying Better Flies*. A former editor of several angling publications, Art is currently an instructor of writing and literature at Tri-County Technical College in South Carolina.

He reflects, "The best fishing, like the best reading, is private and quiet and unhurried, so that the person doing it has time to enjoy the act itself while also absorbing impressions upon which he can reflect for years."

The Novitiate's Tale

Excerpt from
The Night Gardener

MARJORIE SANDOR

At the south end of Darby, Montana, right before the speed limit goes up and the Bitterroot River comes back into view, there's a Sinclair station with a marquee that looms like wish fulfillment. All in capital letters, like the message DRINK ME on the little bottle Alice finds, this marquee reads: DIESEL, UNLEADED, FLIES.

What is it about the prospect of trout fishing that turns the novitiate's simplest act—that of buying a couple of flies or a new leader—into a quest, a rite of passage? There was a long riffle just upstream from Darby that looked magical to me—it had to be full of rainbows—and waiting for the time to get there, I hungered for it as unrequitedly as I do for certain film stars and countries I'll never get to: secretly, with idiotic surges of adolescent chills and fever.

Practically speaking, I needed a leader. I strode to the screen door of the Sinclair station, heavily booted like any hero, but faintly aware of my relatively small size and deep ignorance. The whole business seemed a dazzling path to certain failure: wrong fly, too hot a day, too cold, wrong spot, wrong way to fish the right spot—infinite and thrilling were the ways.

In a small room beyond Wheat Thins and Jim's World-Famous Jerky, a man waited behind a glass case of flies, reading the newspaper with the tricky nonchalance of all guardians of the dreamworld. A few packets of hooks and spools of fishing line hung on a pegboard. The whole thing looked preposterously spare and antimysterious, like a false front.

The man smiled when I asked for a tapered leader. "Just startin' out, are we?" he said. "You don't need it. You'll do fine with plain old monofilament." And he brought down a spool of what looked to me like purple sewing thread.

"I'd really prefer tapered leader," I said, in the hushed, careful voice of someone asking for groceries in a foreign country. He, in his turn, waved his hand casually in the air, as if my remark were utterly irrelevant.

As I took the monofilament and two locally tied nymphs, he followed me out and told me not to go to that dumb fishing access point—the place'd be crawling with tourists. He drew a spidery, complicated map of a secret hole no out-of-towners know about, which I could only get to by trespassing on a local rancher's property. "He doesn't mind," he said, and tipped his hat. As he followed me to the screen door he added, with a dreamy air, "You'll learn the hard way on that monofilament. Believe me; when you get back to tapered leader, it'll seem like a breeze."

Suffice it to say that though I fished the wrong spot all day, with the wrong line and the wrong fly, the Bitterroot itself, with its willow-shaded margins and islands, its riffles and runs and promising boulders all just out of reach, made failure seem both a reasonable and sublime occupation: ambition, particularly, is a sin against the abiding rush of a river. But I'll confess, I wasn't even in the water when I thought this; I was still standing in the high grass before barbed wire, preparing to crawl between its thorny knots, thinking this was no ordinary fence but the door into the unknown world in all good stories, where spiritual journeys always start. Even the little scratch, the bit of blood on my arm, seemed right and necessary.

This feeling carried me straight through to the next day, north on the Bitterroot highway into Missoula, where, in a slightly clearer but no less literary frame of mind, I found a bona fide fly shop. Of course Missoula has at least a half dozen, all thriving, but this one had a proprietor who, through the big plate windows, bore a striking resemblance to a dear old friend of our family's, Uncle Maury, who in his lifetime had loved fishing and literature with equal passion. He'd point a finger straight up, as if testing the wind, and quote somebody dead—for instance, Jean Cocteau: "The greatest beauty," he'd say, "is the beauty of failure." This made my parents nervous: it was un-American to embrace failure. But he gave me my first great books, among them *Moby-Dick* and Turgenev's *Sketches from a Hunter's Notebook*.

I looked at this owner innocently eating his corned beef sandwich and saw destiny in the coincidence of his familiar bald spot, his heavy glasses, his capable, square-fingered hands. No one else was in the shop for the moment, and when he saw me, he beckoned me in and spoke in a voice as miraculously gruff and East Coast as my old mentor, and took me around to all the cases, shaking his head grimly at my plain old monofilament and box of tattered wet flies while I privately misted over with nostalgia. In real life, I was apparently staring at some little hooks tied with red and gold thread, and he waved his hand disparagingly. "Sure," he said. "That's the San Juan Worm, and it works just fine, but as a beginner, what you really want is a dry fly, so you can see the trout come up for it. That's what'll knock you out."

So I bought from him a half dozen dries, a tapered leader, and some 6X tippet, all the time feeling a kind of warmth spreading in me, a great access of trust, of *home*. He threw in an extra Parachute Adams and a map of Rock Creek with his own favorite spots circled here and there. "Don't fool around up there," he said sternly. "Just stop at the first access point you find." Now, I thought, *now* I'm on track. But as I left the counter, I saw him turn with great comic enthusiasm to two young men who had just entered the shop. To him, I was no hero at all, just one more dazed novice with shaking hands and weak terminology. God only knew what he was telling them now.

Back in the car, I fought the urge to go home, to give up the quest for now. But in my hand I held the map of the next mystery: a world-class fishery I'd never seen. I had the right leader, the right flies, and only twenty-six miles to go. I followed my guide's directions unswervingly. I stopped at the first access point and read the water; I even got my leader a tiny way out. No hits, but it was enough just to know I had tapered leader now, and after a few hours, I was sweetly exhausted by my little progress. The day passed beautifully, uneventfully, in that narrow canyon of building clouds and slate-colored water, a cool wind coming down the valley as the summer took its own first, minute turn toward fall. I'd been there to see it go, and this felt like enough adventure for one day.

It was then, in the cool of late afternoon, in a dark little glade into which leaves dropped with a living patter, that I sat down on my tailgate and set my keys beside me where I could not possibly forget them. I had begun to eat my Wheat Thins when I heard a thrashing in the woods behind me. Into view came a short heavyset man with a red beard, an invader lumbering toward me with spinning rod and cooler. Behind him trailed an ancient, bent woman in giant rubber boots, a long wool shirt, and a kerchief around her head—a dream-babushka straight out of Turgenev's *Sketches*. She had the look of the old crone in fairy tales, the one who delivers the crucial if cryptic message, or opens the right gate, hitherto unnoticed. But no. The babushka retreated into the forest, and the man lumbered closer. I was pulling off my hip boots when he began to speak in a garbled voice, with an accent deeper than Deep South. He wanted to know how I'd done, what I was using.

"Parachute Adams," I said. He smirked and sprang the latch on his cooler, where a twenty-inch brown trout lay cramped and faded against the dirty white. He addressed me again in that ferocious accent.

"Juh bring yer bait?" he asked.

"Illegal here," I said coolly.

"It's just un expression," he replied, rolling his eyes a little. "I mean yer bait box with yer Muddler Minners and yer big Woolly Buggers. They're only eatin' the big stuff now, and they're hidin' in the troughs. Din't juh notice the eagles?"

I looked politely into the sky, took another Wheat Thin. He rocked on his heels and snapped the cooler shut with a little violence. He was, I suspect, a man who did not like mysteries, particularly.

"Yer fixin' ta leave yer keys," he said, pointing down at my bumper.

I tried to make the best of it, tried to convert this bleak moment as quickly as possible into story. This would be the nadir, this the dragon and the darkest moment of the heroic cycle. But I couldn't; I was depressed as hell. Something about the fading light, the dead fish in the cooler, the reminder, smack in the middle of a lyrical analysis, of the ugly side of failure: the trout lying trapped and flatly dead between his condescending teachings and my stubborn ignorance. It was too dark to go back out into the river again, and he stood there, quite clearly waiting to see me leave, as if he'd been sent to take up the last available light. The river was aloof now, cool and secretive, no risers, not a ripple in the troughs, the eagles gone up to their roosts.

"Well, I better get goin'," he said. "Don't forget them keys."

I waited there until I could no longer hear his boots crushing the brittle leaves, until I could no longer see his white cooler, that awful beacon, floating backward through the darkening woods. When it was quiet, I got back in the car and headed out Rock Creek Road, back toward Missoula. But I couldn't believe the story was over, so bleakly, hopelessly, finished. I was starved for a better ending. And lo, as if in answer, there rose up before me the Rock Creek Fly Shop, which, in my haste to get streamside, I'd missed on the way in. At the very least, I told myself, just use the bathroom, grab a soda, ask what these guys would have used.

I stumbled in, Eve expelled from the river for not knowing that the trout were lying in the troughs because of eagles, and eatin' only Muddler Minners. I nodded at the man behind the counter and tried to look like I knew my way around, but

"Lady," he said. "If it had teeth it would jump up and bite."

"Just tell me where it is," I said tensely.

He pointed behind me.

When I came out of the rest room, he smiled. "You look tired," he said. "What were you using—I hear they're pulling in the big browns like nobody's business!" I shook my head and he slapped his hands on the counter. "You were using what?" he said. "What joker told you to use a dry on a day like this?" He paused dramatically, hand on the phone, ready to dial 911. "It's only big stuff now, they're only eatin' big stuff." Again, the sad shake of the head, the unspoken message that if I'd only asked him first instead of the Guys in Town, I'd be rich with fish—hell, Missoula's twenty-six miles away, what do they know?

It occurred to me that I should stop taking advice for a while, that all advice was suspect, hopelessly rooted in some deep and complicated tangle of pride and secret regret that rose up to meet the susceptible customer with her own deep and complicated tangle of pride and secret regret.

But the proprietor had stopped talking, and was looking at me as if I'd asked him a deep theological question. "Wait a minute," he said. "Come with me." He beckoned me away from the counter and the cases of flies, around a corner to another room entirely—one I would never have guessed was there. In this room a potbellied woodstove hissed and crackled. A family was seated around the stove: two brothers in red flannel shirts and jeans were cleaning their guns; a young woman, with cheeks flushed from the heat of the stove, was knitting; a baby, also red-faced, with its knitted cap fallen low over one eye, lay regal and stunned in its swaddling.

The proprietor seated himself at a round table piled high with yarn, feathers, fur, and thread. "Here we go," he said. He wound red chenille around the shank of a hook and burned both ends with a match. "I call it the Poor Man's San Juan Worm," he said. "It has no class, but when all else fails—"

I didn't leave right away. I held myself still, welcomed, if not into the life of the river, then a step closer to it. It was like falling into a fine old painting of peasant life, where there's sunlight drifting down from some window you can't see. The dog sleeps, the hunters pause over their guns, the baby lies amazed under the golden light. We are at the beginning again, with Rock Creek just outside, moving swiftly through its canyon as the dark comes on in earnest. Cocteau would approve, and so would Uncle Maury: by failing to catch trout, look at the gift you've been granted.

Never mind that on my next visit to Missoula, the owner of the fly shop there would look at my San Juan Worm and say accusingly, "Where the hell did you get this? It's all wrong. Who made it?" My host at Rock Creek must have known this would happen, because as he handed me the finished fly, he smiled the brief, cramped smile of the failed artist, the wise teacher.

"Just a little present," he said. "Since you tried so hard. Just promise me you won't tell the guys in Missoula who made it. They'd have my head."

Marjorie Sandor is the author of three books, most recently the linked short story collection *Portrait of My Mother, Who Posed Nude in Wartime* (Sarabande Books, 2003), for which she won the 2004 National Jewish Book Award in Fiction. Her essay collection *The Night Gardener* (October 1999, The Lyons Press) won an Oregon Book Award in Creative Nonfiction in 2000. Her essays and stories have appeared in such publications as *The New York Times Magazine, The Georgia Review,* and *The Southern Review,* and have been anthologized in *The Best American Short Stories 1985* and *1988, Best of Beacon 1999, The Pushcart Prize XIII,* and elsewhere. In 1998 she received a Rona Jaffe Foundation Award for fiction. She lives in Corvallis, Oregon, and teaches fiction writing and literature at Oregon State University.

Excerpt from *An Even-Tempered Angler*

LOUIS RUBIN JR.

The real test of which kind of fishing one prefers above all other forms is probably that of the association of ideas. When you hear the word "fishing," what image comes into your mind? Doubtless for the trout or salmon fisherman the picture that "fishing" conveys involves standing, feet braced against the current, in a stream of cold rushing water, up to one's waist and with the water swirling outside one's waders, while expertly dropping a dry fly across fifty feet of water so that it settles without a ripple upon the surface where a trout has been feeding.

For the black-bass fisherman, the image that is summoned by the word "fishing" must be the exploding force of a huge largemouth—a lunker or hawg, the B.A.S.S. Masters call it—as it breaks the surface of the lake to grab a plug tossed skillfully to within a foot of the bank, and the tautness of the monofilament as the rod is lifted to halt it.

The offshore fisherman, moving along the edge of the Gulf Stream in a powerful boat and taking the light swells easily, must surely dream of the leap, high above the spray, of the billfish while the fisherman strains to hold the bending rod in its socket. For the inshore fisherman trolling for kings and big blues, there is the moment when the rod bends in a wide bow, the click mechanism on the reel rasps and the drag hisses as the line is stripped from the reel, followed by the rush to pick up the rod and to feel, transmitted along its length, the plunging weight of a big fish.

For myself, however much I enjoy those kinds of fishing, and however much I crave going after flounder with live shrimp in the tidal creeks of the coastal salt marsh that I have watched and loved watching since my boyhood, the word "fishing," uttered abruptly and without particular context, means something else.

It is the month of August, in Gloucester County, Virginia. I am anchored in a motorboat in twenty feet of water, inshore from the red nun buoy opposite the Naval Weapons Station just upstream from Yorktown on the York River. An hour earlier the buoy was slanted upstream from the force of the incoming tide; now it floats upright. I have caught a half-dozen good gray trout, and I am waiting for another, but there has been a hiatus in the fishing. I know that other fish will come along presently and am content to wait.

Everything is still. The gulls are at rest. They are perched on the stakes of an old fish trap in toward shore. The grass of the tidal marsh, the foliage of the trees on the shoreline beyond them, a quarter mile away, are in full green. Yet there seems in that greenness shading that is too fulfilled for the green growth of the spring and earlier summer, a ripening beyond the point of greatest strength and beginning to shade into decline.

There is the sound of a boat, a gasoline engine over across the way. A white boat, low and slender, is easing downstream—a crab boat heading home after working upriver. So far away on the water is it that it seems to have no wake, no waves, sliding across the water as if in a tableau. The sky overhead is remote and endless, a blue canopy with indifferent clouds.

A breeze picks up, lightly patterns the surface of the river into lines and shapes. The slight waves come slapping against the sides of the boat, making a low, hollow tapping sound. A gull lifts itself from its fellows and swings off in a wide arc; its white wings propel it across the river toward the shore. Its sharp cry interrupts the silence as it trails off, disappears. There is crying among the remaining gulls, but not one rises to follow.

The calling subsides, the gulls sit quietly and wait. The breeze falls off. The surface of the water is still. The crab boat is so far away that its engine makes no sound at all. All things are at rest.

It cannot last. It must not. The tide must change, the wind pick up, to blow away the stillness, the gulls rise to their scavenging, the world get on with its affairs. Soon we will be leaving for home, and the green of the marsh and trees will turn yellow as the summer sun recedes and autumn comes.

Not once does the season stop, for all that it seems now to suspend itself. It was passing by all the time, and what seems at rest is only the momentary consciousness of its movement on its regular, methodical course. As surely as the gull rises into the air and swerves away, the tide is flowing and the earth tilting away from the sun.

Yet they seem to have stopped this day, as if the summer, and the season, and the sun were like a steel ball rolling up an incline, propelled by its own momentum, further and further—until the force of inertia moves to equalize the momentum, and asserts itself, and prevails.

For a moment, before the downward plummet, at the very top of the ultimate forward ascent, the one force is countered by the other, and summer seems, here on the river, to have stopped in midflight.

It is then, just then, that another fish bites.

Louis Rubin Jr., a native of Charleston, South Carolina, has been principally a teacher, editor, and literary critic, but among his writings are books, articles, and essays on boats, trains, baseball, journalism, and fishing, including *The Even-Tempered Angler.* He lives near Chapel Hill, North Carolina.

Getting Hooked

ROY ROWAN

*"Man is a rope stretched between the animal
and the Superman—a rope over an abyss."*
Friedrich Wilhelm Nietzsche (1844–1900)
Thus Spake Zarathustra

Anyone who has never battled a bull striper all alone on a beach may not understand the closeness it's possible to feel to a fish. The instinctual strand that can bind a human and an animal doesn't stem simply from the striper's enormous size. Or even from the fierceness of the fight coming from the other end of the line. The connection is more obscure, born out of respect for a creature that has eluded net, spear, and hook for fifteen or even twenty years.

After the initial electrifying jolt—a strike so hard and unexpected the rod almost flies from your hands—comes a primordial message from your quarry, as clear and challenging as any emanating from a human mouth. Only this message is passed through the pulsating monofilament line, into your two hands, up through your arms and neck and directly into your brain. Its meaning, nevertheless, is brutally clear.

"You and I, Mr. Fisherman, though temporarily tied together, are engaged in a deadly duel of endurance that only one of us can win." Right away you're aware of the striper's vast capacity for courage and determined will to live, the same powers that propel people through a long and successful life.

The strange sensation of closeness felt with this fish is amplified by the fact that no other human is there to intrude on the battle. No fellow fisherman around to shout advice or encouragement. No beach walker strolling idly by to stop and watch if you win or lose. And most important of all, no tenderhearted preservationist present to suggest releasing your prize, if it's ever yours to let go.

As the big bass strips off line, swimming furiously to break free and spit out the unchewable plastic minnow hooked in its mouth, a single thought seizes your mind: "Can I stop this fish's surge before it snaps my line?" Carefully you tighten the drag, listening apprehensively for the staccato *pop* that would signal victory for the fish.

Your eyes are riveted on the spot in the flat sea out beyond the surf where the taut line slants down into the water. The surface around the line suddenly bulges, then erupts in a shower of spray. Striped bass don't usually jump. But for a few seconds this one hangs acrobatically in the air before splashing back into the water. You wonder if you and the fish are still connected—whether you're both still linked, physically and yes, mentally.

The answer comes quickly. An angry yank almost rips the rod from your grasp. You can feel the fish's rage. It, too, probably thought for those few instants while flying through the air that it was free.

At least you've glimpsed your prize—wide black stripes imprinted on a field of shiny silver scales. Old Linesides, as the species is nicknamed. The leap, however, seems to have strengthened the bass's resolve. The rod butt is now digging painfully into your groin, your left hand cramped from cranking the reel without gaining line.

You shout tauntingly at the fish, "By God I've got you! You're mine, you sonofabitch!"

No reason to swear at this noble beast just because he's showing the same strength and fortitude we admire in our own. But the curse words pop out.

Once again the bass is zigging and zagging wildly through the water, still very much in control of the fight. It's the wide caudal fin, rooted in a muscular tail, that enables it to change direction and accelerate so rapidly.

Few other fish are capable of making lunges, leaps, runs like this. But then the inshore turbulence that most big fish avoid is where stripers are at home. It's their playground as well as their feeding ground. If you watch closely, sometimes you can actually see stripers frolicking in the rips and tides, and racing through the arcs of breaking waves. They may lack the sustained swiftness of sharks, tuna, and other open-ocean predators, but their bodies are flexible, built for maneu-verability and the short bursts of speed needed when searching out a meal close to shore.

Without warning the line goes slack and you're now sure that you've lost your prize. "Crank fast," you say. Dripping monofilament piles up on the reel until a heavy tug tells you your fish is still there.

"Move back. Take a few steps up onto the beach," you tell yourself. "Try to turn this big boy around before he empties your reel." But the fish stubbornly refuses to turn. The reel sings and all your regained line is gone.

It's not exactly sympathy for the fish, but there comes a moment of hesita-tion in the battle when you momentarily wonder if this gallant fighter doesn't deserve its freedom. Its extraordinary strength and valor have already given you a year's surfcasting excitement even though the close connection with it has only existed for a matter of minutes. It's the quest, not the kill, that's the real reward in seeking to outwit a wild animal. Foxhunters thrill to the chase, not to shooting sly old Reynard once he's cornered.

These thoughts evaporate quickly. The taste of firm, mouthwatering fillets, grilled to perfection over a charcoal fire, replaces any generous, life-sparing feel-ings. Especially when you spot a dorsal fin slicing through the water like a knife, a signal that the big fish may finally be weakening and ready to surrender.

The trick now is to nudge it into a wave and let the force of the water wash the heavy body ashore. But it's still too game to come willingly. Instead, it bursts out of the water again, standing on its tail and shaking its head, resisting surrender.

Noticeably, though, strength is seeping from its body. Its zigs and zags are slower. And you can tell from the weaker pull on the line that it's probably too drained for another run or dive. But bass, like humans, can still generate an extraordinary exuberance when their lives are threatened.

Suddenly its surface thrashes pose other problems. Will the plug be ripped from its mouth? Will its sharp fins or tail slice the line? Even in its weakened state, you know that the odds favor the fish.

Just when you're wondering how to bring it in a heavy roller engulfs your prize and it disappears in the boiling surf, only to reemerge tumbling toward you in the shallows a few feet from shore.

Lying on its side, exhausted, the bass is even larger than you thought. Its head is huge, the size of a dog's. The green-spotted plug that it mistook for a mackerel protrudes from its mouth like a fat cigar. You wade out into the water and slip your hand under a gasping gill and drag the spent fish up onto the beach. The fight is finally won and the big striper is yours. But do you really want to destroy this magnificent creature?

At this moment it's impossible not to think of the frailty of life, and how it can be snatched away by a whim of weather, disease, or even by diabolical human nature. Holding life-or-death power over another creature is an enormous responsibility, especially when that creature is lying helpless at your feet awaiting your decision.

Fortunately for stripers big and small, it's a decision surfcasters don't often have to make. As one outdoor writer aptly put it, "The beauty of this form of angling is that it's possible to go for long periods of time without catching a fish." Or as another surfcasting aficionado admitted, "I go to fish. Not to catch fish." For me the joy of just being alone, surrounded by nature and immersed in my own thoughts, is the real reward of surfcasting. My deepest moments of understanding come unexpectedly when I'm communing with the sea, my mind dwelling on life's many mysteries.

For this reason angling enthusiasts from the days of Izaak Walton have claimed that fishing is not simply a sport, but a religion. If this is so then surfcasting, with its own devout followers, should be recognized as an important sect.

Our morning devotions begin at daybreak in the great high-domed cathedral where the fading stars and ghostly glow of last night's moon are the candles soon to be extinguished. But before the sun's fireball rises out of the sea and sets everything ablaze, we surfcasters breathe in the new day's coolness and contemplate the good fortune that has brought us to the ocean's edge.

It is only after such a moment of reverence that our ritual begins. Almost mindlessly we check the grip of our waders on the slippery stones underfoot, open the wire bail of the spinning reel, whip the long fiberglass rod forward, and send a shiny lure affixed to the free-spooling monofilament flying off to kiss a wave.

Barely has the lure hit the water than in our mind's eye we can see the silvery flash and flying spray of a striper or blue striking the plug. It's the excitement of a strike that keeps us repeating cast after cast, although deep in our subconscious we know almost every wave is empty—devoid of fish, or at best containing one that has already feasted on so many menhaden or sand eels, its appetite is sated.

That's why the high priests of our sect who have written such how-to tomes on surfcasting as *The Salt-Water Fishman's Bible* preach infinite patience. They realize there are many more productive ways of fishing.

Trolling or jigging from a boat begets more blues, bass, and bonito—even an occasional weakfish, as the beautiful speckled sea trout are called in the Northeast. Bottom fishing off a dock or jetty can yield a mess of blacks, fluke, or flounder.

But then surfcasters are not usually out there foraging for food. Most of us are more meditative than we are meat fishermen.★ We are made happy by the mere motion that sends our plug arcing through the air, and by watching expectantly as it skips back over the wave tops.

"Hit!" we murmur. "Hit!" This little word is our mind-numbing mantra. It doesn't matter that almost every cast is fruitless, completed without a hit.

Skunked is one of the most common words in the surfcaster's vocabulary. Only in recent years have I discovered that the solitude that goes with being skunked is catching—though in a different way than the catching of fish. No telling what deeply suppressed thoughts or secrets of nature will tug at my mind on those days when I'm swinging that rod back and forth without a strike.

Waves, especially, stir my imagination. On windy days with the sea slapping hard against my waders I sometimes wonder where they came from. Did they originate on the shore of some far-off continent thousands of miles of ocean away from where I'm casting? The idea of the kinetic energy in a wave traveling so far before it is dissipated by hitting my body conjures up unsettling thoughts of a personal connection with the universe that is always mystifying.

★My use of the term fishermen, rather than fisherpersons, is intended to include both male and female anglers.

Clouds, too, catch my attention, but in a more reassuring way. With fish on the brain it's not surprising that so many clouds take on a piscine appearance. Sometimes it's a mackerel sky, resembling the mottled back of that species, which strikes me as a sign of good luck. More propitious are the long, strung-out cumulus formations in which I can distinctly make out the broad tail, eyes, nose, and underslung jaw of the striper I'm hoping to catch. Instinctively I sense that these cloud-stripers swimming across the sky are a good omen, indicating the imminence of a strike.

Surfcasting can induce a kind of coma, erasing all thoughts about nature—and everything else for that matter—while keeping the brain in neutral. In this blank state of mind, if some simple physical diversion is required, I'll engage in a little contest with myself by trying to cast farther and farther out to sea.

We surfcasters assume that as in life, the big fish are just beyond our reach, which usually is not the case. Bass, in fact, cruise so close to shore they often resist lunging at a lure until the final few yards of a retrieve. And even if they all spurn my plug, sensing it's indeed a fake fish, this doesn't stop me from going out again the next day.

Of course the thrill of marching home with a fat bluefish or gorgeous striper in hand is not to be lightly dismissed. The hunter's triumphant return is a familiar scene in history, recorded all the way back in the earliest cave paintings. But for me bringing home a fish is simply a bonus. The solitude of surfcasting is my main enjoyment—to be savored like a fine wine or a fragrant flower.

Roy Rowan was a foreign correspondent, writer, and editor for *Time*, *Life*, and *Fortune* for thirty-five years. He is the author of eight books including the critically acclaimed *Chasing the Dragon*, a memoir about Mao's revolution that has been optioned by Hollywood, and *First Dogs*, which was made into a documentary and aired on the Discovery Channel. His latest book, published in 2006, is *Throwing Bullets: A Tale of Two Pitchers Chasing the Dream*.

A Single Step

GEORGE REIGER

Once, while poking along the recently flood-ravaged banks of Rock Creek in the District of Columbia, I came across two men and a boy fishing by the dam below Oakhill Cemetery. When I asked the age-old question, "How's fishing?" their replies were sufficiently evasive to encourage me to linger.

Sure enough, first the boy, then one of the men, got bites. They flicked their rod tips as nonchalantly as possible, but the resulting liveliness of their lines made further subterfuge futile. Each landed a channel catfish of about a pound and a half. When I asked whether they'd caught others, pride overcame discretion, and each angler hoisted a stringer of channel cats, bullheads, and sunfishes.

Meanwhile, not many yards away, car-imprisoned commuters crawled by, unaware of our presence, eyes fixed on the bumpers and tail-lights of the vehicles ahead of them. If and when Washington commuters go fishing, most drive to the trout streams of western Maryland and Pennsylvania; or down to the salty waters bracketing the Delmarva peninsula. Although many of their children become fishermen in their own right, who's to say they're more worthy anglers than those who learn their craft by the less than pristine waters of Rock Creek?

Non-anglers assume that fishing is entirely about catching fish. Catching is important, of course. It's all that matters to beginners, and if veteran anglers didn't at least occasionally find their quarry in a feeding mood, they'd take up some related pastime, like the study of plasma physics. But veterans also know that as we grow older, fishing becomes as much about ritual and memory as putting new notches on the reel.

Many non-anglers, especially those who've come of age in the past quarter-century, think fishing is a spectator sport dominated by tournaments and dependant on high-tech equipment. Yet even competition fishermen know that angling means participation, not voyeurism, and that the most successful anglers have knowledge and special skills superceding gadgetry. Ultimately, each and every fishing trip begins with the individual making a single step from the shore into the water, or from the dock onto a boat, where he or she hopes and expects the anxieties of ordinary life to seep away on the current and tides, allowing him or her to become someone better.

Herbert Hoover observed that all men are equal before fish, and surely the boy with a menial summer job, casting into the dawn, believes that something wonderful is about to happen; the woman whose reality has not quite matched the bright expectations of college is renewed by the sight of birds far out over the waves; and for the troubled man, each moment of fishing dilutes his old sins and fresh suffering.

Philip Wylie once wrote that all anglers are philosophers, not because of our alleged patience—the usual explanation—but because we understand, even as children, that angling is lifelong recreation. Whitewater kayaking and mountaineering are sports for youth alone. Time may alter the kind or quantity of angling we do, but it never ends our opportunity. The old man casting over a darkening pool and the white-haired lady watching her sand-spiked rod nod to the surf are only variations on the little boy who once chased suckers in the shallows or the little girl who collected shells along the beach. The ghosts of who we were commune over increasing seasons with whom we are today. We're humbled by this, and some are even made wiser by the eternal nature of the fact that angling—like every epic journey—begins with but a single step.

George Reiger is Conservation Editor of *SaltWater Sportsman* and Conservation Editor Emeritus of *Field & Stream*. These reflections are adapted from an article he wrote for the May 12, 1974, issue of *Potomac*, the Sunday magazine of the *Washington Post*. His books include *Profiles in Saltwater Angling*, *Fishing with McClane*, *The Bonefish*, *The Silver King*, *The Striped Bass Chronicles*, and *Wanderer on My Native Shore*. He lives betwixt the Chesapeake and the Atlantic on the Eastern Shore of Virginia.

Like Father, Like Son

STEVE RAYMOND

Something magical happens the first time a father puts a fishing rod in his son's hands and leads him to trout water. It happened to me when I was five years old, going on six, and now I have seen it happen to my own son at the same age.

I hope he remembers it as well as I remember that first trip with my own father. It was a spring morning and the air had never been so clear. We followed a dirt road toward far mountains that stood out so vividly it seemed as if the horizon had been ripped along its edge. The road wound through pastures where white-faced Herefords grazed behind split-rail fences, then climbed into aspen groves and pine thickets where the ground still was wet with dew.

We came to a bridge over a small stream and my father stopped the car. The bridge was just a pair of heavy planks and the stream was hardly a stream; I could jump across it easily on my short, five-year-old legs. But it was filled with trout, which was the reason why my father had stopped.

The trout had run up from a nearby lake and now they were spawning. Some of them were longer than the stream was wide and it was difficult for them to maneuver in the close quarters between the banks. But they went about their business purposefully, the females probing the gravel with their tails to prepare their nests while the males slashed and fought for the privilege of pairing with them. It was a fascinating sight, unlike anything I'd ever seen, and it prompted a feeling of awe and respect for trout that is with me still.

Later we drove on to Big Bar Lake, our destination, and spent the night in a log cabin on the shore. The next morning there was bright frost on the meadows and a thin layer of ice around the margins of the lake. Fire crackled in an old wood stove in the cabin and the sweet smell of alder smoke soon mingled with the odor of frying bacon. Breakfast was a hurried affair and then we rushed down to a leaning dock where a rowboat was waiting. My father took the oars and pushed off onto the still surface of the lake. When we were out far enough he took a fly rod, worked out the line, then placed the rod in my hand. "Hold tight, son, or the fish will take it from you," he warned.

We rowed slowly across the lake, and I held tightly to the handle of the long bamboo rod, trailing the sinking line behind the boat. The line slanted gently away into the depths and I wondered what was going on down there, and whether any trout could see the bright fly at the tip of the leader.

Soon enough one did, and the rod suddenly came alive in my little hand, throbbing with a strong, electric pull. Instinctively I thrust it back at my father, who took it and played the fish to the side of the boat. It was a foot-long trout, all bright and gleaming silver and quite unlike the dark and ruddy fish I had seen spawning in the stream. And it was a small matter that my father had landed it; I had hooked it, so it was "my" fish, and I proudly proclaimed it so while Dad grinned from ear to ear.

My father and I fished together many times thereafter, but never quite as often as we would have liked. He was an Army officer, a career that left few opportunities for fishing, so the opportunities took on added importance when they came. Always there were elaborate preparations—food to be bought, sleeping bags and bedding to be aired and packed, fresh flies and leaders to be purchased, maps to be studied, plans to be made. But my favorite time was when we took the tackle out to see what things needed to be repaired or replaced.

Each item had its own special feel and scent. The reels were cold and solid to the touch and held braided silk lines with a strong aroma of linseed oil and silicon dressing. The bamboo rods had a musty scent mixed with a lingering odor of varnish, and the long brown shafts felt smooth and strong. We would join the sections together to test the fit, then flex the rods in the air and imagine them bending under the weight of a heavy fish. The fly boxes held a kaleidoscope of colors and textures and the names of the patterns were nearly as exciting and colorful as the flies themselves—Colonel Carey, Black O'Lindsay, Alexander, Nation's Special, Cummings Fancy, Rhodes' Favorite, Lioness, and others whose names escape me now.

Finally, when all was ready, we would pack the car the night before departure, and I would toss and turn in bed and be up well before the dawn, waiting impatiently until it was time to go. Usually my mother or one of my uncles or a fishing companion of Dad's would come along.

But on the last trip it was just the two of us alone. We didn't know, of course, that it would be our last trip together. We set out with the usual bright hopes, and Dad wore the happy look he always had when going fishing. It was not the best fishing we ever had, but neither was it bad, and on the last day we fished into the twilight in a driving rain until both of us were soaked. My father was shivering when we started back to camp, and by the time we reached it he was trembling uncontrollably. I built a fire, wrapped him in a blanket and made some soup and gave him some. After a while he seemed all right again, but it was the first time I had ever really worried about him.

I was 17 then and just about to start college, and back in Washington, D.C., they were cutting orders that would take my father to Germany. We saw each other only a few times after that, and there was never enough time for fishing. And then he suffered the heart attack that killed him.

Now his old reel sits atop my bookcase, the pungent smell of oil and dressing having long since faded. His old bamboo rod stands in its case in the corner, the luster long gone from its varnish. His old flies are carefully put away, but their colors, too, have faded over time.

But the memories remain—recollections of sunlit days and days of rain, of full creels and empty ones, of misty mornings full of promise and evenings spent cleaning a catch by lantern light. Remembered too are his lessons about what knots to tie, how to gauge the wind and light, and where to place the fly. But the brightest memory and the best lesson was one he taught subtly, a little at a time. Call it an attitude or feeling, a sort of inner excitement that returns each spring when the green buds burst open on the trees, the mayflies hatch, and trout begin to rise. It's that and more—a kind of understanding and appreciation that fishing is one of the very best things that ever a man can do, and trout fishing is the very best of all. It is one of my father's most precious gifts to me, and now I hope somehow to impart the same feelings to my son.

His name is Randy, the same as his grandfather whom he never had a chance to know. He is a strong and sturdy boy with a quick mind and many interests, of which fishing is one. It is not something that he has ever been com-pelled to do, nor has he ever been told that he should want to do it. It has been offered to him as an opportunity that is available whenever he wishes to take advantage of it. And often enough, he has.

The first time was at Dry Falls Lake. It was a spring morning, but a very dif-ferent one from the long-ago day when I "caught" my own first trout. The sky was dark and streaked with lightning, the wind was cold and strong, and rain came in hard bursts. Randy was bundled up in heavy clothing that made it dif-ficult for him to move, but he was at my side when I hooked a husky little trout and passed the rod to him. He squealed with delight when the fish jumped, then cranked the reel so furiously he nearly wound the fish up to the top guide of the rod before I could stop him. It was a proud moment for him, but an even prouder one for me.

Not long after that he asked if he could have his own rod, and I gave him one my father had given me, along with an old reel and a line. Soon he asked to learn to cast, and I have tried to show him how—sometimes to our mutual consternation, but sometimes, when all goes well, to our mutual delight.

Watching me tie flies one night, he asked to be shown the secrets of that art. Now, with a little instruction, a hand-me-down vise and hand-me-down mate-rials, he is tying his own, which get a little better all the time. He has yet to take a trout on a fly he tied himself, but surely that day is not far off.

Some years ago we bought an old cabin on the North Fork of the Stillagua-mish River, and when Randy watched me wade the stream he asked to follow suit. Not yet, I said; you're not quite old enough for that, and besides you have no boots or waders. But then a friend gave him a pair of children's-sized hip boots, and I no longer had a good excuse.

So on a summer day I helped him into the boots and strapped them to his belt. Even though they were children's size, the boots were too long for his short legs and they hung loosely in accordion pleats. Undaunted, he walked with me down to the river, and I showed him how to slide his feet over the slippery rocks, how to plant one foot firmly before moving the other, and how always to keep his body turned sideways to the flow. Then he put his warm little hand in mine and held tightly as we started out across a side channel to a small island. We reached it safely, waded back, then crossed again. In all, we waded the channel six times before Randy decided he had finally had enough. "Dad, I think that was the funnest thing I ever did," he said.

I thought it was one of the funnest things I'd ever done, too.

Each of these things has pleased me, as my own childhood fishing exploits must have pleased my father. But what a boy does is not always an indication of what he will do when he becomes a man, and there have been times when I have wondered if Randy's interest in fishing is a permanent thing or merely a passing fancy.

And then, last year, I think I got my answer.

Randy was eight then, and decided for the first time to go fishing by himself. He donned the hip boots—they fit a little better now—put his rod together, attached the reel, and threaded the fly line through the guides. He chose a fly without asking my advice, knotted it to the end of his leader, walked down to the river and waded alone into the same side channel we had crossed together a couple of years before. He found a spot to his liking, worked out line and began to cast, while his mother and I settled down to watch from among the trees on the high bank above the river

Soon we heard his shout and saw the rod bend in a pulsing bow.

I saw the look of joy upon his face, and understood.

"He's hooked one," his mother said.

"No," I told her. "I think maybe it's the other way around."

Steve Raymond is author of nine books on fly fishing. He was also editor of two angling magazines, *The Flyfisher* and *Fly Fishing in Salt Waters*, and has written for many others, including *Sports Illustrated* and *Fly Fisherman*. He was also an editor at *The Seattle Times* for thirty years. He lives on Whidbey Island in Puget Sound.

Alaska

JOHN RANDOLPH

Catching a Pacific-salmon grand slam (king, chum, sockeye, silver and humpy) is one of fly fishing's lesser known, and least attainable, holy grails. Lesser known because few of us have taken even one of the five Pacific salmon species on a fly, and most who have consider them to be dead-fish swimming by the time they reach the headwaters of the Northwest rivers and the Great Lakes.

That makes the grand slam (taking all five species on a fly) a dream. And, with the destruction of the North American rivers, there are few places in the world where a salmon grand slam *can even be attempted*. Still there remains western Alaska, and especially Bristol Bay, the mother lode of Pacific salmon. It's possible to enter heaven on these waters, because in summer pinks, chums, kings, and sockeyes run into the same or nearby rivers, and early-run silvers can provide a chance for a catch of all five species on one trip.

But there is a better goal. It's a cinch that if you catch all five salmon species, some of them will be logs, near the end of their run and approaching death. In some watersheds the runs overlap, but they are not simultaneous. Better to go for two or three of the salmon species near the salt, while they are fresh with sea lice still clinging to their sides. They are salmon that take you down into your backing and send you stumbling along rivers, dashing through a myriad of fish from seven in the morning until one the next morning. If you are one of those shuffling, half-crazed fly-fishing troglodytes, you should depart from Alaska with sated eyes and sweetly aching arms. You will be convinced that you are no longer an epigone, a second-rate follower: You have joined the Tenth Legion. There just remains that one hyperion fish.

There are a number of camps and lodges *near the mouths* of the great salmon rivers of the Bristol Bay-Kuskokwim area that have all five salmon species passing their doorsteps each summer. The trick is to hit the rivers at just the right time—when the right salmon are just in from the saltwater. They quickly turn color in the spawning rivers and their attention changes existentially, from moving and taking flies to regenerating their kind. The fresher the fish, the more savagely they take the fly.

Jim Teeny and I made plans to fish the Kanektok River, a tributary to Kuskokwim Bay on the edge of the great Yukon-Kuskokwim Delta. We would fish out of the Duncan camps on the lower river, 15 miles up from tide water. Our trip would begin on July 9, the tail of the king-salmon run and during the arrival of the chums and sockeyes. There would still be fresh kings in the river, and we would have leopard rainbows and Dolly Varden as finger food. The salmon would be sea-bright and full of fight and suckers for the fly.

★ ★ ★

Fly fishers are tackle junkies. In our quiet, reclusive hours at home we hallucinate the dreaded breaking of a knot, or being spooled by a mythic fish. We obsessively, secretively, rig lines to probe the watery depths, where no commercially made line can reach.

As my Alaska experience expanded, I had become increasingly paranoid about what I took for tackle and flies. I made special plans for this trip for giant kings and other strong salmon that seldom rise for the fly and the right lines and rods headed my list of weapons. I had learned through sad experience that when fishing for Pacific salmon you must fish bottom or a life trip can turn into exercises in frustration or, worse, panhandling companions for spare parts.

I spent days scheming the line strategy and rigging—a complete 10-weight shooting-head system from 200-grain to 800-grain, with a shooting-line rigged with a whipped loop for fast changes. To that I added a Teeny line system, from T-200 to T-500. To complete my sinking-line system, I added Uniform Sink 8- and 10-weights and two sinking-tips—one fast-sinking, the other slow-sinking.

For fishing the surface, I included three weight-forward floating lines—two 8-weights and a 10-weight. Then I sat and carefully itemized the minimum line system I consider adequate for Alaska salmon fishing. I clucked "there" with self-satisfied approval. I tied and tested the backing-to-line and line-to-leader knots and clucked again.

King salmon are tough fish to beat on a fly rod. I estimated that I could survive with an 8-weight, 4-piece travel rod for the chums, the rainbows, and the sockeyes, but I'd need a 3-piece, 10-weight for the kings, which would average around 20 pounds and run as high as 50. I knew that I'd break at least one rod, so I took two 10-weights, an 8-weight, and a 5-weight for grayling.

I also obsessed about my flies, and when Carl Richards described his near-birth experience with a lemming hatch on the Good News River, I added a dozen mouse patterns to my Clouser Deep Minnows, Teeny Nymphs, Woolly Buggers, egg imitations and Muddlers, all heavy-wire patterns except the mouse. I planned to fish on or near bottom 80 percent of the time.

Yes, I would need a quality reel with a good drag system and a minimum of 200 yards of 20-pound backing. I would still be taking a chance with a 50-pound king. A reel that would take 200 yards of 30-pound backing plus the fly line would be ideal. It could handle all the salmon, and particularly the kings. I included in my gear two lightweight saltwater reels (one with 200 yards of 30-pound backing and another with 200 yards of 20-pound) and a 5-weight trout reel for rainbows and grayling.

★ ★ ★

When you fly over the Kilbuck Mountains, heading west toward the Bering Sea on Alaska's western littoral, the mountains fall away and a lake plain rises like a green carpet dotted with sapphires to meet you. In a small plane you feel diminished by the sight, and as you approach the Yup'ik village of Bethel, you realize just how remote from civilization you are. Down there a Stanley Kubrick-style hospital sits like a large, partially squashed, metallic yellow banana amidst a cluster of shanties. A lonely five miles of paved road runs through the village founded by the Moravian missionaries in 1884. Its buildings are constructed on posts to survive the permafrost. It looks healthy but tentative and alone perched there on the edge of one of the world's largest river deltas formed where the 2,000-mile Yukon and the 800-mile Kuskokwim rivers become neighbors.

Life on the delta was always tenuous for hunter gatherers, but the lake-filled plain is one of the world's great waterfowl nesting grounds, and the salmon runs of the two rivers made life possible for the Yup'iks, who believed that the earth was created, or scratched, by a great raven who carved out the gorges of the Yukon and Kuskokwim rivers, lakes, and streams with its talons. About 10,000 Yup'iks, the largest ethnic native concentration in Alaska, inhabited the delta at the time of the arrival of white man in the last century. Today 16,000 people live in Bethel.

The Kanektok slides out of the Kilbuk Mountains, across the ancient Kuskokwim flood plain and into Kuskokwim Bay. Its graveled runs are spawning grounds for all five Pacific salmon species. One hundred and fifty miles to the west lie Nunivak Island and the Bering Sea. The Duncans lease sport-fishing rights on the river from the Yup'iks of Quinhagak, the native village near the river's outflow into Kuskokwim Bay.

In late June and early July, when the kings are in the river and the chums and sockeye are arriving, the Kanektok buzzes with urgent, purposeful life. The Eskimos pound up and downriver in family boatloads, netting and drying fish for winter food in their summer camps. They pass boatloads of white sport fishermen in search of fish for fun.

And the river is so full of fish. The long holes near the tidewater hold great congregations of silver salmon, all preparing for the move upstream to spawn and die. The kings are a dominant presence. They appropriate the water they want, and the smaller chums, newly striped with watermarks, move aside for them. The sockeyes, slim and shining like highly polished torpedoes, lay up quietly in the sloughs and then swim upriver in great V-shape wedges in the half-light of the arctic summer nights. The fish are in and everyone is fishing, including the occasional bear, whose prints mark sandbars and whose scent turns the camp dog into a barking, schizophrenic canine.

There are so many fish and fishermen that you metamorphose into a round-the-clock predator, chasing them frantically until, exhausted, you drop. Then in a few brief hours you rise, eat, and go out again, hunting big, bright fish, fighting them passionately, searching for that obsessively imagined Great One. You see, sight-fishing to Pacific salmon is an intense visual and emotional feast for excited nerve endings, like sight-fishing to double-digit bonefish on an undisturbed ocean flat.

All the king-salmon pools are within 15 miles of camp, and where the salmon lie each year on their movements upriver is predictable unless the river floods in runoff and changes its familiar bottom geography.

You motor to the Ten Minute Hole and as the guide drifts the boat through, you stand on the deck and search for the large rust-green shapes of the kings resting on their upriver migration. You sight-fish to the shapes as you stand on the sand-and-gravel bars and cast the heavy lines upstream of the brown-green forms barely visible in the green-gray water. Casting the lines is relatively easy; casting them long requires skill. The 27-foot tapers built into running lines must be slung with a smooth, high delivery, the excess line held in your line hand as loops that shoot as the heavy taper pulls them up into the guides. The head must be the right weight of sinking line for the speed and depth of the water, for when the head hits the water it must sink quickly through the current so the fly reaches bottom as it approaches the fish. The fly must bounce or crawl across bottom or the king will not grab it.

If your eyesight is good, and you use high-quality polarized glasses, you can spot the movement of the fish's head when it takes the fly and the line goes tight and you lift.

The king may hesitate momentarily, not realizing that it is hooked, or it may charge off and into the air or simply turn and begin a long, unstoppable run downriver, quickly into your backing. You yell "Boat!" and the guide kicks the broad, shallow-draft jet sled off the bank and the two of you chase the king through the long riffle water and into the next pool. Hopefully, if the fish is not too large and ocean bound, the fight will be waged there. With kings, as with tarpon, it's the size of the fight in the fish not the size of the fish in the fight.

When it is finally beached, the king will average about 20 pounds, but there are much larger shapes in the pools, and the shapes keep changing from day to day as newcomers arrive and depart for the upriver spawning gravel. When the shapes are of the brightest silver, and large as well, then the fishermen and guides become very excited: a large, bright king is the main event in this fly fishing.

★ ★ ★

Chum salmon come in two runs. The largest, the summer run (fish averaging seven pounds), arrives in early June and continues until mid-July when the fall fish (averaging eight pounds, with fish up to 15 pounds) arrive. In the long pools they occupy the same water as the kings, and when you fish for one, you fish for the other. And, like the kings, the chums take flies fished on bottom.

Chums are powerful fish for their size and when sea-bright they fight doggedly with vicious rolling and thrashing leaps. They take the same flies as the kings— brightly colored patterns (especially pink) tied on heavy wire. One day a green Teeny Nymph may work best, the next a pink deer-hair Polywog waked across the surface turns them giddy; the next day a black or red fly incites a suicidal grab. Which color today? Let's huddle and compare flies: only trial-and-success will tell.

The concentration required in this sight-fishing is exhausting. Haig-Brown described it in his book *A River Never Sleeps* as fishing to the ripples made by moving schools of fish. In the Kanektok and some other Alaska rivers, when the water is low and clear, you spot holding fish and fish to them. It's like saltwater-flats fishing, except you stand for long hours in one place working the fly carefully to one giant pod of fish. By noon your arms ache from maintaining a sustained predator's crouch and the fatigue of standing and fighting fish extends down your back and into your legs. Line burns crease your fingers; your eyes ache, and your forearms are tight from strain.

The right presentations require the utmost effort and attention, but the hookups and the fights are pure avoirdupois—dogged heavy-tackle battles between brute fish and man. For relief, you turn your attention to the gentle side-water, where the sockeyes are laid up waiting for the light to fall to begin their runs upriver. You creep along the banks and watch the bright finning salmon in the aqua-green, deep pools, knowing that tonight after supper you will fish for them on their migrations.

As the sun drops, the fish become more difficult to spot in the surface glare, so you fish carefully and instinctively to where they have been, and must still be. You fish urgently because the boat ride upriver for supper is approaching.

★ ★ ★

In the arctic twilight, the sun slides slowly toward the horizon and the salmon move. Below camp, where two flows converge, exhausted fishermen meet to fish the midnight run. Sockeyes ripple the surface in a long, slim backeddy. They are stacked in a little Grand Central Station of soft water, schools coming and going in a vast upstream evening push of fish. Jim Teeny waits for them and fishes a Nymph Tip line fixedly like a pointing bird dog approaching a holding pheasant. The line moves imperceptibly in its quiet drift amidst the myriad sockeye, and he lifts and yells: "Fish on! Chromer!" In my half-sleep a half-mile upstream from Jim, I hear him exclaiming over another chrome-bright fish and I toss on clothes and stagger downriver to join the joyous hunt.

Some sockeyes leave the backeddy and, in schools, follow a leader over the four-inch-deep riffle bar. Standing at the head of the riffle, you can see them coming in a wedge-shaped ripple moving in the water's midnight surface glare. You cast with a sink-tip line, leading the wedge so the fly drops and intercepts the fish as they move upriver in the shallow water. The line hesitates, ever so slightly, and you lift and feel fish. A sockeye runs and jumps and jumps again and again.

You catch sockeyes there, with leopard rainbows and chums, until 1 A.M., until your arms and legs can stand no more. Only then, limp with the hunter's catch-sated fatigue, are your thoughts more on the cot in your tent than on fish. You must sleep. But . . . just one more tug.

★ ★ ★

The leopard rainbows are dry-fly light-rod candy in the rivers that drain to the Bering Sea. No one has explained why their markings are so brilliant. They are true river rainbows, not ocean-going steelhead. And they are suckers for the little lemmings, mice, and voles that inhabit the banks of their rivers and occasionally tumble in and struggle to swim.

Under pewter-gray skies, Brad Duncan skulls the driftboat downriver, holding while we drift-and-shoot the banks with mouse patterns. The water is cold, about 50 degrees, and the rainbows are sluggish and strike short. We adjust—leaving the fly, twitching it—and they take.

"When the water temperature rises five degrees, they'll take hard and you'll have thirty-fish days," Duncan says.

The river braids and in the side-channels we walk and wade and work the alder sweepers, stalking the lemming hatch. When the rainbows come, they attack the fly, suddenly shooting out from under the brush, and are instantly air-borne. After the large brutish salmon, they are luminous, like celestially marked rainbows leaping on dark Montana days.

★ ★ ★

The mind must slowly accept a return to civilization. The adjustment com-mences on the last day on the river, when you urgently search the holding runs for the largest king salmon you have ever seen. When the shape appears, unex-pectedly where there had been no rust-colored apparition before, your stomach tightens and you peer hard at the image—disbelieving. It cannot be *that big*— one fish. Perhaps there are two there, side-by-side in a pair. No, no, it's one fish all right. But, God, it's got to be 50 pounds!

Wade close. Carefully. Get positioned just right, just downstream of the fish so you can hit the bucket, that sweet little slot in front of the fish's nose, with the first cast. Cast way upstream ahead of the fish so the fly will tick bottom as it approaches the shape. There! No, not quite right. Cast again. And again.

The minutes and casts string out. You are ready to resign—the ache in your arms and back is too much. One more cast.

There! There!

The head moves. The fly stops solidly. Then the bottom moves; the shape is underway. This weight comes from the center of the earth. Line peels off the reel. The fish runs away across the river. And then . . . Oh! leaps in full-bodied, eye-level salmon bravado.

"Is that your fish?" Roger yells. "He's big! Boat!"

We are in the boat and away . . . helplessly following. The fish leaps again; it drafts on the downstream currents backward into the lower end of the pool; it jumps again—it's a female! Then it turns and heads downriver. She will do what she will. There is no stopping her charge. We can only follow and regain backing when she—oh, please!—comes to rest with a pod of kings in the next pool.

She hesitates and I can put pressure on her, standing back from the shore with the rod bent double, the line stretched taut like piano wire. She dislikes the pressure and turns downriver.

"Boat!"

Once she has her body into the current, the fight is all her way and we must follow—down into the next pool, and the next, and the next. She does not jump any more. She knows now that something serious has begun—a fight for survival. I can gain line when she holds, but I cannot turn her head or move her body weight sideways. I'm irritating her, and when she holds in the current, I can only sap her strength by pulling her hard sideways. I must not give her rest. She must *feel* defeated before she *is defeated*. She can sense my fatigue through the line. I can feel her existential determination, and when she sulks and rests, I can almost feel her heart beat.

I know her life history—her mother dropping an egg into the gravel to which she is now headed to drop hers; the egg hatching in early spring; her tenuous wiggle emergence as a fragile swim-up fry; her gradual metamorphosis into a gaily colored smolt; her joining with others of her kind, the cloudlike young-of-the-year school that will drift its way downriver to the sea; her two- or three-year odyssey in the sea; and her urgent return to her square-yard of clean gravel where this all began.

My odyssey as a fly fisher has taught me that the odds of her making it this far are in the millions to one. Now only I stand between her and her final genetic ritual, her grotesque physical deformation, and her death spasms in a quiet river side-channel, where only a hungry bear may notice, inspect her briefly and splash off in search of better fish to eat.

★ ★ ★

"You've got to beat her before she reaches those root wads. See them down there at the end of the pool?" Jimmy shouts. The fish is tired. I can feel her fatigue, and I can see that her shape flounders a little when I give her the rod butt and strain the line until it sings. Will the knots hold? She flounders back toward the current, and I lose 20 feet, then 50 more. She's going to make the root wads.

"Boat! Boat, now!" Jimmy yells. "Too late! She's gonna snag you! Boat!"

"Damn, Jim, she's in the wads."

In the boat, beside the wads, I can peer down and see the line and leader all tangled in the roots. Frustrated . . . desperate . . . I plunge into the water and pull and lift on the line.

"No! No! John. Do it from in here, in the boat. We can free it!"

It's hopeless. The line will not come free. In a last, desperate, effort, I wrap the line around my hands and haul with all my might. It comes free from the top roots, but there are others. I haul hard again.

"No! You've got her! That's *her* down there. See!" Jim shouts.

Deep in the blue-green water, at the base of a root wad, lies a shape.

"That's her there, John. Lead her downstream. Don't let her have her head or she'll dash in and break you off. We can land her there, on that beach down below. See it? It's just right!"

I lead her gently downstream away from the wads. She swims sluggishly toward the large flat. Her weight is still so heavy that I can only watch line peel off the reel again. But this time she turns into the quiet water beside the flow, and as I tumble from the boat, I know that the end is very close. "Please don't let the knot break now," I whisper. "It's been an hour and a half and a mile of river. How long can monofilament and a 10-weight three-piece last?" The truly large fish are usually lost with the leader at the rod tip-top.

Jim shouts staccato instructions. "She's tired. Get farther back on the beach! You can turn her now! Once she's turned, keep her coming. When she feels the stones on her belly, she'll bolt, so be careful she doesn't make a sudden move and break you off. If you get her far enough up on the gravel, she'll turn over on her side. Then she can't swim; we've got her. Keep backing up! Reel! Keep the pressure on her!"

She feels the pebbles on her belly, and she bolts in a weary, inertial-more-than-energy-driven dash for the main current. For the first time I can stop and turn her. She comes to me . . . she comes. The pebbles tickle her stomach, but she does not have the energy to turn and run. Her jaw slides up on the shallows and she tips on her side, and Jimmy and the guides and the other fishermen are with her. "There!"

I can touch her now for the first time. When I grasp the hard muscular wrist of her tail, my hand cannot completely encircle it. She is strong, firm, full-bellied and cold in my hands. I can lift her only momentarily. She is the largest freshwater fish I have ever held. Her sides are already turning reddish brown. Her eye is a black like onyx, celestial. As she revives in the current, I can feel her full strength . . . pulsing, reviving. Then I feel something tight within me release, as though a heavy stress had been lifted from my heart. I relax and exhale deeply.

She quivers anxiously; she needs to be off upriver. She is determined—strong again. It cannot be that this bright living thing will spawn, deform and quickly die. She seems immortal. I slowly, reluctantly, release my grip on her tail wrist. She senses freedom . . . and she charges away, sending rooster tails across the shallows as she heads for the main current.

She is gone. I have her here, still with me.

The Yup'iks believe that to fish for fun is a sin: Fishing must be for food. This is not sin. This is communion.

John Randolph has been editor and editor/publisher of *Fly Fisherman* magazine since July 1978. He has fly fished around the world and in most of the United States. His books include *Becoming a Fly Fisher* (Globe Pequot/Lyons Press 2003), *Fishing Basics* (Prentice-Hall, 1981), and *Backpacking Basics* (Prentice-Hall 1982). He lives in Harrisburg, Pennsylvania.

Excerpt from
The One That
Got Away

HOWELL RAINES

No, I was oppressed by the sheer weight of something more personal—my own amateurishness in the face of this new kind of fly fishing. I had gotten cocky about my ability to catch trout and bass, including some large ones. But in saltwater environments, the heavy rods and lines, the persistent winds, the greater distances needed even in routine casts—all these factors converged to form a nexus of neuromuscular chaos. Whenever it was mentioned that I had written a book about fishing, I made a point of telling people that my skills were modest. Then I would pick up a rod and prove it.

But hell's hammers, I didn't want to think of myself as clumsy, either. Somehow the abundance of Christmas Island, where it is possible to catch plenty of easy fish, sharpened the contrast between those fish and the hard ones that Lefty or the other experts might catch. I'm talking about the ghostly torpedoes you sometimes glimpsed on the turbulent rim of the islands, where the easeful shallows brushed up against the fertile, brutal surge of the blue Pacific. I particularly liked these ocean flats, which were bands of shallow, protected water between the coral reef and the shore. It is an environment of great violence, beauty and motion: gulls, terns, pipers zipping by within inches of your head, angelfish and blacktip reef sharks at your feet, and always the big combers marching in to die in shuddering explosions against the coral ramparts of the barrier reef. Fishing those flats, with the cannonade of the waves always in your ears and the spirals of white spume leaping incessantly toward the sky, was a little like standing behind a fortified line during a battle, protected improbably from a world of violence that stretched to the horizon. In those spots, if you trained your eyes on the area where the clear water stranded off into the deeper green underbelly of the incoming waves, you'd see the most intimidating bonefish, the sovereign loners, a full yard long, which didn't need to slide into the kneedeep flats to nibble little stuff. In their passing, these fish put me in mind of what Isak Dinesen said about elephants. They moved along as if they had an appointment at the end of the world.

In the precincts of such fish, one day Tabaki spoke.

"Big bone. He's coming along the edge of the deep water."

Sure enough, moving steadily through the green murk was a gray shape five or six times the size of the fish we had been catching in droves in a long march across an amiable flat.

"You can't reach him from here. Let's move out. Don't splash."

We took an intersecting line to try to get ahead of the fish. It was coming steadily on an unveering course, out there in about four feet of water.

"Cast now, as far as you can," Tabaki said, in that voice guides use when they suddenly care whether a particular fish is caught. It is a voice very different from the one they use when they are saying, in effect, you paid your money, here's your shot, I do this every day.

He was watching the relationship between my false casts and the fish. On the fourth or fifth stroke, he said, "Let it go."

I did. To my surprise, the fly landed in the edge of the deep water. Maybe my best cast ever. Not dead-on, but plausible.

"Let it sink," Tabaki said. "He might see it."

I let it sink without hope, satisfied simply that the cast had not been a humiliation.

"Now, strip, strip," he said.

Dear hearts, I wish to tell you that this lordly fish swung toward the fly as inexorably as doom's pendulum, not hastening in the least until the last instant, when it closed on the fly in a rush and took it and was the biggest fish of our trip and one of the biggest ever taken at Christmas Island, where a seven- or eight-pound fish is a large one.

I wish to tell you that and I suppose I could, but it did not happen.

The cast was not quite good enough, or my luck was not the supremely obliterating luck you need to make up for a cast that is not quite good enough. A few times in a fishing life that kind of luck will come along, but it did not come to me on this day in the Republic of Kiribati.

Nor was my casting good enough for the other edge-cruising gorillas we spotted on the ocean flats where the big ones would from time to time come looming along under the combers. Just as well, Tabaki explained, since a bone-fish that strong and that close to the reef will simply bore over the edge and cut you off on the coral and that would break your heart more cleanly than a bad cast. I would have been willing to take my chances on that kind of heartbreak.

Howell Raines is a Pulitzer Prize-winning journalist and former executive editor of *The New York Times*. He has written four books, including *Fly Fishing Through the Midlife Crisis*, an autobiography that chronicles his lifelong passion for "a higher magic called fly fishing" and what he learned there.

Sacred Eels

JAMES PROSEK

We have not attained to the full solution of the exceedingly difficult eel problems, but the steady progress of the last twenty years is full of promise for the future . . . Altogether the whole story of the eel and its spawning has come to read almost like a romance, wherein reality has far exceeded the dreams of fantasy.

—Dr. Johannes Schmidt, 1912.

My early encounters with eels were awkward, confused. My friends and I caught them by accident while fishing for trout or bass with worms. We never stopped to admire them; we were too shocked by their energy, frustrated by our inability to hold onto their slimy bodies, and just wanted our hooks back.

One December in Italy eight years ago, I stood at the edge of a lake next to my friend Larry Ashmead. A line of slender poles was sticking out of the water along the shore. A man nearby said the poles marked traps for catching eels, and I began to tell Larry what little I knew of the life history of freshwater eel.

Like those slender fish on the other side of the Atlantic, the eels in this lake were born in the middle of the Atlantic Ocean, somewhere east of the Bahamas, maybe several thousand feet deep. The discovery of the eels' spawning place was made in the early 1900's by the Danish oceanographer Johannes Schmidt, who caught thousands of specimens of the larval stage of the eel in fine mesh nets in an amorphous region of the North Atlantic, several million square miles, called the Sargasso Sea. Observing these larvae, only a few millimeters long and a few days old, drifting in the surface of the ocean currents, Schmidt concluded that the adult eels had recently spawned, somewhere beneath his nets. News of the find, one of the most exciting in marine biology in the twentieth century, was published widely, in such magazines as *National Geographic*, in 1913, and the journal *Nature*. But it soon became clear that although Schmidt had solved a part of the "eel problem," he had merely stoked the fire. Although they knew at the surface where the eels spawned, no one had witnessed the adults spawning. It became then, perhaps, an even greater marine mystery.

Before the twentieth century, scientists both amateur and professional had concocted numerous explanations about how eels reproduced, many of them harebrained: that they were generated from horse hairs, or drops of dew, that they mated with snakes on the banks of rivers, or emerged from the carcasses of dead animals or the mud. It was not even known whether eels were asexual or had gender and reproductive organs until Sigmund Freud as a young medical student published the first paper on the location of the eel's gonads. As it turns out, the reproductive organs were virtually invisible until the fish began its journey in the sea. The larval stage of the eel—which looks nothing like the adult itself, but more like a leaf-shaped fish with fangs—was indeed known for centuries, named its own species, *Leptocephalus breverostris*. But until two Italian biologists in the late 1800's observed these fish metamorphosing into eels we didn't know the eel had a larval stage at all. Schmidt was determined to find out where these larvae, caught in the open ocean, came from. But even after Schmidt's discovery of the general vicinity of the Atlantic eels' spawning place, to this day, no one has witnessed an adult eel spawning in the sea, or seen an adult eel much beyond the river mouth on their way to the spawning grounds. His findings merely opened a larger can of eels.

"After the young are born in the ocean as little leaf-shaped fish," I said to my friend Larry, "they are spread randomly by ocean currents to the coasts of the Atlantic. After twenty years or so in freshwater, the adults return to the ocean to spawn and then die."

The eel is one of the few fishes that are *catadromous*—that is, it spends its adult life in freshwater but reproduces in salt. This life history is the opposite of that of the salmon, for instance, an *anadromous* fish, which spends its adult life in the sea but reproduces in freshwater. There are several other populations of catadromous eels around the world that spawn in other oceans but carry out very similar lives to the Atlantic eel.

Larry found all this hard to believe. Until his moment of doubt, I hadn't really stopped to consider what the eels went through to get to and from the small brooks and lakes where they spent their adult lives. The place where they would reproduce, and probably die, was thousands of miles away.

Some weeks later, Larry came across a 1941 story by Rachel Carson from *Under the Sea Wind*, called "Odyssey of the Eel." It is a tale written largely through the eyes of a female eel named Anguilla (the genus name for catadromous eels), inspired by Schmidt's discovery. The story begins by describing juvenile eels swimming to a small body of water called Bittern Pond, two hundred miles from the sea, "like pieces of slender glass rods shorter than a man's finger." And then, one dark rainy night in autumn, many years after she first entered freshwater, Anguilla leaves the pond, beginning her long journey back to the Sargasso.

Anguilla is drawn almost magnetically toward that place of warmth and darkness hundreds of feet below the surface of the ocean where she was born. Beyond that, the author imagines the rest, because once Anguilla leaves the mouth of the river, her life in the ocean is entirely a mystery: "No one can trace the path of the eels that left the salt marsh at the mouth of the bay on that November night when wind and tide brought them the feeling of warm ocean water—how they passed from the bay to the deep Atlantic basin that lies south of Bermuda and east of Florida half a thousand miles."

We don't know much more of the eel's life history today, nearly a century after Schmidt's discovery. What remains consistent about the eel is its ability to avoid our gaze. That ultimately was what attracted me to the eel.

It's not easy to get to like, or to know, the eel. It is dark and slippery, and not particularly beautiful at first glance. For me, the eel began as an idea. The idea was of the unseen journey, and the eel's intangible determination to reach a destination, a destiny that ends with death, and life. I'm still trying to figure out what to do with that idea, and whether trying to make sense of its ethereal qualities would somehow break the beauty of its incomprehensibility. In the course of my time spent with eels, I met other people who were as interested in eels as

I was, people whose lives cross paths with the eel. Fishermen, scientists, slippery lovers of darkness themselves, who I began to call, in jest, "eelians."

Many eelians live lives like the eel, unseen, quiet, under the radar. For me, the unexpected paths that led to these people became wrapped in the original idea. One, Ray Turner, an eel fisherman of the Catskill Mountains in New York State, became a kind of prophet to me, who spoke in aphorisms that appeared alternately meaningless and prophetic, depending on the circumstances and delivery. "It's not the journey, it's the road," he once told me. Or, "Art is reality out of proportion." But the elusiveness of the eel was its beauty.

All around the world, the eel inspires fear, awe, and respect. Humans seem to have some visceral reaction to this minimalist fish, as they do the snake, a tempter of the innocent and virginal, an erotic symbol, a food source, a god. In some cultures the eel fills both the well of human spirituality and the stomach. The spawning areas and much of the life history of the world's catadromous eels is still a mystery, one that may be, as the indigenous people of New Zealand believe, best left unsolved. But it would be unfortunate if the opportunity to know the eel became lost. All around the world, catadromous eel populations are in serious decline. The causes are many and not always easily defined. If we do lose the eel, however, before we witness its spawning or know more about what fuels its determination to make the journey, or how it navigates in its migration, then, as the poet Wallace Stevens once wrote, "farewell to an idea."

I began my work on eels around 1998, and, as is the case when I dig into a topic, I mentioned my interest in eels with anyone who came within talking distance. I brought up eels in conversation with family, editors, artists, therapists, my barber, and one day with a friend named David Seidler, a screenwriter friend in Santa Monica. He asked me if I'd heard of the sacred eels in New Zealand.

I had not, nor had I read anything about how important eels were to the culture and traditions of the Maori, the native Polynesians of New Zealand. There was, I would discover, a reason for this—Maori stories and traditions are passed on orally, and only between Maori.

As I found out on my first visit to New Zealand a few years before, a post-college trout-fishing trip with my friend Taylor, the Maori are genial, but don't go out of their way to share anything. Taylor and I saw Maori men in bars after their long days at work in the sawmills or slaughterhouses, but not much more than a grunt or nod passed between us. We trekked on Maori tribal land, hiked trails through old growth forests, fished crystal clear rivers with tall fern trees shading emerald pools, caught trout introduced by the British, and hung out with naturalized British people. But overall, the experience, though visually and physically fulfilling felt superficial. I left New Zealand feeling empty, knowing that I was glimpsing only one small part of that country and little of its soul; in other words, its people. It was the first time in my travels that a pretty landscape was not enough for me.

As David told me more about the giant eels in New Zealand, I remembered then, while eating lunch on the bank of a remote river on that first trip with Taylor, that a slender dark shape, five feet long and big around as my arm, had come out of the shadows to eat a piece of the sandwich that I'd thrown in the water. I saw it so briefly that I wasn't sure I'd seen it at all. But as David spoke over the phone, it registered in my mind that the big dark fish had been perhaps the only native fish I'd seen on that trip, an eel.

David told me that it is a tradition of the Maori to keep ponds with sacred eels. The Maori feed the eels and protect them and in turn the eels protect the *iwi*, or tribe. The eels can be huge—six, seven feet—and feed right out of one's hands. The Maori say some of these eels are over 300 years old.

David, who grew up in America, knew the land of Kiwis from his years living there married to a Maori woman named Titihuiarangimoana, whom he met while working for a television company in Australia. His marriage gave him access to a world usually closed to *pakeha*, or white people. His introduction to the New Zealand wilds, or "bush" as it's called, was through fly-fishing for trout with a Maori man named DJ.

"I've seen some *huge* ones while trout fishing, mate," David said. "I was fishing in this mountain lake one day, wading through the shallows and went to step over this big log when . . . the log moved! It was a giant eel—big around as the fattest part of my leg. There was no stream running out of the lake, so I don't know how this eel would get to the sea to spawn, but they say that some small eels get up to high lakes when there's a typhoon, and they'll stay up there, some-times over a hundred years, until the next big typhoon comes and washes them down the mountain."

David sent an e-mail to his friend DJ on the North Island in autumn of 2002, inquiring about eels on my behalf. DJ said he knew a thing or two about eels, but would try to find someone who might have more to say than he did on the importance of eels in Maori culture. Eventually, it was decided that the best person to lead me around New Zealand in search of eels was a twenty-three-year-old half-Maori woman named Stella August. Stella had just finished her graduate work at Waikato University in Hamilton. The subject of her thesis was the spring migration of glass eels on the Tukituki River, which flows toward to the eastern coast of the North Island, near her family's tribal land in Hawke Bay.

A few e-mail correspondences later, Stella agreed to set up an itinerary for me and to be my eel guide on a trip to New Zealand. Our trip was scheduled for February of 2004, summertime in the southern hemisphere.

In the meantime, in my research, I came across some Polynesian myths that involved eels, in the work of Joseph Campbell. Campbell explains in his book, *The Masks of God: Creative Mythology*, how the creation myth in India involving the snake made its way through Indonesia and was eventually inherited by the Polynesians, who replaced the snake, which was unknown in the islands, with the indigenous eel. "East of Indonesia, Melanesia, and Australia, throughout the island-studded triangle of Polynesia—which has Hawaii at its apex, New Zealand at one angle, and Easter Island at the other—the mythological image of the murdered divine being whose body became a food plant has been adjusted to the natural elements of an oceanic environment," Campbell wrote. "The voluptuous atmosphere of the lush Polynesian adventure will be different, indeed, from the grim holiness of the rabbinical Torah; nevertheless, we are certainly in the same old book—of which, so to say, all the earliest editions have been lost."

In several stories throughout the region, particularly in Samoa, a small eel is taken as a pet by a girl named Sina. Sina raises the eel in a coconut shell until it becomes too big, at which point she lets it go in a spring, but continues to feed it. One day when she's bathing in the spring the eel tries to pierce her vagina with its tail. The eel is killed and the head is buried, where a coconut tree grows. The nut of the coconut bears the mark of the eel's eyes and mouth. The story of the eel as a creature both loved but feared, and as a kind of detached phallus with a mind of its own, is consistent throughout the region.

Another Polynesian story, of which there are many variations, concerns a monster eel called *Te Tuna*, and the seduction of the god Maui's wife, Hine. Campbell likens Maui to a kind of Hercules of Polynesia. When Maui finds the giant eel Te Tuna in bed with his wife one night, he cuts off the eel's head with a hatchet. In the story, the head of the eel becomes all the saltwater eels of the world, and the tail becomes all the freshwater eels of the world.

It is not surprising, perhaps, that in the South Pacific region the word for eel, *tuna*, is a synonym for penis. There are many variations of stories of eels seducing women by a spring while their washing clothes, or in their sleep, as well as stories of eels as monsters, but I found nothing specifically about the Maori and eels, or about sacred eels at all, until I stumbled onto the works of Elsdon Best.

Best was born in Tawa Flat, New Zealand, in 1856, the son of British immigrants. He is considered to be the foremost ethnographer of Maori society, which was diminishing rapidly even in the late nineteenth century. In his work, it is evident from the sheer proportion of pages devoted to the eel in his book, about two-thirds, that the eel was once the greatest inland food source for the Maori. He listed over two hundred local Maori names for the freshwater eel in his *Fishing Methods and Devices*. If the number of different words used to describe the nuances of an object in a language—like snow to the Eskimo—is evidence of its importance in a culture, then this fact alone, for me, confirmed the importance of eels in Maori life.

It was also in Best's work where I first read about the Maori monster called the taniwha, which most commonly takes the form of a giant eel.

In *Maori Myth and Religion Part II*, Best describes how Captain Cook, on his third voyage to New Zealand in 1777, gave us the first written record of what the natives there called taniwha: "We had another piece of intelligence from him, more correctly given, though not confirmed by our own observations, that there are snakes and lizards there of enormous size. He described the latter as being eight feet in length and big around as a man's body. He said they sometimes devour men."

Best, commenting on Cook's account, points out that the Maori man telling the story to Cook would certainly have known a lizard—though no eight-foot lizards exist in New Zealand—but would have never seen a snake. What the native described to Cook was the longfin eel of their freshwater rivers, *Anguilla dieffenbachii*, capable of growing to eight feet long and confirmed to live well over eighty pounds and a hundred years. Best also wrote that large eels were sometimes tamed and regularly fed. Offerings were sometimes made to these eels, and thought to be "sacred," they were respected like gods.

These Polynesian myths and traditions in the works of European writers, as they related to eels, were interesting to me, but at times dry. This was in part because the people who recorded them were not the authentic tellers of the tales. There was no Polynesian Homer to write them down. The soul of these stories was yet unwritten, was still in the minds of Maori elders in seaside and mountain villages in New Zealand. Because they were nature-based stories, they felt deflated and pale when told outside of any other context than the environment they came from. I slowly learned when I returned to New Zealand, the dangers that face the so-called pagan faiths. If the nature was endangered, the culture and ideas were as well.

Stella August was twenty-four years old when I visited New Zealand in 2004. Her mother is British, and her father was Maori. Stella's mother left home when Stella was nine, and she lived with her younger sister Wiki and their father on their tribal land on Kairakau Beach, a remote windswept coastline at Hawke Bay. Stella learned of her affinity for the sea and rivers through her father, and it was the sea that took him in a boating accident when a rogue wave overturned his skiff. He drowned, just off the beach near their home. Stella was sixteen at the time.

When her father died, Stella contacted her mother and asked if she would return to their tribal land to live with her and Wiki and help out on the farm. The mother had not set foot there since she'd left, years before. She agreed to return and has lived there ever since, tending to a herd of sheep and cows with her boyfriend Ray, and the help of cigarettes and cold Lion's Red beer to pass the time.

Drinking was just another part of living out there, a good hour and a half from the nearest supermarket.

Since Stella's father died, the elders of Ngati Kahagnunu had looked after her. Because of her love for the sea, she studied marine biology in college on a fellowship from her *iwi*, Ngati Kahanunu. When I met up with her, she had just handed in her master's thesis, was working part time in a coffee shop, and was organizing what she'd termed an "eel adventure" throughout New Zealand, for me.

Our scheduled meeting point was a Burger King on the second round-about in Hamilton about a two-hour drive south of Auckland. She was wearing board shorts and a sweatshirt with surfer logos, and would not look directly into my eyes.

"You brought the sun," she said.

It had been raining for three weeks straight and New Zealand waterways had experienced some of the biggest floods in a lifetime. It was good weather, I supposed, for an eel.

We talked briefly about our itinerary there in the parking lot. Toward the end of our trip, I'd arranged for us to stay at a fishing lodge on the Mohaka River called Poronui Ranch. "That will be a good chance for us to sit down and make sure we both know where we're coming from," Stella said, with slight severity. "About what you're going to write."

I assured Stella that I would be sympathetic to the Maori culture. But she worried me when her tone turned defensive. She mentioned that the stories we would hear during our eel adventure were the "intellectual property" of her people. The Maori people had a right to be wary, even protective—the English colonists had lied to them, stole their language, customs, their spirituality (replacing it, with mixed results, with Christianity), and land. The latest assault in the eyes of some Maori, was the success of the film *Whale Rider*, about a young Maori girl learning the indigenous customs from her grandfather. Hollywood had made all kinds of money on this "intellectual property," and the Maori people hadn't received any measurable compensation. It was clear that Stella was conflicted about being my guide. She seemed happy that I'd shown interest in learning about her culture and sharing it with whomever cared to read, but also reticent about making known what was sacred and very personal, and being paid, though not much, to do so.

The movie *Whale Rider*, Stella agreed, was actually a very realistic portrayal of modern Maori life, especially in the instance of a young girl inheriting the culture from her reluctant grandfather, who traditionally would have passed that knowledge orally to a boy. But the boys in the modern Maori culture had no patience, they had attention problems, were fidgety, and more often than not got into trouble with drugs and alcohol. It was young women like Stella and her sister who were inheriting the faith and staging a cultural revival.

"I'm here," I said, repeating sentiments I'd shared in numerous emails over the previous months, "because of a genuine fascination for a very strange and fascinating fish."

She paused before answering. "Well, you and I are alike, then," she said. "But I didn't always like them. Eels. When my father brought them home, I wouldn't go near them. But my interest in fish is definitely because of my father."

A lot of people were suspicious of me, Stella said, when she rang them up and told them she wanted to bring an American by to do research on eels in Maori culture. "The first thing they said was, 'Why does he want to know?' They've got a lifetime of experience, which traditionally is shared with those in their *hapu*, or sub-tribe, within the iwi. They're suspicious of science."

"I'm not a scientist," I protested.

She knew that, she said, but there was something she wanted me to understand about her culture. "I went to this big eel conference where the leading eel experts in New Zealand had gathered. Don Jellyman, a *pakeha*, probably the most famous, he's at NIWA"—the National Institute of Water and Atmosphere—"and was delivering a paper on his attempts to track eight large migrant eels from the river mouth to their spawning grounds with radio transmitters. He explained that all sign of the radio transmitters had been lost once the eels reached the edge of the trench off the east coast of the South Island. When Don sat down, Kelly Davis, who I hope will be available to see us, got up to represent the Maori. He addressed Don directly, saying, in front of everyone, 'Why do you need to know where they go? The juvenile eels come up the river in spring, the adults migrate out in the fall. My people have known this forever. What good will it do the fish to find the house where they breed?' Don was speechless."

I listened. And I learned not to assert too much, to ask too many questions, and to listen as best I could to what these individuals on our eel adventure had to share. Not an hour went by that Stella did not remind me that we would be meeting with the most knowledgeable people on eels in all New Zealand, that

I was privileged to have time with them. As she advised, I had brought *koha*, or personal gifts to give to them all: small art works I'd made, signed books.

Over lunch at her flat, Stella told me more about her love of eels, and about the time she spent with them. "Why do we have to try to understand everything that isn't understandable? Everyone wants to unlock everything. I'm conflicted because I'm Maori: I don't want to know where they go, and yet I've studied their movements in the rivers in a scientific way."

Our conversation returned to the idea of the taniwha, that important element of Maori stories. In the *Reed Dictionary of Modern Maori*, the translation of taniwha is "water monster, powerful person, ogre." It can make itself known at certain times to certain people, sometimes to warn them of danger. Stella pointed out that the most common form in which a taniwha shows itself is an eel. Usually a large eel.

"If you spear an eel that's a taniwha, or catch it in a net, it will cry like a baby or bark like a dog, or even change colors," Stella said. "If you killed a taniwha, you'd have a *matuku*, or curse, and start going crazy, like you're possessed."

In that case, she added, it meant you had broken *tapu*—something sacred, or off-limits.

Three weeks later, Stella and I were huddled in a tent, stranded in the bush with DJ. He had taken us up a small tributary of the Mata River he called Stony Creek, in the northeast corner of the North Island, so we might fish for trout and search for the big eels that often live in the headwaters of streams. The creek was in a remote piece of tribal land, thick with punga, the exotic looking New Zealand fern tree, the fronds of which hung over emerald plunge pools inhabited by large trout and eels. We'd been dropped off via helicopter four days before. In a driving rain, the river in the canyon rising, we waited for the weather to clear so we could be picked up at the appointed time. A day later, we were still in the tent, wet as water rats, hoping for a break in the rain so we could try to start a fire.

After four days in the bush, DJ was just starting to get comfortable enough with me to tell me what was really on his mind. He was, like all Maori I had come into contact with, a little reserved at first, even intimidating in his silence.

His stature was imposing, tall and thin with dark skin, but strong, like a Native American cowboy. He had a long sage nose and a casual swagger and wore a silver pocket watch in a leather sack on his belt. The rain let up and, toward evening, the sky began to clear. Relieved that we'd probably fly out in the morning, we slipped from our tent, stretched our legs, and, after some effort, got a fire started.

DJ pulled out his skillet to cook the two remaining steaks we'd brought. "I've seen some crazy things out here," he said, poking the fire, making a spot over the coals for the skillet to sit. "But it's more the things I've felt and haven't seen that stick with me."

DJ started to talk about the skillet and its history. He called it his family heirloom but with his Kiwi accent it sounded more like "hair-loom." His short "a" and "i" sounds were long and drawn out, pronounced like "ee"s. I asked DJ if he had any stories of taniwha. I was eager to know more. But, as I was learning, he wouldn't be rushed.

"This was my dad's skillet," DJ said. "Most of the places I take people fishing and hunting in the bush are places I went hunting with my father as a boy. If I'm in an area I don't know I ask local people in the pub, the bros, or I have a yarn with the publican. I never take my white clients along, 'cause if I do, the bros won't talk. They won't even move their leeps, mate." DJ stoked the fire with a stick. A cool wind blew down the river valley.

One time, he said, he was up in the bush with friends on horseback, pig hunting. "We'd camped under this permanent shelter that heed been there foreever. We'd had a long day of hunting and we were cooking a big feed and all of a sudden the bush weent silent. You normally hear all these noises, the crickets and that, like now. Well, it all weent quiet, and then the horses started acting up, and then the dogs weent balleestic. We're told, you know, don't ever camp on the track, you're neever supposed to, but we deed, we were set up right on it." DJ flipped the steaks.

"I'm always trying to reason, and I thought, there's a logical reason why the horses are acting up. An expeerienced horseman could ride up in the dark and spook the horses. People do it all the time. It's possible. I waited for that horseman, but he neever came."

Stella asked if he had grabbed a gun.

"What good's a gun?" DJ asked. "I was in my sleeping bag with the top pulled over my heed. And then come this roar. I don't know how to describe eet, and I never heard eet since, and I'm not superstitious, but I have no way of explaining eet. Eet was like a jeet eengine, and loud, like deefening. I don't know what to call it, like a taniwha or what."

DJ split the steaks three ways and we sat on logs and ate. We made the fire bigger and were soon dry. To hear a personal taniwha story from DJ made me think. This wasn't a dry story told by a European ethnographer, it was an account told in the element from which it was derived. And the impact of the experience was as loud as the monster in his story. It was more impactful than a ghost story at a campfire, because you knew for sure by his tone and serious-ness that DJ had experienced it, and had no logical reason to explain it. But in his spirit, in his Maori spirit, he believed it was a taniwha.

DJ knew I'd come to New Zealand to learn about eels in Maori culture. He'd been waiting for the right moment to tell me his version of things.

"The way I see eet," he said, salting his steak and taking a bite, "there are three players in a New Zealand river: the rainbow trout, the brown trout, and the eel. The eel is the cultural factor. The eel is the Maori factor. The trout is the British colonist. Everyone forgets about the eels because you don't see them. They're out at neeght mostly. You don't see the eel, but he's theere, and he's releentless in his eefforts to catch the trout. He's always stalking them. Ultimately he's the survivor. He can take the other two out eeny time. He might wait years to catch theem. 'Til they geet old and weak. The eel's got time. The eels been theere long before the British put theem in the rivers," DJ threw the gristle from his steak in the fire, "they'll be there eefter. We call that *morehu*, the survivor."

DJ's was a common sentiment among Maori in the early twenty-first cen-tury. The culture, buried underground for the better part of a hundred years, was re-emerging with a vengeance, and sometimes with some resentment for the descendents of the British colonists. The eel, I would come to find, was not only "sacred," but one of the most important creatures in Maori culture for a host of reasons—the lubricious creature seducing the wife of gods, a synonym of the penis, a protector, and the main traditional food source for the inland Maori. But most importantly, the eel was a symbol of what we were losing, the world over—that the loss of nature would equal a loss of culture, especially indigenous "pagan" culture, a loss of connection to the earth, and loss of soul.

This new world was not one I wanted to live in. And I began to rethink the assumptions I'd made about indigenous people from the things I'd read in the work of Campbell and Elsdon Best. I'd treated the stories about taniwha in the way that they were presented, as myth. But from the seriousness of tone in my conversations with Stella and DJ and others, I was finding out that what I had perceived as "mythology" was indeed very much a part of the spiritual reality of the Maori. And in many ways, the eelian thinking about nature, as an idea that couldn't be, and didn't need to be, pinned down, that would persevere, began to make a lot of sense.

As far as spirituality went, the idea at the source of, for instance, the Christian faith was much more portable and versatile than the core of the nature-based faith. The success of the Christian "myth" it occurred to me, sitting in that tent in the rain, listening to DJs story, was its versatility, malleability, and portability. The Christian religion was based on the belief that the son of God, in human form, came to earth to take away our sins; this can be understood by any human anywhere in any environment in the world. The concepts of the Christian religion are promoted both in buildings built by people and in the open air. The difference with a nature-based faith like that of the Maori (and other indigenous peoples around the world) is that once you lose the Nature that the spiritual system is based on, you are also in danger of losing spirituality. If the eel is endangered is the Maori sense of spirituality also endangered? If a young Maori boy does not see a giant eel, is not awed by that six-foot writhing pile of muscle, can he have faith, truly, in a taniwha? What has happened to a large extent in the Maori culture is that the British immigrants began to destroy the foundation of the Maori faith. The Acclimatization Society (the established Department of Wildlife if you will) introduced trout to make the streams friendly for settlers from England, and they trapped the large eels, leaving them stranded on the bank, because they saw them as a threat to the introduced fish. Kelly Davis, an old Maori I spoke to later in the trip, said that he used to walk the banks of the river with his dad, kicking these large stranded eels back into the river. The British knew the quickest way to eradicate an indigenous culture, remove the creatures that are spiritually and gastronomically closest to them.

The end of the eel for the Maori (and the whale and the kiwi) was the end of an idea. It is precisely what the Europeans did to the American plains Indians when they slaughtered hundreds of thousands of Bison. Is there a connection between the loss of such natural wonders in New Zealand and the disillusioned youth of the Maori, especially the boys, who are turning to drugs and mischief instead of nature? When their energies and aggressions are not spent running around fishing and hunting do they turn to hostility? Toward their spouses, toward the government, toward everything? What becomes clearer and clearer to our 21st century society, with all our wisdom and reason, is that, although it is harder to imagine myth as a spiritual reality, we do need some form of spirituality. I found when I was in New Zealand, that when I let my "reason" fade, and imagined a giant eel living in a deep pool, one that warned off children from a dangerous current, or protected the surroundings of a place, or heard stories of areas of forest that were sacred, where there is a spiritual silence, where "no birds sing," I felt whole, I felt motivated, and I felt human.

James Prosek is a painter, writer, and documentary filmmaker. He became passionate about fish at the age of nine, when his early paintings of birds became fish. His eight books include *Trout: An Illustrated History* and the children's book *A Good Day's Fishing*. His work has been shown in New York City, Sante Fe, and Philadelphia. His documentary about Izaac Walton won a 2003 Peabody Award. His most recent book and first novel is *The Day My Mother Left* (spring 2007). He finds fly fishing "a great vehicle for getting into nature. It has a low impact on the environment and is a way of exercising humans' predatory urges without killing anything."

The Island

MARGOT PAGE

The Atlantic Ocean off Cape Cod is virtually boiling with fish, the brownish striped bass rolling slowly on their sides as they gulp the bait they have trapped on the surface. A layer of bluefish slash just underneath. A glint in the high summer sun, seagulls hover excitedly twenty feet above the water, one to a fish, dropping to the surface when they see a choice available morsel of baitfish.

Gleeful shouts pepper our twenty-one-foot craft as we stagger for balance in the pitch and rock of the waves. The fish move toward us and then away in predatory packs, marked by gulls and the agitated surface. In between frenzied moments of their activity, we wait at attention, scanning the surface of the water intently, heads swiveling. We're not looking at one another: all eyes are on the gulls and the water. We hold our fly lines at the ready.

Tom and I have brought Brooke along—now seven and a half, too smart for empty promises, too young for no reward—with the tantalizing promise of a boat ride to a tiny "desert island" off the Cape.

Our captain is Tony Biski, a burly, enthusiastic convert to fly fishing, about which he says, "Fly fishing is an art, something to do while you're fishing." Today he is taking us to the flats off Monomoy Point, the thin finger of sand pointing south from the Cape's elbow, home to seabirds, dunes, and many sea disasters of yore. But while we're coming off the high tide, we detour to The Rip where he's just received radio reports of blitzing fish.

My arm is firmly around Brooke's tubby, colorful life preserver. Her Barbie dangles from her hand as we skim over the high tide that covers the miles of

undulating white sand we will later walk. Approaching the ocean side of
Monomoy we can smell the distinctive oil slick produced by baitfish being
shredded, and see gulls circling and diving—two sure indicators of large groups
of working fish.

While Tony controls the boat, trying not to drift over the path of the fish,
we swiftly lift our rods out of the keepers. Within a couple of casts, Tom hooks
and lands two fish, and then—after a drawn-out fight into the backing—lands a
twenty-pound striper. I, too, quickly hook a heavy fish and can feel him shaking
his head against the line. Pulling him in, we see the flashes of blue—he is a large
bluefish—just before he shakes himself one last time and bites off my tippet with
his razored teeth.

We wait in a momentary calm, and Tony repositions the boat to where the
gulls are working. The brown rolls start in waves towards us, a liquid earthquake,
the gulls again fluttering above. Not used to a stripping basket, I have elected to
leave my line free and as a result familiarize myself with every protuberance in
Tony's boat. As I am having trouble casting any distance with the nine-weight
rod into the wind, Tony suggests I use his eight-weight with a sinking line.
Instantly my range improves and the deep ache in my shoulder disappears, but
because of my excitement, I still cast badly and miss.

Seeing striped bass in such healthy profusion after the decline of the 1970s
and 1980s is wild and exhilarating. They arc in chopping circles, swirls of beige
backs breaking the surface as they twist and turn in deceptively lazy, vicious
packs. Daytime fishing is, obviously, different from night fishing, because here
you can see the fish moving up from the murky depths or prowling along the
surface. You can see the take or kick yourself about what you're missing.

Of course, night fishing has its particular compensation: the sea's neon phos-
phorescence lights up the stripers as if they're electric.

And then there's always the indigo night.

★ ★ ★

By this time, Brooke's patience is beginning to fray. We have sold this expedition to her based on an island of sand and that is what she wants to see

right now. Nearly an hour of this pitching and rolling is enough. She begins to complain. "You two are fishing maniacs," she cries with only marginal humor.

Fish are boiling towards us again and our attention is diverted from her crisis. We cast furiously into the watery chaos, hooking or missing as the case may be, forgetting about the small, unhappy member of our quartet. Soon, we hear the sound of pointed foot stamping, harrumphing, and covert groans. We are too preoccupied to respond. Tom hooks a huge striper and our yells of delight set Brooke off in the opposite direction. Never one to hide her feelings, she shouts loudly, "I WANT TO GO TO THE ISLAND NOW!" But my attention shifts to Tom whose face is wreathed with joy as the giant bass runs down into the depths. He sets about bringing it in. Brooke will have no part of it. "NOOO MORE FISSSHHHHINNNGGG!"

To fend off impending disaster, Tom, at the same time he reels in his prize, launches into a long and complicated story involving a cockatiel at a pet store that has amazing adventures. As soon as she hears the magic words, "Once upon a time . . ." Brooke instantly settles into her rapt listening mode, but she is still suspicious enough of her good fortune to give no quarter. When Tom pauses to reel and pump the line and marvel at his luck for a few seconds, Brooke registers immediate vocal displeasure, and Tom resumes, seamlessly, the meandering thread of his story. When the fish is landed and released, the cockatiel's saga continues through my search for my fish ("No, Brooke, we can't leave until Mommy gets *her* fish," Tom explains.)

Mercifully, I finally hook and land a small striper, about twelve pounds, that takes me into the short backing. Tony, the captain, has been feeling the strain. He flicks a drop of sweat from his brow and grins happily. We take a couple of photographs, release the fish, and Tom gives me a kiss and formal congratulations on my first daytime striper. Brooke is moaning insistently. We zoom quickly back to the flats where the tide is receding.

"You've been spoiled, Margot, really spoiled," Tom teases with satisfaction. "You've seen it as good as it gets."

★ ★ ★

The high tide is on the wane, leaving crescent pillows of fawn-colored sand islands that turn white as they dry. On the horizon the emerald dunes that line Monomoy lend the seascape dimension and color under the reassuring blue dome of this enormous summer sky. Old fishing weirs spike in the distance, like startling, thin, tall fences sticking out of the ocean, grandfathered down in families through the area's salty legacy.

We jump out of the boat into knee-deep, clear ocean water. I strip to my bathing suit and anorak and wade over the firm flats, grateful to sink my feet into the fine, sugar sand. If you didn't know *you* were on the Massachusetts coast, you could be persuaded this was the Caribbean, so clear is the water, so smooth and white the sand.

In the distance, Tony stalks the flats like a muscular, nut-brown bear, his keen green eyes looking seaward always. Over on the other side of the island, Tom has flipped his stripping basket over his shoulder and is heading away; in one hand he carries his rod and with the other holds the hand of a little girl with a blonde braid who wears a shocking pink bathing suit and carries a bright blue pail, both colors visible at long distance. They range further, getting smaller and vaguer, one looking for shells and crabs, one looking for fish. Ocean treasures.

When we leave later that afternoon, Tony tells me he has named this little island for Brooke.

★ ★ ★

Several days later, Brooke is invited to play at the beach with friends. At this point in our vacation week, I am numbed from the medical problems of my father, a widowed stroke victim, who lives on the Cape year-round. We have come to visit him only to discover him in medical crisis. Though I have other things on my mind than fishing during this short reprieve from my unofficial nursing duty, I am drawn—hollow as I feel at the moment—to the water. We go again to the sea.

This day we hit low tide right on the nose. Tom and I are now enjoying the company of two Tonys, our captain again, Tony Biski, and our artist friend Tony Stetzko, who in 1981 held the world's record for a surf-caught striper (seventy-three pounds). The sheet of water on the flats we had skimmed over three days

ago has now receded, leaving acres of white, rippled sand. Before Tony B. fin-
ishes anchoring the boat in the remaining tide, I plunge into the clean, warm
ocean, readying my rod with one hand and adjusting a waist pack around my
neck with the other. Shouted instructions drift on the wind behind me as the
two Tonys rig up their tackle. Tom is out of the boat too, ranging wordlessly and
rapidly out to the far flats through the knee-deep water. Tony S. strides out
through the water calling eagerly to me, "You're too far, come in on this side of
the slough, they're all in here." A pause, then a shout, "LOOK AT THEM . . .
SEE THOSE HUGE SHADOWS, THERE THEY GO!"

Behind me there is a close splash, and I hear it and Tony doesn't. I whirl and
see the boil and cast and instantly nail a large creature. Plunging, the beast runs
out for a while, then eventually turns and bites the hook off.

We wait and shuffle along the slough, this being apparently a slow day on
the flats, and Tony teaches me: *See the birds working over there, see the dark edge near
the light band, that's where they're coming in, going after the bait, pushing them toward
the beach. They like to rub their bellies on the sand, so they come in shallow. They're
coming right in.* OH, LOOK AT THEM, OH HERE THEY COME, GET
READY, GET READY, THEY'RE MONSTERS, OVER HERE, RIGHT IN
FRONT OF . . . (cast, cast, cast, strip, strip, strip).

OH . . . *Oh . . . oh . . . there they go.* . . . Tall and lean, Tony has long, dark
Botticelli curls and a small, somewhat dashing scar on his cheek from a boating
accident. A friend to all, he boyishly strides the Cape beaches like a great,
excited heron.

We walk along the exposed tidal flats of this broad ocean floor, following
the little rivers that flow through channels in the dead-low water. Stripers, blues,
and maybe bonito are cruising along these miniature rivers, the Tonys explain to
us, dining on nature's conveyer belt of sand eels and baitfish.

We come to the convergence of tidal flows where we catch a tidy number of
stripers, fishing our striper patterns like nymphs, releasing them all after admiring
their size or coloration. Someone brings me a live sand dollar to admire—I had
only ever seen their bleached skeletons—and I place the brown-flannelled disk
back in the ocean to, I hope, find a mate and make more sand dollars.

Then we amble back to our original starting position before the quickly
incoming tide dissipates the still-feeding stripers off Brooke's Island's shores.

While we walk back, Tony S. tells me how once he was so excited casting to a night blitz of fish that he dislocated his shoulder—which didn't deter him from completing the evening's fishing.

Now *that's* a fishing maniac.

★ ★ ★

By the time we reach the island, my intense need to catch fish has subsided. I have another mission.

After casting without success for a while, I wade back to the anchored boat by myself, grab a sandwich, soda, and a towel, and run back over the humped sand bar to where my carefully placed rod is about to get engulfed by wavelets. Safely repositioning it in a cradle of dark seaweed near the apex of the island, I spread my towel on the white sand of this crescent island and eat my lunch.

In the distance stand the optimistic, hazy figures of the men poised at the ready in the shimmering ocean. Around me, dunlins and yellowlegs twitter and scurry. As I relax, only the sound of the waves and the wind and the birds fill my ears.

Now it is time. I am overwhelmed trying to spread myself around to all those who need me—my father on the Cape, my husband and daughter, my work. Two households to run, an expanded team of nurses and home health aides' schedules to keep track of. How to keep my father safe and honor his wishes to stay at home when he needs twenty-four-hour care?

At this moment, I just want to run away. The nightmares of aides not showing up have made even my nights heavy. I can't get away from the image of my father's jaw clenched in pain, the helplessness of his frail body. The stuffiness of that old, hot, whaling captain's house.

I wait for the weariness, the confusion, the sadness to be washed out of me by the only salve I know.

The sand crystals coat my hand where it lies on the beach, the terns mew and cry, the sun warms my shoulders. There is a deep throb of a boat on the horizon and the sound of the waves' nurturing constancy as they throw themselves on the beach one after the other. Here, on this little island, miles from the mainland, there is no talking, no demands, no decisions I have to make. I am responsible, at this instant, only for myself. Not a human figure in sight except for the three sympathetic and somewhat protective men who have brought me here and are now gathered on the faraway boat to eat their lunch.

This is my oasis. Brooke's Island. The island of a young girl in a pink bathing suit with a bright blue pail, her blonde hair shining like a beacon.

Here, a bit of wonder returns to pierce my depression. Here, the breeze begins to blow and cleanse. The distant thrum of the boat engine, the calling of the plovers, the sandpipers, the steady fall of the waves, start to nibble at the mounting chaos of schedules, urinals, pain control, and emergency trips to the pharmacy for gauze, saline, rubber gloves, and medicine. I stand up and walk the receding perimeters of this white crescent island, now a mere patch curving out of the encroaching, resolute ocean. I mark off my territory, reclaiming myself from within my father's slow demise. No one is watching me, I am alone. My companions are back out on the flats, ever hopeful, ranging like a small pack of benign wolves.

He's suffered enough. Twenty-two years of paralysis.

★ ★ ★

The rivers of salt water are now slowly narrowing the spit of white sand. Little lapping rivers turn into wide ones, then become bays, and then merge with the ocean. Soon the foam will touch my toes and I will move further up the island.

I can't fill my mind enough with the seascape, the radiating light, the liquid sounds of the sea. But random thoughts intrude: images of the icy February ocean ahead. Worries from life back in Vermont. How in an hour we shall have to leave and I fear I won't be able to return to fish these flats for another year.

Eight long-necked cormorants skim low over the water's surface. They line the tidal islands, some with wings extended, frozen in mid-flap as they dry their feathers. Sandpipers hurry by me along the water's edge like race walkers in the park, beady dark eyes darting nervously. It's gratifying to note their healthy populations.

All of us have our own rivers, I remind myself, with their own beginnings and end-ings. I am alone on mine, as is my father. I stand in awe of the wonder of circumstance and the mysteries of our lives.

Tom splashes over with a bottle of mint iced tea and some sugar wafers. "They're *killing* them out in the rip! Wanta go or stay here?"

I elect to stay and he and the two Tonys speed out toward the Atlantic with lots of large hand-waves and big smiles.

I look around. Now I can be by myself on the planet, for this briefest of moments in time. Maybe I'll be lucky and they'll forget me and so I'll have to spend the night on the island.

This idea makes me excited and nervous.

I will bundle up in my windbreaker and towel. I have a Tootsie Pop, Snapple, and a pack of Kleenex in my waist pack, along with a juicy book, pen, and fat notebook. I will watch the glorious Cape Cod sun go down on my now-tiny island of twenty square feet. Then I will huddle and wait for the Perseid meteor shower, the silver dashes flashing so fast in the inky canopy you're not sure you even saw them.

With my rod and only one fly, I will catch a small bluefish, eat sushi, chew on some seaweed. Suck on the last of the lemon drops. Morning will come, a sunrise of indisputable hope and renewal. The striped bass will roil in, just for me, and I shall cast, catch, and release these great creatures from the ocean. Later in the day, the Coast Guard will pick me up on my deserted island, sunburned, thirsty, and I shall have been cleansed by the meteors, the salt winds, the cry of the terns. My fears of death and loss will have been swept away, and I will be ready to return to my father.

I am alone. Peace wraps me like an airy miracle. Slow and light.

★ ★ ★

Some time later, the wavelets converge and move more rapidly up the white sand, devouring several inches a minute. I notice an insistent tone to the waves as they get closer. I pick up my gear and move it into the very middle of the exposed sand with a faint feeling of alarm. My crescent island is becoming a fingernail. I am under the assumption that this island stays dry but we are still two hours away from peak high tide. What if this is an abnormal tide? What if my whole island gets swallowed and my companions haven't returned?

I succumb to a brief moment of panic and then happen to glance over to a corner of the island where two seagulls are standing on a tiny crescent island of their own. At the same instant my eyes alight on them, their sliver of sand is being washed over by the first waves. The gulls, looking calmly out to sea, stand knee-deep in the rising tide and then confidently strut about their drowned island.

Again, I patrol my island as the tide comes up. I can measure its width in number of footsteps. And as I walk, I notice that I am not altogether alone. A strange speedboat with one lone occupant has been making a couple of large circles around my island, watching me with craned neck, I now realize. I mildly speculate on what kind of weapon a graphite fly rod would make.

As I complete my tour with hands clasped behind my back, watching my feet making prints in the sand, Tom and the two Tonys suddenly appear, surfing in fast to the island on a big boat wake with anxious looks on their faces. It turns out they couldn't see me from afar, and when they finally spotted my vertical figure on the horizon, it looked as if I was engulfed by water, with that lone boat circling like a shark.

I also learn that my island does *not* remain dry at high tide.

We head for home. The guys are still talking with fevered interest about where the bass are, what and why they do what they do. Tony S. enthuses about plans to bring a mask and a raft the next time, so he "can swim down one of the rivers of eel grass *right next* to the bass." As we gather speed, I look behind me at Brooke's Island. A vessel in full sail moves majestically behind it as the slim patch of sand disappears in the waves.

We hit the rougher water, banging and slamming hard into the waves, the wind whipping strings of my hair into my mouth. Each hard satisfying crash pounds away the remnants of my depression. The pointed white nameless ghosts of a sailing regatta line the haze on the horizon. One has capsized.

Suddenly we are at the harbor mouth. Tony B. cuts the throttle.

The island is nearly underwater by now, but it is a comfort to remember that the tide will eventually turn.

Margot Page is a nonfiction writer/book editor living in Vermont. The author of three books on sport—*Little Rivers: Tales of a Woman Angler, Just Horses,* and *The Art of Fly Fishing*—she is the former editor of the quarterly journal of the American Museum of Fly Fishing and the granddaughter of the legendary writer/editor Sparse Grey Hackle. She began her fly fishing career in 1983 working in the New York publishing offices of Nick Lyons. She thinks that rivers, oceans, and all the creatures that live therein, are the coolest things Mother Nature ever invented. Mountains, too.

A Disappearing Act

CRAIG NOVA

The pleasure of going into a grouse cover with a shotgun, as Ortega y Gassett says in a little book called *On Hunting*, is that the hunter escapes everything and, for a moment anyway, he is only alert. He isn't reflective, isn't calculating. He isn't worried about his taxes, or the leak in the roof at home, or his kids' SAT scores. He isn't even concerned, really, if his dog is staunch and careful with the bird it's pointing. This alertness is pleasurable because it is a reminder of what it was like to live before human beings had consciousness. Having had this experience, I can say that is very pleasurable and haunting, too, since to be in this state is to be completely aloof from everything but the physical.

In fishing there is a similar pleasure and one that is even more intense, and I like to think of it as the instant when everything disappears. Here is the way I have experienced it.

I was fishing a northern stretch of the Connecticut River, not far from the Canadian boarder. It was evening, and the surface had a green satin quality in which the flowers on the bank appeared as white smears. Some pale mayflies were on the water, a cream variant, I guessed, and I was casting one of these into a silvery run that was at the head of a pool. I was standing in just the right spot, since I could see the fly as it came out of the fast water and then, with a kind of languid movement, it floated on the shimmering surface. The fly slowed down, didn't drag, and just hung there as though suspended between the green of the water and the green of the trees and bank. It was right there. Then it was gone.

I have noticed a small lag in my understanding at this moment. Maybe it is the difference between the alertness of watching and the alertness of having to take action, but in the instant when the fly disappears, I have the sensation that everything else does, too, and for a brief period, so brief as to be maddeningly illusive, I seem to exist in some state that is nowhere at all. It is that same nowhere that is part of those most pleasurable parts of life: inspiration, the moment when understanding is just about to arrive, the second before everything makes sense, the time when people realize that they are in love. Then the world reasserts itself. The river reappears, and the line becomes taught. The electric, trembling fish makes itself apparent. You tighten the line and start playing the fish, too concerned with that to give the moment you have just been through a second thought.

But later, in the car on the way home or in a bar that I find to have a beer (and where I can feel the first warmth of a sunburn) I have the recurring sensation of that time when the world seemed to reboot. It is a small thing, or so it seems, just an instant, but I often think that a large part of the pleasure of fishing is right there, in that place that you can't see and can never quite get your hooks into. It is, or so it seems to me, part of the illusive quality of all pleasant things, the essence that, because it can't be summed up precisely, always eludes us. But that doesn't mean it isn't there, and sometimes I think this pleasure is a sort of invisible substance, a delight that makes itself apparent in one of those short lived moments. At these times, I think we are all in it together: the fish, the moment, and the fisherman.

Craig Nova has written eleven novels, including *The Good Son*, *Trombone*, *The Universal Donor*, and *Cruisers*, and an autobiography, *Brook Trout and the Writing Life*. He has received numerous awards, including a Guggenheim Foundation Fellowship and an Award in Literature from the American Academy and Institute of Arts and Letters. His short fiction has appeared in *Esquire*, *The Paris Review*, and in *The Best American Short Stories*. His work has been widely translated. He is currently the Class of 1949 Distinguished Professor of the Humanities at the University of North Carolina.

A River of Child

SETH NORMAN

Sophia Mariah will get no pastel waders, at least not her first pair, though I may throw a Pink Lady into the mobile of flies which will circle her crib. Imagine that construction urged into motion by the nursery breeze. Better yet, consider that among her first views of the world will be a hatch presented from the trout's point of view . . . how can she go wrong? It will seem only natural to a child so imprinted when someday I explain her origins:

"Daddy sent his sperm a-spawning on the Lovely River Mom. Oh, the way was long, the journey difficult, but at last one brave sperm nestled in Mommy's redd. He shared with her a secret code, then signed a sacred pact, sweet girl. And if you'll check Clause 32, section 4) b, you'll see it requires you to tie a dozen midges today, size 22, before you go to school."

Sophie will *want* to tie those midges, of course, knowing that half are for her. She will likely delight to pin a few on Barbie's vest, crying gaily, "Oh Dad, can I also practice my reach casts tonight? And *please, please, can* I take some leeches to class, for Ms. Carson's show-and-tell?"

Never mind spelling and social science: I'll encourage excellence in Entomology, Ichthyology, and Physics of Casting. And certainly one must learn to read, in order to appreciate Lyons and Leeson and Roderick Haig-Brown.

Balance, you see. That's what I'll strive for.

Naturally it's impossible not to think of my daughter exploring a stream. Images of children and water—deep eddies and bright riffles, the edges of ponds—swell in my mind with a sentiment which defies cliché: true wonder never feels cheap. Nor can a kid's curiosity sit subject to ordinary judgments. In the days when I fished for food my stepchildren would demand I bring the catch home whole, so they might examine each organ I removed. "That's his heart? That's his guts—what's inside? Is that a *snail*? What happens when you cut open its eye?"

One stormy night when Cathy was seven or eight, she insisted on holding a flashlight and umbrella, to watch as I cleaned live young from a viviparous perch. I worried that the sight of fry babies would appall her, but no, she was merely amazed. Her credibility would only stretch so far, it turned out. Neither she nor her twin Eric—not even older brother Marc—would believe the whopper I told about the lives of flounder. "A fish's eyes can't *move*, just because it gets older! That's impossible!" Cynics, so doubtful . . . and ten minutes later I caught the twins trying to adjust their own baby browns in a mirror. "See! It just doesn't work!"

It's possible, I know, that Sophia will have an entirely different world view from mine. Acorns may fall close to oaks, but they roll. One hunter friend of mine has a daughter, now a woman, who was apparently *born* vegetarian. And I do worry about aberrations in Soph's gene pool, given that her mother considers carp "cute" and leans toward the idea that worms, while loathsome, should have the right to vote, at least in primaries. "That's not *rabbit* fur?" she will demand, sighting me at my vise, her outburst catching the attention of Blossom, our house bunny. Then I must launch a long story about road kills, respect for resources, et al. Mom-to-be will glare, then show her true colors when she lifts my best peacock plume for some pointless vase arrangement. Already we argue about proper care and handling. "I don't care *how* Hopis carried their babies," she snapped last week, "Sophia's not going anywhere zipped into the back of a fishing vest!"

So much for my patented Pupae Pouch. And I bet I hear no end of objections to her first float tube, no matter how neatly I sew around the rubber duck's little head.

Still, I'm confident that Daddy's girl will shrug off Mom's provincial attitude, educated as she will be from toddler-age to casting tight loops, wasting no wraps, keeping the hook-eye clear. Sophie will see TV only as an excuse to sit tight at the vise, baseball as good training for overhead casting, wild dancing as practice for wading too deep. And what a treat for the neighbors, that first Halloween, when she drifts down street dressed as a stonefly nymph! Neat little antenna, ostrich-herl gills and tail-gills out to there . . .

There's a more serious side to all this, of course. Already I worry more about the future, what opportunities it will hold, how I might assure these. I cringe to imagine the two of us standing beside some river or lake as I mouth dread words I've heard too often—"You wouldn't believe how good this once was." So it happens that, even in the midst of developing new family consciousness, scaling down my life to tend closely the immediate world my daughter will enter, I have also the compulsion to make larger things right. The sight of mother-to-be's profile will, suddenly, prompt me to write checks to my favorite conservation outfit, for example. At times I'm likely to consider new equations, as in, "If the Trinity River gets the water it needs this year, how many steelhead will return the first seasons Sophia's ready to throw a seven-weight?"

The present's exciting, the future holds questions . . . but I also find myself angling in memory, upstream, toward the headwaters of my own life. There's gray at the edges of early images, a certain stillness. Sadness, also: Sophie will never fish for porgies with Grandpa Charley, wondering about the Cossock edge to his eyes, smelling on his neck the good brown scents of beer and tobacco and sweat while tracing on his knuckles scars from a knife fight in Harlem. Nor will she ever hesitate on the edge of sleep, riding home from Lake Pleasant in a '65 Ford Galaxie 500, face pressed to the bench seat back, watching my father's eyes as he watches the road and feeling as about as safe as anybody can in this life, gloating to hear him say, "You know there's really no need to tell your mother the part about the snake." I'd hoped to have Andre Puyans teach to her tie—even grinned, anticipating a nod from the Master's leonine head as she whip-finishes a loop wing while he watched . . .

Not to be. There's a limit to what we pass on; and some things just pass away. Other adventures await, unknown today, soon to become memories in their own right. Not all will be fine: together we will know harm, as well as a host of firsts, biggests, bests, even a few years of "remember when?" I'll be ready and eager, probably flush with platitudes: Fight the good fights, Sophia, for our forests and fish. Watch your shadow on the water. Listen to your mother, and don't tell her about the part about the snake.

In the meantime, Sophia? Stay limber, in that warm pool you drift. Flex those tiny digits. Your new eyes will see marvels, I know, but these old ones with which I'll watch you with such excitement . . .? Ah, well, they're having a few a problems with size 22 midges, these days. But that's only one reason I'll tie the flies of your mobile larger than life.

Seth Norman's reporting on police corruption led to the Jane Harrah Award, a Golden Medallion, and nomination for the Pulitzer Prize. He has written for most national fly fishing magazines—also *Gray's Sporting Journal, Outdoor Life,* and *Field & Stream*—is Books Editor for *Fly Rod & Reel,* Master of Meander for *California Fly Fisher,* author of *Meanderings of a Flyfisherman* and *The Fly Fisher's Guide to Crimes of Passion.* He adds, "I've always sought excitement in fishing, also diversion, solace and, once, sanctuary. . . . In fly fishing I've found special friends, perhaps because our stylized blood sport attracts people of unusual quality and character, committed to codes and ethics and honor . . . also to exquisite and frightening nature. A fine lot of fine eccentrics, to be blunt."

From Birth

JAKE MOSHER

This was the second time in less than three minutes that the game warden had driven over the culvert, and the big rainbow trout on the end of my hand line was getting as nervous as I was. He darted across the pool, holding in an eddy beneath the fluorescent pink sign tacked to an overhanging alder which declared his stream off limits to fishing during the spawn. I could feel him down there, throbbing against the monofilament, wondering when he would begin his acrobatics, a show certain to draw further attention from the already-suspicious warden. Reluctantly, I unwound a dozen coils of line from my hand, letting it spill over the edge of the culvert, watching from within its confines the reflection of the green Chevy that had stopped on the road above.

I hated to give that fish any slack, but without it he was sure to explode. I'd fooled him with the nightcrawler, letting him take it deep in his mouth with the weighty tug only a large fish is capable of, careful to set the hook delicately, planning to play him cautiously until I could ease all four, exhausted pounds of him over the lip of the culvert. I figured the warden had seen my bicycle in the red osier patch a hundred yards downstream and it didn't require a leap of faith on his part to realize some bad boy was fishing nearby, three weeks before the season opened. He hadn't counted on me hiding in the culvert, however, braving northern Vermont's icy April runoff, so for the moment, as long as the barbed, number 4 hook held and the rainbow didn't begin jumping, I was confident I'd get away with it. Confident I'd be the only boy in town with a last name other than Royer (a family whose skill at catching spring-run rainbow trout was unparalleled and who would approve heartily of the tactics I was employing), to come home that day with one of the French Canadian red-stripes on leave from the deep waters of Lake Memphremagog for a few weeks to ensure that each spring more of his kind would make the southern pilgrimage up Vermont's rivers and streams. If I had my way, by god, this was one trout that wouldn't resume its Quebec residency.

★ ★ ★

It seems like a long time ago now. Hell, it *was* a long time ago. I haven't fished for spring rainbows or any other kind of trout in Vermont for more than ten years, haven't ridden a bike in twice that long, and have managed to put approximately 2,323 miles between me and that warden. I'd have put more, but I like southwest Montana better than all points west, so unless we annex British Columbia—a proposition I could no doubt readily recruit local help with—this will have to do. And why not? Memories of my first decade in Montana glide through my head like the upper Missouri I live on in May when she's running bank-full, swift and clear, the mirror opposite of her lower, lethargic self. They are memories of midnight, October browns, mountain goats blending with alpine fog along the high lakes where they drink as I fish for cutthroats, of September meadows full of the musk of elk and foot-long brook trout slapping at grasshopper flies they've torn the hackle from, and of the quiet solitude unique to a big river you've got to yourself in the moments just before sunset. Sometimes, they run with memories much older.

★ ★ ★

My parents named me for the northern Vermont outlaw fisherman, Jake Blodgett. Robert Frost might have said that in doing so, from the time I came out of the womb and scrutinized the hospital room—looking for a place to wet a line, my father says—I was destined to have a healthy disdain for authority, a stiff, left jab, and an innate sense of where to catch a trout. It might have been set in stone from the moment my birth certificate was filled out or, more likely, I think, it was a combination of nomenclature and upbringing.

My father started taking me fishing with him before I was three. Some of my first memories involve dangling in his backpack, bumping across brown fields not yet free of snow, turning my face sideways into the collar of his wool coat so that out of one eye I watched lichen-covered stone piles, tall stalks of mullein, unyielding even to Vermont's long winter, the woods line of budded maples where I first felt the throb of drumming grouse wings, and the cut of softwoods that marked the course of the stream we'd fish. It was there, in the shade of a hemlock, that I caught my first trout. I remember feeling the wondrous tug of life on the end of the line, lifting five inches of flopping brook trout out of the water, watching—with both eyes this time—as my father broke its neck, blood dotting the snow in a pattern I could trace to this day. It was my introduction to the country philosophy that some of god's creatures were put here because quite frankly with a little salt and pepper they, like my first fish, taste pretty damn good.

My only memory of Jake Blodgett comes fast on the heels of that trout I caught just before, against his doctor's advice, he spent two weeks fishing for spring rainbows, contracted pneumonia, and passed from this world into one where I suspect, as he was so adept at doing here during prohibition, he must once again smuggle whiskey. I remember sitting on his lap looking up at the whiskers on his face, into eyes that met mine with approval, and would continue to do so as long as I never released a fish, backed down from a fight, or had much good to say about any officer of the law. I trust that in the thirty years since then I haven't disappointed him greatly.

My boyhood passed in a whirlwind of fishing expeditions and mythical stories about my namesake, landmarks all over northern Vermont existing to lend credence to the fascinating tales. Here was the covered bridge he'd sat submerged beneath with a trunkload of white lightning as the revenuers' lights shined above him, this was the store where a surly clerk was hauled over the counter and suffered Jake Blodgett's trademark punishment of having his face rubbed raw on his wool coat, there was the dam where all it took to procure three or four limits' worth of fish was a "little charge" of dynamite, and the winding dirt road where, when late in life Jake finally attempted to get a legal drivers license, he took the test examiner for a wild ride at over 100 miles an hour. Between stories of bear hunts, whiskey running, and fist fights, my father made sure that we never let a warm, May rain go to waste—even if it meant me dodging school for a day—that by the time I was ten I could cast a dropper fifty feet off a split-piece bamboo fly rod, and that I understood there were times when I might have to "slug" someone in the stomach in order to reach a better understanding.

★ ★ ★

On the edge of my youth, as Vermont teetered on the edge of a new era in which people like my namesake—and to a certain extent myself—are not tolerated, I found myself hunkered down inside a culvert, raging that I'd just given a hell of a trout too much slack. Through the "cold, blue" eyes my father had recently told me that I had to be careful how I looked at my school teachers with—named for Jake Blodgett or not he was growing weary of trips in to meet with the principal—I stared at the reflection of the warden's truck. I stared hard, willing him away into my past where he blends with the sweet taste of that rainbow and times when I learned a great deal about being a man and a fisherman. They are lessons that have stood me in good stead in Montana, though I'm half ashamed to say I release virtually all fish I catch these days, am something of friends with an Idaho game warden, and confine most fighting to a boxing ring. Still, there are times—

★ ★ ★

The steelhead had come into the river early, arriving in February, threading their way upstream between cuts in shelf ice, resting in deep seams where they would postpone their odyssey until the sun hit and warmed the water each day. I had already picked up two of them on eggs, great males pushing the 40-inch mark with hooked jaws and sea lice on their gills. A pair of fly fishermen in the head of the pool were grumbling. Loudly. I was certain I'd heard "goddamn" and "bait fisherman" in the same sentence, and I wasn't happy about it. One of them began working his way downstream toward me, whipping his Winston as though he was driving a team of unruly mules, round, red face glistening with whatever he'd smeared on it to help ward off the cold. I watched his weighted nymph whistle closer, slipped it as it came for my head, letting it lodge in the canvas shoulder of my beat-up Carhartt work jacket that I'd been logging in. Like a big brown going for a mouse, I had his leader and then the main line, stripping it off the reel hand over hand until fifteen yards of it hung at my feet. It broke too easily, weather-checked no doubt from lack of dressing and exposure to sunshine, drifting slack before me like the line from so many years earlier in the culvert. Not at all careful how I looked at him, I asked if he'd like it back and several things happened at once. A tom turkey across the river, aware that daylight was finding his perch earlier than a month ago, gobbled, the sun rose, the fly fisherman nodded, and I grinned.

"Then come and get it," I said. A dimension away, on another early, spring river, I suspect Jake Blodgett had already sized him up. Filson wool, Simms waders, bulbous nose. He wasn't going to take time away from his own fishing to watch this one. Besides, I'd released my two fish and he was mad at me.

Jake Mosher lives in Southwest Montana near the headwaters of the Missouri River. His work has appeared in *Outdoor Life*, *The New York Times*, *Yankee*, and *Bugle*, and he has written two Montana-based novels, *The Last Buffalo Hunter* and *Every Man's Hand*. He has fished and hunted all over North America, working as a logger, freelance journalist, blaster, prizefighter, and big-game guide. He continues to live in the tradition of his namesake, happiest in wild country with his fly rod or rifle.

What's in a Name?

HOWARD FRANK MOSHER

"Name children some names and see what you do."
"Maple," Robert Frost

It was the summer of 1969, and I had just made a monumentally foolish mistake. Imagining that there were shortcuts to learning how to write and publish fiction, I accepted a creative writing fellowship at the University of California at Irvine and lit out with my wife, from our home in Vermont, for the Pacific coast. Along the way, we fished. We fished in the Upper Peninsula of Hemingway's Michigan, in Norman Maclean's Montana, up in the mountains of Alberta. We fished in Washington and Oregon, and then we hit southern California, where there were no trout, just automobiles and palm trees.

One afternoon a week or so after we'd arrived, I stopped at the intersection of Hollywood and Vine, where a man in a gorilla suit was busily directing traffic. A guy in a phone company truck pulled up beside me. He must have noticed my green license plate because he rolled down his window and called out, in a deadly serious voice, "I'm from Vermont, too. Go home while you still can."

So, missing the mountains, the farms and the woods I'd begun to write about, and, not least of all, the fishing, that's exactly what we did. Three days later we were back in northern Vermont. I had no writing degree, no job, no prospects. There were two small consolations. We'd gotten home just in time for the fall brown trout run, and the brook trout fishing in the beaver bogs was just starting to pick up again.

"What have you done for work before?" Jake Blodgett asked me on the morning after my somewhat less than triumphal return to New England.

Standing on the falling-in door stoop of the tall, white-haired logger and former whiskey runner, feeling his pale-blue stare cut through me like a chainsaw, I admitted that all I'd ever done was to teach school, but hearing that he needed a helper, I was hoping to get some "real-life" experience.

Jake thought about this proposition. Then he said, "Well, schoolteacher. How much would you want for pay?"

Now it was my turn to think. Finally, I said that I'd never worked in the woods before, and suggested that Jake try me out for a few days, then pay me what I was worth to him.

"That wouldn't be much," he said, and it wasn't. But for the rest of that fall and on into the winter, I worked with Jake, up in the mountains near the Canadian border, skidding the logs he cut out to a clearing with his ancient lumbering horse.

After work and on Sundays, we fished the brooks and rivers of the border country. When the lakes froze, we went ice fishing. Over lunch in the woods, and on our fishing expeditions, Jake told me stories of his wild, Prohibition-era days, running Canadian booze, making moonshine, outwitting game wardens. He was the best fisherman I'd ever known, with a sixth sense of where trout lay and how to entice them to strike, and a sixth sense, too, for telling a good story. During the course of that fall and winter, the Vermont woods became my graduate school, Jake Blodgett my literary mentor.

One day in a snowstorm he asked me if I'd ever write about his life. I told him yes.

Jake nodded. "Well, schoolteacher," he said, "then you better get on with it."

I love Labrador. I love its big, wild lakes, its unexplored whitewater rivers, its northern lights flaring up pink and silver and blue across the entire night sky. Most of all, I love its brook trout. In 1992, my 20-year-old son, Jake, and I stood by a nameless Labrador river we'd walked over a nameless mountain to reach. I was upstream from Jake a hundred yards or so, and we were both catching brookies from three to five pounds, as fast as we could land them.

"What have you got on there?" I called out to Jake over the rapids. "A whale?"

"No, a two-pound brook trout," he called back.

"That's no brook trout. That fish you're fighting is huge."

"Oh, that," Jake said. "That's the twenty-pound lake trout that has my two-pound brook trout in its mouth and won't let go."

Thinking how much my son's logger-whiskeyrunner-fisherman namesake would have enjoyed being here to see this, I began to laugh. Jake, in the meantime, handed me his fly rod, walked into the river, wrapped his arms about that monstrous laker and picked it up out of the rushing water, with the brook trout still in its jaws.

At that moment, I had a father's, and a fisherman's, epiphany. I realized, standing in the last wilderness of eastern North America, one hundred miles from the nearest settlement, that like his namesake, my son was attuned and connected to big woods and wild rivers, and the wild animals and fish that lived in them, in a way I could only marvel at. That, too, would have delighted my old bootlegger friend, and so would Jake's reply when I asked him what he was going to do with his unusual two-for-one catch.

"Put them back where they belong and fish some more," Jake said, and that, of course, is just what we proceeded to do.

Howard Frank Mosher is the author of eight novels, including *A Stranger in the Kingdom*, *Waiting for Teddy Williams*, and *Disappearances*, which has just been made into a major motion picture starring Kris Kristofferson. He has received many literary awards and prizes, and lives with his wife of forty-two years, Phillis, in Vermont's fabled Northeast Kingdom. He writes, "I love to fish for trout because through my line, leader, and fly, I feel connected to the beautiful places where trout live and to the family members and friends I have fished with for as long as I can remember."

The Surrender

BIL MONAN

Late March 1945

This war was all but over. You could tell by the arrival of staff officers on our line. They usually appeared in pairs, stepped out of their jeep, looked officious, and, if they were lucky, would be shelled by less then accurate German mortars. They would then quickly remount and run like hell to the rear all the while congratulating themselves on getting the combat infantry badge and perhaps the Bronze Star.

My platoon, all of twenty men, more like a glorified squad, had been dug in along the edge of a stream in western Austria for four days. It was a luxury of sorts, since it was unusual for us to be so static. Everything was moving fast and resistance was sporadic, but still lethal, and none of us had any urge to be the last casualty. The one good thing was that it appeared the Germans felt the same way, overall. We had been sent forward to this stream, the Erlauf, near the town of Scheibbs, to ensure that the bridge was secure and to hold the position until we were relieved. The Germans fired a few mortar rounds and a volley of machinegun fire to let us know they were indeed on the other side, but had since been silent.

I looked down the line where my men had dug in and could only see brown piles of dirt with eyes—mud soldiers. At this point you could probably throw seed on them and grow crops. No longer did they have names. It was just "You, You and You, over there," "You and You, that way," and "You, stay here." To my men I was just "Lieutenant." Only Sergeant Malvani had a name and it was "Conductor."

He was an unlikely sergeant—scrawny, short, wore glasses, and had very long, elegant fingers. He had been a concert violinist back home and had been 4-F'd early on, but after Normandy and all the losses, well, the draft board decided he was just perfect. We called him the "Conductor" after he lost two fingers to shrapnel somewhere in the Ardennes and upon discovering his loss, he remarked that his violin days were over and he would become a conductor, and never spoke of it again. It was what made him such a good sergeant; he just adapted and made stuff happen.

We weren't all that similar, Malvani and I. He was actually a city boy and relatively sophisticated, and I was just an ROTC graduate hailing from Westkill, New York. The only symphony I had ever heard was the thunder in the Catskills and the tumbling of water over rocks on the Willowemac. We were similar on one account; we had both been promoted primarily for surviving. The only thing that bothered me about Sgt. Malvani was that he wore a helmet where a bullet had entered the left side of his helmet and had somehow miraculously spun across the front casing exiting through the right side.

I said to him, "Sergeant, you need to dump that helmet, it only reinforces the men's belief that their leaders have no brains."

"Well . . . me accepting these sergeant stripes just proves they're right."

I just left it alone but it gave me the creeps. It then struck me that it really was quiet. I mean, I was actually thinking. I could not remember a period of time over the last year that my brain wasn't being banged from one side of my skull to the other by artillery fire. I decided to peak over the edge of my fox-hole to scan the other side of the stream. I saw nothing moving, which was normal. You never saw anyone out front, alive that is. What I did notice was the stream.

To my left it made a broad turn back towards the German lines, where it channeled deep and close to a steep rock wall. As it flowed towards me it straightened out and formed a nice flat pool about fifty yards long and fifty yards wide, where both of our lines faced each other. The stream ran down to my right under the bridge and faded into the darkness created by a canopy of over-hanging trees. The milky, green-tinged water ran fast and cold. The Esopus, back home in the Catskills, had the same look in early spring and I began to see in each pocket of water and riffle a place where, with the right presentation and the right fly, a nice brown trout would come roaring out of the water. I started to see Junction Pool at Roscoe, where the Little Beaverkill merges with the Willowemac and where the late evening hatch would emerge and all hell would break loose as trout gorged on green drakes or blue quills or usually something else that I never could match.

Now, you would expect most men in my situation to be thinking of women, but most of us had lost our libidos somewhere on the first hundred yards of beach in Normandy, or in the hedge rows or on the Rhine. Thoughts of trout I could handle. I remembered my dad teaching me how to fly-fish on the little Westkill, which ran right behind our house. The first trout I caught on a fly was a beautiful twelve-inch native brook. I used a brown dry-fly. My dad didn't have any names for the flies. He just said, "Match the damn color as best you can or make something up that's black with a little red on it." And that's what we did. Working in our garage at night pulling feathers from grouse capes, cutting up deerskins, and even slicing little chunks of wool from our socks, we would make our flies. My mom thought we had a terrible moth problem.

I was really tuning out as I thought about Fir Brook and how my dad and I would head up high when it had rained causing the Willowemac and Beaver-kill to run fast and muddy. The Fir was a small stream, hard to fish, and it dropped into a small gorge that required you to commit most of a day working small pockets of water behind boulders and little waterfalls. We would use about five feet of line and just flick it over a rock, into any likely spot and the brook trout would strike like piranha on a wounded pig. We only used tiny black ants; since the average trout was about eight inches. I do believe a pig cast just right would have provoked those greedy little brookies to strike.

My reverie was aborted by a sharp slap to the back of my helmet and a voice so close to my ear that the strident whisper sounded like shell fire, saying "Wake up Lieutenant, something's moving across the stream!"

I stared hard across the stream and noticed pieces of loose shale and dirt slipping down the face of the embankment from a thick hedge. A German soldier slid down the bank and took a few tentative steps towards the edge of the stream.

Sergeant Malvani raised his M-1. I grabbed the end of his rifle and said, "Hold off sergeant, when have you ever seen a living German out front? They haven't shot at us for three days. I think he is making a point. Tell the men to hold their fire."

Sergeant Malvani looked at me like I was insane, but waved down the men. We waited and watched.

The soldier righted himself with some difficulty; apparently he had a bad left leg. He proceeded to remove his helmet and camouflaged poncho, then quite deliberately folded the poncho, neatly laid it on the gravel streambed and placed his helmet on top.

He wore no insignia, but it was obvious that he was an officer. How I knew, I couldn't tell you, he just held himself in a way that one knew. Most line officers, myself included, had discovered long ago not to wear anything that might distinguish them as an officer. Snipers made short work of you if you did. He was unarmed and wore the uniform of the Wehrmacht, not the SS, which was a relief in some ways. Not that the Wehrmacht didn't try to kill you, they just seemed more like us, less fanatic. He was a handsome man, stood about six foot, lean, but there were not many fat soldiers these days. He was an older man, late forties perhaps, at least that was my perspective, since he had graying hair around his temples kind of like my dad. He then turned back to the bank, reached up into the hedges and proceeded to pull something out of the bushes.

Once again Sergeant Malvani raised his rifle and once again I pushed him down.

I said, "It's not a rifle he's getting Sergeant."

"What in the hell is he getting?" replied Malvani.

"It's a fly rod."

"Well, I'll be damned," Malvani exclaimed. "He must be shell shocked."

"No, I think he's just tired of this war and like I said, I think he's making a point."

Again, we just waited and watched.

There was a certain planned choreography to the officer's actions. I suspected he knew that his life depended on carefully orchestrated movements so everything he did seemed to flow with a cautious slow motion. Reaching into his field jacket he produced a green felt Tyrolean hat. There was a pheasant feather stuck in the hatband and around the sides there were a number of trout flies hooked haphazardly into the felt. He pulled off a fly that looked like some kind of streamer. All I could see was a flash of whitish silver with a blackish body. He tied the fly to his leader then stuck the hat on his head, reached into his tunic again and removed a pipe. With deliberate nonchalance he tapped the bowl on some rocks to remove the old ashes, filled the pipe, lit it, and with obvious enjoyment took a few puffs. Picking up the rod, he stepped to the edge of the stream while stripping off line, and started to false cast to extend the line out over the stream. All this orchestration came to an abrupt end on one of his back casts, when the fly ended up snagged on a low branch jutting out from the hedge line behind him. Apparently, he was out of practice.

I heard a not so smothered laugh next to me. Malvani thought it was funny. I mean, so did I, but being a fisherman I couldn't help but feel sorry for the man. It's okay to snag when you are by yourself but to have an audience can be demoralizing. It's kind of like being in a spelling contest in third grade and you find yourself in front of all your peers and parents and you misspell a simple word like "castle," which I did.

Retrieving the fly, the fishing soldier dressed in combat gray, black boots and green hat, went unperturbed about the business of catching fish. The birds started moving, and perhaps Malvani's laugh allowed everyone to exhale, for the air seemed relaxed and alive again.

He worked to my left, casting up and across where the stream made the turn towards the flat water in our front. His streamer fell lightly on the edge of the far bank. The lure caught the current where the last bit of rapids tailed into a softening pool and just as the streamer reached the apex of its turn in the current a roiling of water marked the strike of a hungry, brown trout. With little fanfare, but with elegant precision, the soldier worked the fish to his boot. The fish was about twelve inches long and plump. He picked it up, broke its neck and plopped it on the gravel bar near the bank. The man knew how to fish. He worked the water with such effortless skill that he caught fish after fish in every likely spot. The fly went exactly where he wanted it to go. Using a series of long casts, roll casts, even short whip like backhand casts when he wanted to flip it under a low branch or cut under bank, he worked the stream like a farmer gleaning his fields. The trout seemed endless in their quantity and maybe a little stupid. More than likely they hadn't been fished for years and had no experience with a hook, but maybe I was just jealous and didn't want to admit that the man was flat out good. I noticed that he only kept trout of about ten to twelve inches in length. When he landed a few that were larger he gently released them.

I found myself mesmerized and by now he had worked down the stream to where he was only twenty yards off to my left. I could clearly see the streamer flashing below me in the water. I noticed directly below me a fallen tree that had formed a good-sized hole. Swirling in the eddy where the current broke around the end of the trunk there lay a dark shadow of a trout about twenty inches long. Staggered around it hovered a number of smaller trout like P-40 Mustangs protecting a B-17 bomber . . . I guess a flight of Messerschmidts protecting a Junker bomber would be more exact the trout being Austrian. Every time the streamer passed outside the edge of the pool, the large fish would move up to a staging point considering a strike, but then his smaller cousins would race out and attack the fly. This fish was wise. He would let the small ones in their greed go charging off to their demise and he would just slip back and wait. He wasn't in a hurry and he didn't want to work that hard.

I couldn't stand it. The soldier's fly was drifting about one foot short. I stood up!

God does make fools and here I was—a magnificent example. I think Málvani passed out. I was standing up, totally exposed. I don't think I had stood erect for a year. I had come to feel like an ape always running at a crouch. Not only did I stand up in the face of the enemy, I was also gesticulating with my arms. I pointed straight down at the trout and then put my hands about twenty inches apart.

I wasn't shot. The soldier looked up, nodded his head and dropped down a few feet and out into the stream. The streamer drifted perfectly into the edge of the eddy and the old trout went for it. It struck hard. The soldier set the hook and upon feeling the sting the fish broke water and flung itself violently back and forth. It is unusual for a brown to leap much, more a rainbow tactic, but this one did. The battle was waged fairly, the angler giving line as the trout tried to roar down stream. Then keeping pressure, allowing no slack, stripping line, with the rod tip high, the soldier tired the old fish down. He didn't horse it around and brought the fish to heel as quickly as possible. He bent down and with both hands brought the fish up to chest height and held it out to show me. It was a beautiful fish with bright red splotches sprinkled amidst coal black spots all splashed against a greenish, blue-gray background. It was an old fish with a hooked jaw and square head, the brood master of the stream.

The fisherman then ever so gently swished the big fish in the current to revive it and let it go. He stood, looked my way and waved me towards him. Without hesitation, I shouldered my rifle and began to slip down the bank and towards the stream. Sergeant Malvani gave me a hard look and said, "You're not really going?"

I replied with a curt, "yes."

"You're an idiot," retorted Malvani.

I gave him a hard look back.

"Sir."

I met him halfway across the stream where the water came to about our shins. It was so brutally cold that it made your teeth ache. I looked at the bank where he had laid out about fifteen trout and said, "trout." And he replied, "forellen."

He saluted and said, "I am *Leutnant* Franz Meyers."

"Lieutenant Patrick Skimmin" and I returned the salute.

"Leutnant Skimmin, for me this war is over and my men are hungry, perhaps, your soldiers are hungry too?" and he handed me the rod.

"Good," I thought, "He speaks English, they all speak English it seemed, and I can only say, *hande hoch*, or *nicht schissen* in German."

I took the rod, looked at him and said, "Aren't you kind of old to be a Lieutenant?"

"All the young men are buried in Russia. I was invalided for wounds during the First World War, but was called up to form a *Volkssturm* unit to protect my village and this bridge. All my soldiers are fifteen-year-old boys or old men like me. I have no great ambition to die or have my village destroyed for Germany since I am Austrian."

I turned to the stream, stripped line and proceeded to cast, slowly remembering all the mechanics of the sport I so loved. It was the one way I could always find peace and quiet and I had forgotten what that was like. I caught as he did, but made a point to catch twenty-five trout since I had counted fifteen of his. I think we both knew we were lying about how many men we were feeding.

As I laid the last trout on the shore, Franz Meyers came to me and with strict military formality said, "I surrender my weapons, my men and my village to the United States Army, and to you Patrick Skimmin, I surrender the stream and this." He handed me the rod.

Franz turned to his side of the stream and waved *to* the hedges. Within seconds ten gray-clad scarecrows tumbled to the streambed, armed with twelve-inch frying pans, mess kits, potatoes, cabbages and onions. I waved to my men and the same mass scrambling and confusion ensued as my twenty mud soldiers emerged with American cigarettes and chocolate. On that night, on the edge of the Erlauf, we shared a most glorious fish fry. It was here, as it was for Franz Meyers, that my war ended.

Bil Monan is a freelance writer who has written for *Fly Rod & Reel* and other local and regional publications. He was the winner of the 2004 Robert L. Traver award for his story "The Surrender." He currently lives in Alexandria, Virginia. "We are here for but a short while," he says. "Let us be stewards of the land and water, leaving only a small footprint for others to follow, so that they too, may share in the wondrous beauty of this earth."

Winter Fishing— Looking Over My Shoulder

STEVEN J. MEYERS

Nearly every time I sit down to write about fishing a couple of jerks show up in my office. They stand behind me, peering over my shoulders. The one who leers over my right shoulder is a well-dressed, literate snob who's read every book ever written about fly fishing. That's a lot of books. In English, those books go back to the fifteenth century, at least that's where he usually begins the history—with a hip nun from England who knew all about *Fysshynge with an Angle*. The guy looking over my other shoulder leans on me kind of sloppily. He isn't dressed as well as the snob, and he kind of smells. He never reads; mostly, he just fishes. Sometimes it seems like the only time he's off the water is when he's breathing down my neck.

Wait, it gets worse. They don't just stand there. They talk to me.

"Steve, may I remind you, *ex*-trout bum—you have a regular job now and you're almost respectable," the literate one intones, "how can you even think to begin a piece about winter fly fishing without a lovely introductory passage about the joys of good books, the pleasures of cleaning tackle and tying flies during the off season in preparation for the fishing to come? It's what fly fishing writers have done for generations, centuries, actually." I can smell a very peaty, single-malt Scotch on his breath. That's the other thing he does in the winter.

"Spare me," the sloppy leaner (who, I now notice, appears not to have shaved in weeks) bellows, a burp escaping mid-phrase, stinking of cheap beer. *Please*, I think, *tell me it's not Lone Star.* He taps me not-so-gently on the noggin with a long-neck bottle, then takes a slug. It's Budweiser. "Ignore that moron, he's a pompous ass; anyway, that was when they had seasons, when they closed the rivers to fishing in the winter. Bad times. I remember 'em. I used to tie flies in the winter, myself. I used to oil my reels and wipe off my fly rods. Even sunk to reading a book, once, something about a British lady and her gamekeeper. But dammit man, they don't close the rivers anymore. At least not here. Fishing is legal all winter. The tourists are gone. Blue-winged olives are hatching. Shut down your damn computer, get your fat ass out of that chair, screw your deadlines! Trout are rising!"

I have to admit, bad hair, ugly stubble, foul breath and all, the beer drinker makes the better case. There are places where bitter weather, sleeping trout, frozen water and a closed season drive fly fishermen to other pastimes. And there are times, in those places, when a good fishing book or a fly tying vise is as close as a fishing junkie can get to a fix. But this isn't one of those places. Here, maybe not every day—but often enough to make it worth your while to throw on some fleece and go take a look—trout will rise to mayflies or midges in the darkest depths of winter. If you get there, and the trout aren't rising, a deep-drifted nymph or streamer will almost always produce a tug. And even if it doesn't, at least you're fishing.

It's quieter in winter. Flows are low. Rivers don't bounce and burble so much as they murmur. When it snows, it's so nearly silent you'd swear you can hear the flakes hitting the water. Sometimes, it is gray and wet; oddly, those are my favorite days. Often, those are the days when the mayflies hatch. Frequently, those are the days when winter trout appear to be a different species, entirely, from their timid summer brethren. Eager to eat (during those brief periods when they feed), winter trout rising to hatching mayflies readily take a compara dun or sparkle dun. Maybe a Parachute Adams. If it is snowing, they often throw caution to the wind. I don't know why. I have proposed a theory or two over the years. One guess is that heavy snow makes visibility poor (for them and us) and trout feel protected in the same way they feel protected by wind chop on the water during summer. But I don't know. I don't know a lot of things, and like a million other blessings rivers bestow without my understanding I have found it better to gratefully accept those gifts, and admit my ignorance.

Sometimes, when I'm fishing, I feel as if somebody is looking over my shoulder. Sometimes it's my long-dead father. Sometimes it's my son. More often, it's that beer swilling, stubble encrusted jerk who bothers me when I'm trying to write. Sometimes I turn to look. Funny, he's always smiling on the river. His buddy, the literary snob, never shows up at times like this. He's cooling his heals in my office, reading a book.

Steven J. Meyers has written six books including *Streamside Reflections* and *San Juan River Chronicle*. His writing has appeared in *Field & Stream, Fly Fisherman, Southwest Fly Fishing*, and several anthologies. His monthly fishing column "Home Water" (from which this contribution was chosen) appears in *Inside Outside Southwest* magazine. He has been a fly fishing guide in southwest Colorado and northern New Mexico for twenty years. He lives in Durango, Colorado, with his wife, Debbie, where he teaches creative writing at Fort Lewis College. He writes, "I believe there is no better way to become aware of our appropriate place in the larger world than to fish well. Ours is a pastime that requires attention to detail; practice; patience; and perhaps most important of all, an appropriate humility that seems to grow the longer we fish."

Speaking of Spoons

JOHN MERWIN

Spoons are basic, but they're not simple. These hunks of tin, brass, or steel have been tangling in American tackle boxes ever since 1848, when Julio Thompson Buel started cranking out thousands of metal baits from a little brick building in Whitehall, New York, near the southern end of Lake Champlain. Buel received the first American patent for a spoonlike lure in 1854, and spent almost forty years manufacturing a wide assortment of metal trolling spoons and spinners. He never advertised nationally because he didn't have to; the new metal lures became so widely popular after the Civil War that fishermen from Minnesota to Maine were beating his door down for samples.

As the *New York Sun* reported in his 1886 obituary, Buel was more fond of pontificating than pounding out metal blades. The front of his dusty shop was often crowded with would-be customers sitting on plank-bottomed chairs and wooden boxes, listening to a long sermon from "Judge Buel" on his spoons' effectiveness for everything from bass to bluefish. The arguments were both simple and never-ending, and centered on which of numerous spoon designs was best for any particular fish species and under what circumstances. Buel and his cronies had quickly discovered what many modern anglers seem either to have forgotten or never learned: All spoons don't work equally well at the same place and time.

For one thing, different spoon designs tend to be speed specific, producing optimal lure action within a relatively narrow range of trolling or retrieval speeds. And this is because of the way wobbling spoons work in the first place.

All modern spoons are miniature hydrofoils, which is why they wobble erratically when they are retrieved or trolled. If you hold any spoon flat and view it from the side, you'll see that it looks like an airplane wing. Water flowing over this surface generates lift, just as air does when it flows over the airfoil shape of a wing. Because water is about 800 times more dense than air, the lift effect underwater is much greater at slower speeds.

Many spoons are more deeply dished or widest or both at the rear, which is where hydrofoil lift is greatest. This effect lifts or pulls the rear of the spoon out at an angle from its line of travel through the water. When the spoon's tail reaches a critical angle, lift is lost and the spoon stalls, which means it flips back through its original position while still being pulled forward through the water. This hydrodynamic lift/no-lift cycle is repeated quickly as the spoon is retrieved or trolled, and the net effect is the familiar wobble/flutter of your favorite red-and-white classic.

Getting this effect requires some finesse. If your retrieve is too slow, the spoon will just drag through the water with no action or wobble at all. In other words, your underwater airplane hasn't reached takeoff speed. On the other hand, if the spoon is moved too fast, hydrodynamic lift overcomes the lift-and-stall cycle, which causes the spoon to spin wildly around its own axis, and the fish-attracting wobbling effect is lost. This behavior varies according to spoon shape. Lift generally increases with width, so wider blades typically wobble best at slower speeds while slim blades can be worked a little faster. As an extreme example, this means that the red-and-white wobbler you cakewalk down a weedy aisle for pike should be traded for a slim, smeltlike spoon when you start trolling at much higher speeds for landlocked salmon in the open waters of the same lake.

A spoon's weight and shape govern not only its optimal retrieval speed, but also—in the case of casting spoons—its depth. More than forty years ago, when I first started fooling around with ultra-light spinning gear, the big bluegills in Connecticut's Candlewood Lake were suckers for a $\frac{1}{32}$-ounce wobbling spoon tossed with 2-pound-test monofilament in the spring shallows. But in summer, the fish would move to depths of 6 to 12 feet. Here, the little spoon would no longer connect as it planed to the surface with a retrieve of adequate speed. The solution was a spoon of identical size and shape, but double the weight, thanks to a thicker metal. I had to work the heavier spoon a little faster to get the same action, but this inconvenience was more than offset by a dramatic increase in effective fishing depth.

Here again, a thick—read heavy—spoon of narrow overall shape typically runs at greater depths and requires a faster retrieve than one of equal weight but broader shape. Because broader spoons tend to sail off the mark when cast into a stiff headwind or crossing wind, heavy, narrow spoons can offer both better distance and accuracy. For example, although not normally considered a salt-water lure, a narrow and thick ½- or ¾-ounce silver Krocodile spoon can work wonders along the windy Atlantic coast during the fall when striped bass and bluefish are often gorging on young-of-the-year baitfish while completely ignoring the typical surfcaster's assortment of oversized plugs and tins.

Some spoons combine the design attributes of width, length, shape, and weight in very specialized ways. The so-called flutter spoons used in deep trolling for lake trout are one example. Here, ultrathin metal is bent to a long, spoonlike shape, combining light weight with a long profile to produce a slow, rolling wobble that's perfectly matched to the character of slow-moving lakers in deep water. The spoons' light weight renders them useless for casting, but that's immaterial.

There are other factors to consider when selecting and fishing spoons—different colors and varied retrieves among them—but if you pick the right spoon design in the first place, you've won at least half the battle. While spoons are close to being universal lures, old Judge Buel had it right: There's no such thing as a universal spoon.

John Merwin is the Fishing Editor of *Field & Stream* magazine, where this article originally appeared in 1995. He is also author or co-author of numerous books on fly fishing, including *The Beaverkill*, *The Battenkill*, *The New American Trout Fishing*, and *Trailside Guide to Fly Fishing*.

Fishing for American Shad

Excerpt from
The Founding Fish

JOHN McPHEE

Among the spectators on the bridge, a cop appeared. He shouted, "Does one of you guys down there own a green Jeep?"

Ed Cervone shouted back, "Yes, Officer, I do."

"Well," the cop continued, with the slightest pause. "Your wife called. She wants you home. She thinks you're dead."

Laughter on the bridge—9:50 P.M.

It was not true that Marian Cervone was concerned about her husband. By her own account, the man is too unpredictable to worry about. She wasn't worried about Edmund, either. It was my wife, Yolanda Whitman, whose mind had been crossed by the ultimate possibility. This was a few years before the sudden bloom of cellular phones. I had no way to tell her why I was late, and deliberately breaking off that fish never crossed my mind.

Yolanda seems to remember the evening with total recall. For one thing, it was my turn to cook. "By nine o'clock, I was just plain mad," she has said for the record. "You were dithering too long. I was waiting for my dinner. You were taking your sweet time, failing in your responsibilities."

Yes.

"At some point after that, I shifted from mad to concern. You had fallen out of the boat. Gone through the rapids."

The rapids, not far from the bridge, cross a diabase ledge and are tumultuous in spring.

"It was pitch black. Cold. I imagined you with hypothermia in the river. So I called Marian. I told her I was worried because your absence was 'out of character.'"

Marian must have marveled that someone could seriously use a phrase like that about a husband. Marian said she would call back if she learned anything. After hanging up, she called the Lambertville police. She said her husband and son and a friend were out in a boat and had not returned "way beyond the time" she expected them. Would the police check the boat-launch parking lot and see if a green Jeep was there? The woman on the other end of the line said the police surely would.

A while later, the police called Marian, and Marian called Yolanda, who continues the narrative: "While I waited, a tear or two actually squeezed out. I had let myself wander into the impossible. Perhaps I was madder at Ed than at you—who knows? After Marian called back, I was again spitting mad. She said, 'They're still fishing.'"

Two hours, thirty minutes. At last the fish had come up enough in the river so that the people on the bridge caught glimpses of it as, now and again, it canted—silver flashing—and changed direction. We heard them go "Ooh!" We heard them shout, "Wow, what a huge fish!" When we, in the boat, finally got a glimpse of it, we thought it enormous, too. Toward the end, I kept pressing it, tightened the drag even more, a risky, foolish thing to do. I just hoped it would not make a sudden run. If it did so, at least I had turned off the anti-reverse button, and the reel could spin free.

The fish was close now. When it saw the boat, it dived. After it came up, and saw the boat again, it took off for the bottom of the river, slowly to rise once more. At some point in the last five minutes, Edmund tried for it with the boat net and missed. I finally worked it up to the side of the boat. It was still swimming, unspent. It did not roll over. It never gave up. On the second try, Edmund got it into the net, and the dart dropped out of its mouth. He brought into the boat a four-and-three-quarter-pound roe shad.

I still have the dart—secured with monofilament to a small piece of cedar shingle. It was only the second dart I had ever retired. On a bookshelf, I propped it up beside a dart of the same weight and colors, with which, on an upriver day the spring before, I had caught seventeen shad without changing or losing the lure. The chemically sharpened hook was a novelty I had succumbed to in a catalogue. That shipment of hooks was uneven, to say the least. Some of them were so weak they were bent out straight by the force of tugging shad. But not this one. Despite two hours and thirty-five minutes in the shad's mouth, the curve of the black steel looked as it had when I made the dart and festooned it with bucktail in a vise. At home, I studied the fish with a magnifying glass. It had not been hooked on the top of the head or in any other place on the outside. It was not foul-hooked. It was hooked in the roof of the mouth, very near the front, slightly off the midline, to the right. I saw a narrow hole there, and I put a toothpick in it, which did not come through to the outside. The connection of hook and shad had been something like a trailer hitch.

Mindful of the species' paper jaw and its legendary fragility, I would one day lay a shad on a dissecting table at the University of Massachusetts and show Willy Bemis just where my fish had been hooked.

"How would you describe that, Willy?"

"It's the ethmoid cartilage of the braincase. It's the part of the braincase that everyone would understand as, regionally, the nose. One solid cartilaginous structure forms the braincase during early development. This is the anterior tip of it. The brain is back in the center of the head. Most of the braincase is protected by bone, which would make it a very tough place for a hook to latch on to. But once you've got a hook past the bone and into that little piece of cartilage, it doesn't come out. If a hook goes through that, it's going to hook on to the fish in a very serious way. There's no way that fish is ever going to throw that hook."

The monofilament line felt sandpapery. When I took it off the reel, it contracted instantly into coils from a hundred and fifty-five minutes of twisting. A thick mass of bunched contracted circles hopelessly intertwined, it looked like something an owl dropped.

I sent the reel to the Daiwa Corporation, in California, for an assessment. They wanted $54.40 to fix it, because the shad had bent the pinion gear, the shad had bent the drive gear, the shad had damaged the oscillating system and gone a long way toward wearing out the drag system. The reel required two new gears, a new pawl, a new worm shaft, and three new drag washers.

I still have some of the scales. They report the shad's age as three. For a female that young to be on the spawning run is more than uncommon. It's rare. The scales record strong growth in the river in the first summer, as the egg turned into a larva, and the larva into a juvenile. They record normal growth in the ocean in each of the following years. Then they show the shad coming back into the river—two years earlier than most females do.

Soon after that evening in Lambertville, I told this story to Richard St. Pierre, of the U.S. Fish and Wildlife Service. Headquartered in Harrisburg, on the Susquehanna River, he is a shad specialist, who has worked as a shad consultant on the Hudson River, the Columbia River, and the Yangtze. He said that it must have been a letdown for me to learn that the fish was not a striped bass or a sturgeon or a muskellunge "but just a shad."

It was not in any sense a letdown, I told him. I'm a shad fisherman. I was fishing for American shad.

John McPhee, author of twenty-seven books, is a staff writer at *The New Yorker* and a Ferris Professor of Journalism at Princeton University. *The Founding Fish* (2002) is about American shad and combines their natural history with their American history and the author's personal history as a shad fisherman.

Excerpt from "Skelton's Party"

THOMAS McGUANE

Skelton followed watching the drawn bow the rod had become, the line shearing water with precision.

"What a marvelously smooth drag this reel has! A hundred smackers seemed steep at the time; but when you're in the breach, as I am now, a drag like this is the last nickel bargain in America!"

Skelton was poling after the fish with precisely everything he had. And it was difficult on the packed bottom with the pole inclining to slip out from under him.

His feeling of hope for a successful first-day guiding was considerably modified by Rudleigh's largely undeserved hooking of the fish. And now the nobility of the fish's fight was further eroding Skelton's pleasure.

When they crossed the edge of the flat, the permit raced down the reef line in sharp powerful curves, dragging the line across the coral. "Gawd, gawd, gawd," Rudleigh said. "This cookie is stronger than I am!" Skelton poled harder and at one point overtook the fish as it desperately rubbed the hook on the coral bottom; seeing the boat, it flushed once more in terror, making a single long howl pour from the reel. A fish that was exactly noble, thought Skelton, who began to imagine the permit coming out of a deep-water wreck by the pull of moon and tide, riding the invisible crest of the incoming water, feeding and moving by force of blood; only to run afoul of an asshole from Connecticut.

The fight continued without much change for another hour, mainly outside the reef line in the green water over a sand bottom: a safe place to fight the fish. Rudleigh had soaked through his khaki safari clothes; and from time to time Mrs. Rudleigh advised him to "bear down." When Mrs. Rudleigh told him this, he would turn to look at her, his neck muscles standing out like cords and his eyes acquiring broad white perimeters. Skelton ached from pursuing the fish with the pole; he might have started the engine outside the reef line, but he feared Rudleigh getting his line in the propeller and he had found that a large fish was held away from the boat by the sound of a running engine.

As soon as the fish began to show signs of tiring, Skelton asked Mrs. Rudleigh to take a seat; then he brought the big net up on the deck beside him. He hoped he would be able to get Rudleigh to release this hugely undeserved fish, not only because it was undeserved but because the fish had fought so very bravely. No, he admitted to himself, Rudleigh would never let the fish go.

By now the fish should have been on its side. It began another long and accelerating run, the pale sheet of water traveling higher up the line, the fish swerving somewhat inshore again; and to his terror, Skelton found himself poling after the fish through the shallows, now and then leaning over to free the line from a sea fan. They glided among the little hammocks and mangrove keys of Saddlebunch in increasing vegetated congestion, in a narrowing tidal creek that closed around and over them with guano-covered mangroves and finally prevented the boat from following another foot. Nevertheless, line continued to pour off the reel.

"Captain, consider it absolutely necessary that I kill the fish. This one doubles the Honduran average."

Skelton did not reply, he watched the line slow its passage from the reel, winding out into the shadowy creek; then stop. He knew there was a good chance the desperate animal had reached a dead end.

"Stay here."

Skelton climbed out of the boat and, running the line through his fingers lightly, began to wade the tidal creek. The mosquitoes found him quickly and held in a pale globe around his head. He waded steadily, flushing herons out of the mangroves over his head. At one point, he passed a tiny side channel, blocking the exit of a heron that raised its stiff wings very slightly away from its body and glared at him. In the green shadows, the heron was a radiant, perfect white.

He stopped a moment to look at the bird. All he could hear was the slow musical passage of tide in the mangrove roots and the low pattern of bird sounds more liquid than the sea itself in these shallows. He moved away from the side channel, still following the line. Occasionally, he felt some small movement of life in it; but he was certain now the permit could go no farther. He had another thirty yards to go, if he had guessed right looking at Rudleigh's partially emptied spool.

Wading along, he felt he was descending into the permit's world; in kneedeep water, the small mangrove snappers, angelfish, and baby barracudas scattered before him, precise, contained creatures of perfect mobility. The brilliant blue sky was reduced to a narrow ragged band quite high overhead now and the light wavered more with the color of the sea and of estuarine shadow than that of vulgar sky. Skelton stopped and his eye followed the line back in the direction he had come. The Rudleighs were at its other end, infinitely far away.

Skelton was trying to keep his mind on the job he had set out to do. The problem was, he told himself, to go from Point A to Point B; but every breath of humid air, half sea, and the steady tidal drain through root and elliptical shadow in his ears and eyes diffused his attention. Each heron that leaped like an arrow out of his narrow slot, spiraling invisibly into the sky, separated him from the job. Shafts of light in the side channels illuminated columns of pristine, dancing insects.

Very close now. He released the line so that if his appearance at the dead end terrified the permit there would not be sufficient tension for the line to break. The sides of the mangrove slot began to yield. Skelton stopped.

An embowered, crystalline tidal pool: the fish lay exhausted in its still water, lolling slightly and unable to right itself. It cast a delicate circular shadow on the sand bottom. Skelton moved in and the permit made no effort to rescue itself; instead, it lay nearly on its side and watched Skelton approach with a steady, following eye that was, for Skelton, the last straw. Over its broad, virginal sides a lambent, moony light shimmered. The fish seemed like an oval section of sky— yet sentient and alert, intelligent as tide.

He took the permit firmly by the base of its tail and turned it gently upright in the water. He reached into its mouth and removed the hook from the cartilaginous operculum. He noticed that the suddenly loosened line was not retrieved: Rudleigh hadn't even the sense to keep tension on the line.

By holding one hand under the permit's pectoral fins and the other around the base of its tail, Skelton was able to move the fish back and forth in the water to revive it. When he first tentatively released it, it teetered over on its side, its wandering eye still fixed upon him. He righted the fish again and continued to move it gently back and forth in the water; and this time when he released the permit, it stayed upright, steadying itself in equipoise, mirror sides once again purely reflecting the bottom. Skelton watched a long while until some regularity returned to the movement of its gills.

Then he cautiously—for fear of startling the fish—backed once more into the green tidal slot and turned to head for the skiff. Rudleigh had lost his permit.

The line was lying limp on the bottom. Why didn't the fool at least retrieve it? With his irritation Skelton began to return to normal. He trudged along the creek, this time against the tide; and returned to the skiff.

The skiff was empty.

Thomas McGuane is the author of fourteen books, including *Gallatin Canyon and Other Stories*. He has been a finalist for The National Book Award and received the Rosenthal Award from the American Academy. He has written for *Harper's*, *The Atlantic Monthly*, *Sports Illustrated*, and *The New Yorker*. He lives in McLeod, Montana.

The Mayfly

TERRY McCARTHY

I knew a man who took his mayfly fishing so seriously that he would put live mayflies in his bath and then look at them from underneath the water with a scuba mask. He saw nothing unusual about this. On the contrary, he regarded it as sensible preparation, since he would spend the best part of the next two weeks sitting in a boat in wind and rain on the great brown trout lakes in the west of Ireland trying to catch fish that only saw his fly from underneath.

"You have got to get into the trout's mind," he would say, sitting at the bar of the local pub with a pint of Guinness at his elbow. "You have to really see what they see." He would catch mayflies at the beginning of each season for bathtub observation, because he believed the colors of the mayflies, which he broke down into different shades on a palette of green, yellow and copper, changed slightly every year. More precisely, he thought it was the color of the sunlight as refracted through the wings of the mayfly that mattered to the trout. Based on what he saw in his bath, he would tie a new batch of flies and fish them tenaciously for the remainder of the natural hatch. Initially his wife was worried by his eccentric behavior, but over the years of their marriage she became reconciled to this temporary May madness, an affliction she discovered was endemic to many Irish fishermen.

I too share in this affliction. When the word goes out that "the mayfly is up," it conveys to me a sense of urgency that I suspect is something similar to a pregnant woman's feeling of the onset of labor pains. From deep inside, the combined force of personal memories and millennia of species adaptation turns the mind to the hunting of brown trout at that most felicitous time of year when they come to the surface to feed with ravenous abandon.

For three decades now I have made the pilgrimage to the same lake in the midst of the peat bogs and mountains of western Ireland, at approximately the same time of year—the last week of May and the first week of June, give or take a week or two depending on how warm or cold it has been earlier in the season. There is nothing else in the world I would rather do than sit in a boat on that lake in a good south-westerly breeze with a plentiful hatch of mayfly on the water, and wait for a trout to pay me the compliment of gulping my fly.

And what a fly it is, this mayfly: one of nature's most graceful, exquisite and ultimately tragic creations, a favorite of poets and dreamers, a natural for water-colorists. The mayfly, of the order *ephemeroptera*—"winged for only one day"— is a fly that hatches in the morning and generally dies by sunset, its only purpose in life to mate before it expires. Verdi and Puccini wrote operas about life sto-ries like this. No mouth with which to eat, its digestive tract filled with air, the mayfly lives at the apex of sexual desire and aesthetic purity—the ballet dancer of aquatic insects. Up close, its wings are veined like multiple panes of green stained glass, its soft thorax marled with brown and gold, a feature in any jew-eler's window. From afar it is a streak of color, flitting past like a flash of green chiffon on the wind. Or so it seems to me, in idle moments of reverie when the fish aren't taking.

More importantly, in the words of my scuba-dipping friend, what does the trout really see? Following the life cycle, the attentive trout will see the mayfly's grey-brown larval case detach itself from the rock or silt on the bottom of the lake and float upwards, where, a couple of inches below the surface, the subimago will begin to emerge from its shuck. This juvenile will pop up onto the surface and wait for its wings to harden enough for it to fly—a good oppor-tunity for the trout to strike. On a warm day with a big hatch, these flies—we call them duns—look like a flotilla of sailboats, all riding before the wind with their green-yellow sails hoisted upright. The trout, of course, has never seen a sailboat, and is only thinking about the next course in the day's ongoing buffet.

The dun will take off and land in the closest tree or shrub, where it will shed its skin again and emerge as a sexually mature spinner, ready to participate in the mating dance in clouds of other mayflies that gather as the day wears on. Having paired off on the wing, the fertilized female will dip her belly in the water for a bare second to lay eggs, presenting the trout with another brief opportunity for feeding, and then, at the end of the cycle, the sexually exhausted flies will expire on the surface of the water, their wings now completely transparent and their bodies shades of light gray and black. I could compare them floating limply on the water to a pair of kid leather gloves tossed on a polished table, but, as I hear you pointing out, trout don't have hands and so have no conception of gloves, kid leather or otherwise. For the fish, this is the spent gnat, an evening favorite of larger trout, a late supper after a long day of feeding from the surface.

After many hours of contemplation, it became clear to me that my view of the mayfly and that of the trout were always fated to be different. The hunter-hunted relationship is not very conducive to friendship. We don't even live in the same medium—despite attempts to pretend in our bathtubs. But then I realized that there is one unique moment when my world and that of the trout intersect, when I can enter into the trout's mind—and at that precise crossover point is the mayfly. It is the second when the fly that is attached to my line and that I have been watching on the surface suddenly disappears in a boil of water—with a sudden thrill I know that a trout has also been watching that fly, in all its green, yellow and copper glory, and for a brief moment we are united, locked onto the same frequency of perception. And then the mayfly is gone.

Terry McCarthy has been a foreign correspondent in Central America, Asia, and the Middle East for twenty years—between assignments he likes to fish for trout in Montana and in the lakes of western Ireland, where he grew up.

The Haddycall

BRUCE E. MATTHEWS

The story of the Haddycall is the story of family, friendship, fishing and roots—a story shared all over the United States in as many variations as there are anglers to tell them. The Haddycall story happens to be mine. I give it to you as we pass the fishing tradition on to a new generation of earnest anglers, to remember the richness and roots of American fishing we all share and to remind us what could be lost if we are not diligent in our work today.

Like a lot of fish-struck kids I'd grown up rummaging in my dad's tackle box. I'd always noticed this old and scarred red-headed wooden plug and occasionally asked my dad about it. I knew he'd used it fishing for bass in the Kentucky River in the early 1950s. But it wasn't until recently that he gave me the plug and told me his part of the story, which in turn led me to push aside the cobwebs hiding a whole fascinating chapter of southern "roots" lore.

As a young engineer early in his career my dad worked for the Kentucky Stone Company at the Yellow Rock limestone quarry in the hill country of eastern Kentucky. Yellow Rock is located on a bend in the Kentucky River, accessible at that time by boat, railroad, or a long ride on a rutted two-track through the woods of what is now the Daniel Boone National Forest. During the week employees lived on-site in company housing. While my dad worked during the week at Yellow Rock, my Mom and I were home in Louisville. I have vague recollections of chicken pot-pie dinners, listening to Lowell Thomas on the radio, and counting the days until my dad returned.

While my mom and I pined away over chicken pot-pies, apparently my dad was out fishing! Taking advantage of after-hour opportunities, my dad joined up with a couple of guys named Chester and Preacher and learned a bit about how to catch Kentucky River bass.

Chester liked to use a red-headed Piky Get-Um Minnow plug made by the Paw Paw Bait Company of Paw Paw, Michigan. Clearly a Piky Get-Um wasn't Chester's idea of a good lure name, and Dad never heard him call it anything but a "Haddycall."

Dad told me he thought he recalled that haddycall was a local mountain patent medicine that was supposedly "good for what ails ya." So Chester's haddycall lure was good for anything that swam. But that was about all the light dad could shed on its unlikely name.

I could sense there was more to this story. So in a subsequent e-mail conversation with my friend Jim Casada, who among a number of notable things is also something of an expert on southern Appalachian colloquialisms, I asked if he'd ever heard of haddycall. Jim dredged his memory and came up with Hadacol, which he vaguely recalled as a locally popular cure-all from his youth.

I looked up Hadacol on the web, and there it was, bringing the story into focus. According to a 1951 *Newsweek* article:

"What's Hadacol? Well, basically, it's a patent medicine—a little honey, a little of this and that, and a stiff shot of alcohol hyped up with vitamin B. Actually it's a great deal more. It's a craze. It's a culture. It's a political movement."

Hadacol is short for Happy Days Company, the final "L" being the first initial of LeBlanc. Dudley LeBlanc was a Cajun politician tailor-made for Louisiana in the Huey Long era. His entrepreneurship, showmanship, PR savvy and plain old-fashioned hucksterism built Hadacol from a backwoods bayou hip-pocket cure-all to a southern states phenomenon grossing more than $20 million in 1950. LeBlanc was smart enough to ride his product only until the Food and Drug Administration started getting serious in wanting to know more about Hadacol's content and actual effects on users. Claiming sales were going to top $75 million for 1951, LeBlanc sold the Hadacol business to NY investors that summer for a cool $8 million in cash. Not long after, the NY investors went bankrupt amid a flurry of accusations that LeBlanc had doctored the books. The story goes that LeBlanc's Louisiana constituents felt little sympathy for the Yankee buyers.

It seems even the Kentucky River backwater of Yellow Rock had heard of the Hadacol phenomenon in 1952, and so Chester's Paw Paw Piky Get-um was, like Hadacol, "good for what ails ya." That plug carried its story locked up in my Dad's tackle box for more than 50 years. It's now mounted in a shadowbox with a picture of my dad, me and my son Nate—three generations of fishing tradition firmly rooted in our family story.

I presented a different Haddycall to Mike Nussman in recognition of his steadfast and unyielding efforts in the 2005 reauthorization of Wallop-Breaux. That particular Paw Paw was the jointed version, and its painted tack eyes and lip firmly dated it to the '40s and '50s when the Paw Paw Bait Company was among the most popular of the era. It was mounted among rocks and driftwood gathered from Raquette Lake in New York's Adirondacks, where my family has spent summers for more than 40 years now.

Perhaps that dream fish, the Wallop-Breaux, wrapped it among the debris before breaking free to fuel yet more dreams. Someone in the Midwest fished it; it made its way to Mike by passing through the hands of at least two generations. In the way of all fishing lures, it represents the hopes and dreams of anglers all across America, an intergenerational connection and common thread binding us all—and a legacy we can all enjoy and pass along.

Bruce E. Matthews is president of the Recreational Boating and Fishing Foundation (RBFF), whose mission is growing participation in boating, fishing, and caring for the natural resources supporting these activities. Before his recent return to Michigan, Matthews often commuted by boat on the Potomac to RBFF's Alexandria, Virginia, offices from his Maryland home. "For me, fishing is all about family," Matthews writes. "The stories we build by fishing together become part of family history, and their telling is the glue that helps hold us together."

Stepping Up to the Plate for Wild Trout, Clean Air and Wild Places—1% for the Planet

CRAIG MATHEWS

I've never seen anything as drop-dead gorgeous as my first trout; or my last or the thousands I've caught and released in between. That first trout was a brown, nearly a foot long. Its flanks peppered with vivid spots of orange, red and black. I kept it alive in my landing net I'd anchored to the shore by its wooden handle. Every few minutes I would stop fishing and return to my net to examine and marvel at the trout's colors and form. That was over fifty years ago.

Last Thursday dawned sunny and warm, unusual for a November day in southwestern Montana. Because the weather was nice I decided to fish and walked a quarter mile from my home to the Madison River in hopes of finding trout rising to midges. It was Thanksgiving Day around noon and I had a couple hours to fish before friends arrived for diner.

When I got to my favorite pool I sat on the bank to ready my gear and watch for trout coming to the surface for midges. I tied a couple feet of 5x tippet and knotted on a #22 Zelon Midge to the end, all the while keeping my eyes on the smooth water behind a huge boulder for rising trout. I was not disappointed. A few minutes later I saw a large head and tail rise of a wild rainbow trout to a midge. I slid along the shoreline on my butt until I was within twelve feet of the feeding fish. I presented my fly on a short-line pinpoint accurate, upstream cast. By getting close to the rising trout taking tiny midges I could track my small fly should the fish take, and fishing a short line upstream I keep drag at a minimum. On the second cast the fish took and a few minutes later I had the big rainbow in my net.

I kept the beautiful fish in my net in the current for a few minutes admiring its brilliant red flanks, deep olive green back, black spots and white tipped pectoral fins. I remembered my first trout and keeping it in my net fifty years before. As soon as the trout recovered from its wild leaps and runs I released it from my net and watched it swim slowly away and stop behind a big boulder not ten feet away.

The warm noon sun felt good and I soaked it in. Sitting there on the world famous Madison River, watching trout rise, and thinking how lucky I have been to live and work in Yellowstone country, and fish 150 days a year.

My thoughts turned to the many years I have lived here and what clean water, wild trout, and wilderness have taught me; and how much I love and owe them.

I've learned a lot about the wild and native trout I fish for. I've also learned of the groceries fish call food; aquatic and terrestrial insects and more. I learned how to tie flies to imitate what the fish feed on. I learned from angling books written by others, and writing a few along the way myself. And, nearly thirty years have passed since I swapped my badge and gun for a fly rod and traded my police career to become a fly fishing shop owner.

Now, sitting on the bank of Montana's Madison River I thought back to the trout streams back east I'd grown up fishing many years ago. Streams that I tried to find on a trip back to my old home town last year; streams that I could not find because now they run under new shopping malls and parking lots. I remembered headlines from my last visit in my home town paper proclaiming, "the construction boom is great and exciting news for the local economy," like local weathermen exulting over more blue sky and hot temperatures in the middle of a prolonged drought. And as if those reading this great news are people who don't fish, or don't love clean water, wild places, and wild trout.

I closed my eyes, warmed by the sun, and listened to the river's currents babbling along and remembered how I became involved in protecting, preserving, and enhancing wild trout, clean water, and wilderness. Through my love of these I've learned to speak loud, clear, and more often for their protection. I've become involved with groups like The Yellowstone Park Foundation, The Nature Conservancy, Trout Unlimited, The Federation of Fly Fishers, and Future Fisherman and FishAmerica Foundations.

Our business has been honored with conservation and environmental awards for protecting and preserving clean water, wild places, and wild trout.

But, most importantly, to help mitigate any negative environmental conse-quences of our business activity we impose on ourselves an annual tax of 1% of gross sales. We look on this as an earth tax, and proceeds are given to organiza-tions like those above to insure clean water and protection of wild trout and wilderness for all future generations.

In 1999 I was fishing the Henry's Fork of the Snake River in Idaho with Yvon Chouinard, owner of Patagonia Inc. of Ventura, Ca. We discussed how our busi-nesses were dependant on the existence of clean water and wild places and how we shared the personal belief that a healthy world is essential for human survival. For these reasons we support environmental organizations through our businesses.

In 2001 Yvon and I started an organization called 1% for the Planet, an alliance of businesses that pledge at least 1% of gross sales toward active efforts to protect and restore our natural environment. 1% for the Planet now has over 200 members from around the world, and growing daily. We feel it is like an insurance policy that we'll be in business in the future by taxing ourselves for using resources. We have to take action in order to solve our environmental problems by digging into our pockets and stepping up to the plate to protect and preserve clean water and air, wild trout and wilderness for all future gener-ations to have and enjoy. Members of 1% for the Planet understand that the environment is the foundation for all life on earth and that a healthy environ-ment is necessary for all forms of life to have a future.

You might ask, "what does this have to do with me?", or "what can I do?" When you see the logo, 1% for the Planet, you know a truly committed envi-ronmental company that stands up for what you enjoy and love. Support these businesses for the continued health of wild trout, wild places and clean water for all to enjoy, now and in the future!

Craig Mathews, *Fly Rod & Reel* Angler of the Year in 2005, is founder and owner of Blue Ribbon Flies in West Yellowstone, Montana. In 2001, with Yvon Choinard, owner of Patagonia, Inc., he started 1% for the Planet, an alliance of businesses that contribute at least 1 percent of their annual revenues to groups on a list of researched and approved environmental organizations. Blue Ribbon Flies has been given several environmental awards for helping to preserve, protect and enhance western trout waters for future generations. Mathews has fished and studied the Golden Triangle for forty years. He is the co-author of four books, including *Fly Patterns of Yellowstone*, and *Fly Fishing the Madison River*. He has narrated and produced three Telly Award-winning DVDs: *Fly Fishing Yellowstone Hatches*, *Fly Tying Yellowstone Hatches*, and *Bone Fishing the Flats*. His latest DVD, *Fly Fishing the Madison River*, will be released in 2007.

Craig's philosophy of business is simple: "When a business makes a living from a healthy environment such as clean water and air and healthy wild trout populations, that business must give something back to continue that healthy business cycle—sort of an earth tax. This is why our business gives back over 1% of our gross sales to conservation and environmental causes through the 1% for the Planet Club. This ensures that all future generations might fish and enjoy wild places and wild fishes!"

On Norman Maclean

JOHN N. MACLEAN

[Publisher's note: The following article about the late Norman Maclean was first published in 1990 in *Fly Rod & Reel Magazine*.]

Norman Maclean is now 87; ill health kept him from attending the 1989 Theodore Gordon Flyfishers banquet, where he would be presented with the Gingrich Award. Instead, John Maclean accepted the honor for his father, and then read this description of him. When Fly Rod & Reel *spoke with John in November, he said his father had just come home from the hospital after another bout with pneumonia. Though he lives near Chicago, Norman Maclean still keeps a cabin in Montana, about 50 miles from Missoula. He has signed a contract with Robert Redford to film his famous book,* A River Runs Through It, *and production may begin next summer. Negotiations are also underway to publish Maclean's next book, tentatively called* Young Men and Fire, *about a forest fire in Mann Gulch, near Helena, Montana, that killed 13 smokejumpers in 1949.*

When I was a teenager, finally big enough to keep up with my father on the Big Blackfoot River, he and I spent several summers alone in Montana at our cabin on Seeley Lake. We once fished 31 days in a row, filling the cabin's freezer with milk cartons that had big fishtails sticking out the top. There was no catch-and-release ethic in those days, and our idea of conservation was to catch-and-give-away to the non-fisher folk in the town of Seeley Lake, who appreciated the protein.

My father, Norman Maclean, fished with too many great fly fishermen to think he was the best, though at some aspects of the game he was better than anyone he fished against.

Once he had a fish on, he almost never lost it. He was a careful and patient player of trout: The throb of the fish running through the light wand connected him to the natural world he worshipped even as his own father worshipped the natural and supernatural worlds, mingling the two. As you can tell from his book, *A River Runs Through It*, he fished waters deeper than the river in front of him.

After my father finally slid a fish onto the bank, rushing only at the end when the fish tired and its head could be held out of water, he would muse out loud for a while, especially if it were a big fish. He liked an audience, even if only one teenaged son, though it was clear he addressed a broader public even then.

Standing on the bank with the fish in his hand like a teacher holding out a text, he would recount the details of the battle. Inevitably he turned to what his brother and father would have thought if they had seen the show. His brother, Paul, was one helluva fisherman.

His brother told him, he often said in his muse, that there was nobody as good as Norman Maclean at landing a fish, though Paul criticized him for lacking his, Paul's, aggressiveness in going after fish in difficult spots. Paul became a presence with us on the river, a broad-shouldered figure with a slouch Stetson who would stop for a moment to admire my dad for his artfulness in playing a fish, but who was happy in the knowledge that his creel was heavier and fuller, and always would be.

The old man, my father's father, was a Scottish Presbyterian minister who believed that only God and big fish merited veneration. In his muse, my dad wondered what his father would have thought of him; no answer came back. The old man was an austere presence, watching from atop the high cutbanks as we—dad, Paul and I—cast for a prize.

I am sorry my dad cannot be here tonight to accept this prestigious prize. He has become an old man himself now, and at 86 years of age can no longer climb the high cutbanks. But after many years of musing, he landed the big one in the end: He got all the stories down the right way in one place. He has left his own presence in the remarkable book for which you honor him.

Now instead of being only with me when ghosts arise along the river, he will be among us all, as long as men fish and read books.

John N. Maclean's third book on wildland fire, *The Thirtymile Fire: A Chronicle of Bravery and Betrayal*, was published in 2007. Maclean, an avid fly-fisherman, divides his time between his family cabin in Montana and his home in Washington, D.C., where he was a longtime correspondent for *The Chicago Tribune*.

The Once and Future Sport

NICK LYONS

Fifty years ago, I fished with half a dozen different fly patterns and a bamboo rod. I could fish all day on public water and see only one or two other fishermen. There was still an old-world quality to fly fishing, though even then you often heard talk of the good old days, twenty years earlier, when there were even fewer folk on the water and far fewer hatchery trout. Then two changes occurred that jerked trout fishing into a new era: the numbers of fly fishers exploded and the sport was assaulted by new technology.

Bamboo steadily gave way to better and better glass rods, some of which were superb casting tools, and people said the spirit of the chase was lost. Art Flick had reduced the number of necessary fly patterns to a handful; but suddenly there were No-Hackles and Comparaduns, wiggle nymphs, Sparkle Duns, bead heads, wooly buggers, Zonkers, and a score of other styles of fly, and then glass gave way to graphite (which the old guard snidely called "plastic"), and suddenly 7X leaders were strong enough to hold good fish and then even 8X leader tippets were, too. After "The Movie," *A River Runs Through It*, came out, the numbers of fly fishers grew exponentially. There were fly fishers in fashionable clothing ads; celebrity competitions; fly fishers in Fifth Avenue window displays; fly fishing articles in general magazines from *Newsweek* to *Martha Stewart Living*. A lot of old fly fishers, myself included, thought sometimes that the hour of the apocalypse had arrived and our lovely old private passion was now merely a fad.

But there were other changes, too. There was a much greater awareness of conservation in the 1980s; groups like Trout Unlimited expanded from 20,000

members to well over 100,000, and became far more potent in saving and reha-
bilitating rivers; the concept of Catch and Release (growing from Lee Wulff's
wise view that a game fish was too valuable to be caught only once) changed
the numbers and sizes of fish in the rivers and began to change the quality of
the fishing, especially with the new awareness (by fish-and-game departments as
well as by fishermen) that wild trout were much more valuable than their pale
hatchery cousins. The world of fly fishing changed, too, opening new frontiers,
especially saltwater fly fishing but also broader destinations, including Alaska,
New Zealand, and Russia.

Fishing a local creek in the Catskill Mountains recently, I tried to think of
the one way in which trout fishing had changed most in the past fifty years, and
whether I enjoyed my fishing more or less these days. The water was quick and
cold, still a bit high but clear on that bright early-May afternoon. I carried a
light graphite rod that I'd come to love for its authority and durability, and I
used an old reel from the 1940s. My fly line floated high, without being greased,
and my leader was thin and strong. I used a Hair-wing Royal Coachman, with
a golden pheasant tippet for a tail. Once I had used the fly almost exclusively
and I always took a few fish with it. That was before I knew anything about
entomology, which I became hugely fond of and found wonderfully fascinating.
There was something visually satisfying about the way the Coachman rode the
riffles and the hatches hadn't started yet anyway. I was out for one of the first
days of the season and I wanted to catch a few fish, but mostly I wanted to be
on the water.

This little river hadn't changed much at all in the thirty years I'd fished it,
though I had fished it less in the past decade when I sought out the big name
rivers with much larger fish. Now I was back. I remembered that ledge of rock,
the stand of birches, the way the river curved left at the old, drooping willow. I
often had to look harder for that solitude I've always treasured in trout fishing—
but today, not twenty miles from my summer home, the river was for me alone.
I realized I'd grown to love the tools of modern fly fishing, which were splen-
didly made and useful. And though I didn't avail myself of many of the far-flung
angling opportunities throughout the world, I was half convinced that the lus-
cious rivers in Montana and Alaska and Iceland had probably lured a good
number of folk away from my local trout streams. I liked to fish nearby. I liked

to fish close to where I lived, where small dramas had come to mean as much to me big rainbows on salmonflies or salmon that leaped a mile high. Simplicity. Intimacy. Love of the near at hand. These counted potently.

I still preferred a few flies, after years of infatuation with the plethora of new patterns, and a few old tools. A lot had indeed changed but it all seemed separate from me, laid out on a picnic table, the tastiest of it available to me if I wanted it, the rest simply to be passed by.

Standing in that nearby creek and casting up under the willow, I realized that one essential ingredient of fly fishing was exactly the same: it was still a sweet, rhythmic, private activity that gave me immense pleasure. I caught three good browns that afternoon and one five-inch native brookie, a wriggling jewel. It was a lovely day. In which one way had fly fishing changed most? I really had no answer. But if the water holds up and we don't chase crowds and we keep our eyes on why we do it in the first place, the fly fishing can be better than ever.

Nick Lyons is the author or editor of many books about fishing, including *The Seasonable Angler*, *Spring Creek*, *Full Creel*, *Hemingway on Fishing*, and others, along with articles and essays in such magazines as *Harper's*, *The New York Times Magazine*, *Field & Stream*, *Sports Afield*, and *Fly Fisherman*, for which he wrote the "Seasonable Angler" column for nearly twenty-five years.

Red, White, and Bluegill

TED LEESON

No fish stands for American values like the adaptable, enthusiastic, and democratic pan-fish. (They don't taste bad, either.)

Among angling aristocrats, Atlantic salmon have long been celebrated as "the fish of kings," no doubt because the two have so much in common: the aloof arrogance and inflated sense of self-worth, a fussiness about habitat, expensive tastes. And as far as I'm concerned, they deserve each other. Give me a panfish any day—a fish of the people, blue-collar rather than blue blood, a working-class fish, a fish for a great republic. I've never understood how the bald eagle, a scavenger and a thief, could have been chosen as our national symbol, whereas the honest, sweat-of-the-brow bluegill never even made the shortlist. I guess the Founding Fathers didn't fish much.

Panfish, of course, doesn't denote a particular species but a loosely defined assemblage with varying regional representatives—a little like Congress but harder working and better behaved. The core of the group comes from the *Centrarchidae* family—the sunfishes—itself a kind of melting pot whose chief ingredients include bluegills, pumpkinseeds, redears, redbreasts, green sunfish, warmouths, rock bass, and white and black crappies. A kind of odd-man-out, the yellow perch is not a sunfish but no less a panfish wherever it is found. I'm not aware of any single place that's home to all these species at once. They crop up in various mixes and proportions in different geographical areas, and member-ship in the category of panfish (or "bream" or "brim," depending on where you live) has always been a matter of shifting local interpretations, further complicated by a host of colloquial names: shellcracker, stumpknocker, goggle-eye, sun perch, longear, speckled perch, white bass, and so on. In practice, the term ultimately falls into that set of expressions, like "I'll do it in a minute" or "I have strong feelings for you," that are universally understood but not necessarily taken to mean exactly the same thing by everyone.

Fishermen don't trouble themselves much about such discrepancies, instead focusing on the collective virtues of the fish. And foremost among their merits is a relentless availability. Like the other indispensables of American life—duct tape, canned chili, and WD-40—panfish can be obtained virtually everywhere. I've taken them in creeks and rivers, brackish water and fresh, 10,000-acre lakes and quarter-acre stock tanks, old quarry pits, prairie potholes, golf-course water hazards, abandoned strip mines, backyard ponds, irrigation ditches, and once, the ornamental fountain pool behind a fancy hotel. As a group, they are America's most widespread and abundant gamefish. And they are nothing if not game. I've caught them by accident and on purpose, on handlines, trotlines, poles cut from tree limbs, garage-sale spincast outfits, fly tackle that cost slightly less than my car, and every kind of gear in between. I've grabbled a few by hand and (in a mercifully brief period of angling dementia) jigged them up through 2 feet of ice. Equally ready for a few casual casts after work or the formalities of an organized expedition, panfish are a fish-of-all-trades, up for anything, anytime. They are a welcome counterweight to the forces of high-tech angling and a persistent reminder that fishing is finally about fish, not equipment.

Accommodating and enthusiastic, genial and cooperative, panfish are custom-cut for the neophyte. In the angling universe of my youth, they were the force of gravity that held everything together. The ones I could catch whetted my skills and honed my instincts. Those that proved better at being fish than I did at being a fisherman gave me a continuing sense of purpose. Without panfish, I might well have sunk into juvenile delinquency, or golf. The pinnacle of every summer was the day my father, a man who did not readily leave the house, squeezed our whole family into a station wagon and endured the eight-hour drive to a lake in northern Wisconsin. He herded us directly from the car into a rowboat where, except for a few moments stolen to dig more worms, we spent a week or two yarding in unimaginable numbers of perch and rock bass and bluegills. The little ones bit readily. And the bigger ones proved just discriminating enough to teach you something but still catchable enough that you could learn the lesson. At a time of life as yet uncorrupted by a lust for magazine-cover specimens, panfish fulfilled the greatest promise in all of angling—pure action.

We ate them too, by the stringerful, with butter and lemon and onions, fried, baked, broiled, and grilled, and best of all, without guilt. Even today, in a time when quality angling for high-profile species increasingly hinges on catch-and-release, you can still sit down to a plate of bluegills or crappies without the slightest twinge of conscience or the fear of a second-rate meal. They come by their name honestly, for a pan is the highest destiny of these sweet-eating fishes. Bony? Sure, a little. And a steamed crab is mostly shell. Who's that going to stop?

Once you've got panfish in your soul, they never really leave. Not many seasons ago, a friend and I extorted an invitation to a pay-to-play trophy trout lake in the high desert of eastern Washington. The morning's fishing, though not fast, produced some remarkable trout, among the biggest of my life. Noon found us prospecting the lower end of the lake. Approaching deeper water near an earthen dam, we suddenly doubled up—smaller fish, it was clear, but dogged and determined fighters. To our utter disbelief, they turned out to be a pair of identical yellow perch a full pound apiece, with deep blue-green backs and lemon-lime flanks that shaded into fat, cantaloupe bellies. With no real idea how they got there, but a pretty good one about how to get them out, we burned up half a box of trout flies and a whole afternoon happily catching perch in a $200-a-day lake where a 5-pound rainbow scarcely elicits a yawn. That evening when our host, proud of his fishery and eager for a report, asked how we'd done, we just told him, "Couldn't have been better."

And we meant it. In this age of scientific fisheries control, of measurements and projections that produce finely calibrated angling regulations, panfish may well be the last unmanaged gamefish in America, left to themselves, on their own as they've always been and doing just fine, thank you. It's ironic that a whole sector of the fishing industry now thrives on whisking anglers off for remote and pristine destinations to experience sport of unspoiled abundance, fishing "the way it used to be." Any 8-year-old kid with a cane pole, a bike, and panfish in his heart can lead you to just such a place.

And maybe that's what I like best about them: Panfish are the most democratic of gamefish. They do not care who fishes them and bite equally for everyone. They're unimpressed by the cost of your tackle, indifferent to the methods you use, unconcerned about the bait you favor, and sometimes, whether there's any bait at all. Panfish are angling's version of the single-shot .22—sturdy and dependable, workmanlike and unpretentious. If panfish formed a baseball team, they'd be the Cubs; if you could play them on a jukebox, they'd be Hank Williams tunes; if panfish were a beer, they'd be whatever's on sale.

Oh, and there's one last thing. Except for the more cosmopolitan perch, panfish are pure homegrown. Though, like much in American life, they've been exported around the world, panfish are indigenous only to North America, native to no other part of the globe. So picture this for a moment—a red-and-white bobber twitching above the slab of a sunset-colored bluegill. Now there's something worth printing on the back of a dollar bill.

Ted Leeson is a contributing editor to *Field & Stream* and *Fly Rod & Reel* magazines. His books include *Jerusalem Creek: Journeys Into Driftless Country*, *The Habit of Rivers*, and *The Fly Tier's Benchside Reference*. He lives in Corvallis, Oregon, where he teaches English at Oregon State University.

Hard Hands, Soft Moon

SYDNEY LEA

No way, of course, to be sure those sea-run brown trout would have taken the fly. But it does look good, sailing into the brush. I fling the whole box of size eighteen hooks after it, turn around and scream: "This is the worst fishing trip ever!"

Years back, that bass—biggest I'd ever had on a line—charged under the rowboat and snapped off. My tears were furious.

"It isn't a fishing trip. It's our honeymoon." She's succinct, not truculent.

I want to do things my own way: Unsure what might hatch in Spain, I packed my streamside vice, a range of dubbing material, and one of the Darbees' dun necks, so that I might tie what I needed, right on the spot. I am made chiefly of the lust for success, especially with fish and game; the young woman's composure therefore enrages me. That these Orvis hooks are lemons, every one of their eyes pinched and unthreadable, is bad enough. That my new wife should keep blithely and irreverently casting her size twelve Tupp's and should even land several of the heavy-toothed, deep-bodied, slurping trout is intolerable.

Why not look up and notice the skill and ardor of bats, hear the nightly gong from the abbey, of which nothing remains but the bell tower itself? Why not take pleasure in the smell of residual sun in the stones, still warm on the bank? Why not think back just a few days, when in a single weekend I netted seven beautiful Narcea salmon, including that luminous 25-pounder?

It is 1966, I am twenty-three, and I pledge to boycott Orvis forever. (I won't actually honor my vow till a few years later, when the catalogue begins to include more wraparound skirts and cufflinks than outdoor gear.) I whip a sapling with my Leonard rod. I curse the very neighborhood goats, who seem to snicker from the waterside path.

Although these Iberian ephemerids are something like our Infrequens, their fitchy shade has an odd *glint*. I'm prepared, however, having brought along a spool of silver wire that makes the adjective "fine" seem coarse.

Where'd I get this stuff? Maybe from that mail-order outfit in Michigan, the one that stiffed me five bucks for the wood duck fibers they never sent, the crooks.

The fly I've tossed away was sparely ribbed with the wire. In flight, it caught the inchoate moonlight just so. Yes, were I a trout on inland tour, I at least would have leapt at such a thing. Now I must resort to a pale upright, dressed to mid-June Battenkill specs. Hell, though, it looks ludicrous, looks bigger than it is.

Below the covered bridge in West Arlington, that twenty-incher gulped my Hendrickson and ran into a muskrat hole. God, the tricks they'll pull! I actually hated that fish.

Of course this Vermont dun might work if I genuinely wanted it to; but I thrash the water, as if to show the gods what an impossible hand they've dealt. It plain won't *do* to catch a fish.

My wife, knowing me, knows also not to chide, nor to whoop when she nets another thick trout. I crash back up to the rented Peugeot, muttering over my shoulder that it's late, that we face a long trip to our next hotel, in the ancient city of Avila. From the road, I yet hear the *whoomp* of rising browns, the fish I'll prefer, lifelong, to any other. The hell with a salmon.

You're young and relatively poor, and you get to the damned Miramichi just as the heat wave hits. The water goes to eighty degrees, and you beat it vainly, angrily.

But at length my mood lightens, not least at the prospect of Avila, one of whose medieval rulers forbade the spending of more than half a given year's budget on troubadours. My own poetry is as yet unremarkable and unremarked, but I dream naively of improving it just by visiting a place where the art seemed once so crucial.

How lovely the countryside, after all! The aura of moon becomes moon itself, breaking over the Sierras to eastward. How lovely my girl-bride, her face open, unduly forgiving. It is nine o'clock. There'll be a late Spanish supper—unpretentious food, a draft of vintage, intimate small talk—and then a room overlooking the walled town.

Behind us lies the much smaller town of Crado. In the rearview I see its light rising to diffuse itself in the sudden lunar brightness. Ahead, a boar crosses the road; then a fox.

Never mind that the run of hooks was defective. That hatch was perversely copious, the fish big: I have squandered all that, but never mind. Crado wasn't so bad, really. The recollected taste of the hotel's blood oranges stings the place where my jaws meet; the vista from our bedroom was sublime; sweetness from the garden below hung on our bedclothes at dawn.

I have no right to self-pity. Perhaps I get part of an important insight: infuriating experience may in time cede to calm, may even become savory in retrospect. I can't know that I'll learn this more completely by virtue, precisely, of fishing; nor that calm may eventually have a preemptive power too. If I'll only let it.

God damn! This fork in the road doesn't show on the map. Easy, I tell myself. What were you just thinking? There: the mountain range is still to eastward; right is still south, the way to be heading. And all around, rustic families make their bizarre crepuscular promenades. I'll cruise along for a bit, and then, if still in doubt, trot out rudimentary Spanish, ask directions.

That twenty-five pounder thundered up the brawling Narcea till I saw spindle on the reel. Then it raced back down in a far channel on the other side of a bridge abutment. At casual risk to my life—I shudder some now at the wheel—I plunged in, waders and all, swimming across, holding my rod high. Gathering slack on the opposite shore, I thrilled to feel the salmon still there. The chef in Cornnellana would dot the steaks with coarse salt, broil them over oak coals, bring them to our table with fresh greens.

"Where are we?"

"I'll ask," I reply, the road having turned to dirt without my notice.

The Spanish father draws four small daughters about him, as if protectively, but his answer is clear and courteous; the other fork after all—drive six kilometers, then bear left. An hour only to Avila.

I lean out of the Peugeot: "Muchas gracias." The peasant bows, the children titter.

The road grows wide and accommodating again.

Then it's dirt, but still broad.

Then dirt, but narrow.

Then a path.

And couldn't ever find that loaded brookie hole again, back in the woods. Washington County, 1957, year of the killer mosquito.

Seeing a burro ahead, jacked in its tracks by the headlights, I back out, ask another walker, whose family hides among pines.

"Oh no, *señor*, back toward Crado, but turn *right* at the highway—a simple hour to Avila. Very beautiful, grand."

"Muchas gracias," I say. The man inclines his head.

I could simply have gone down a size; the twenties were perfectly fine. Why not? Because I'm pigheaded and spoiled, my purism ruinous, manic. Every cast needn't put Kreh to shame. My every fly doesn't have to rival Whitlock. Even Homer nodded: every sonnet need not be "When in disgrace. . . ." Fish. Write. The world is all before you.

Before me now, however, another burro, wide-eyed in the high beams. Families scurry into the roadside brush like rodents. Through the open window, I hear their sibilant chat and laughter. I'll drive to the best road I can find behind us, keep the moon-bathed Sierras on my right, tending ever south. It has been two hours now, but Avila must be nearby. And those hours have been pleasant, maybe even instructive, the moon turned to the color of that fine silver rib on the discarded fly. I imagine it, cocked on its stiff hackle: the tinsel winks in the gleam amid flowery bushes. I could wish to be a painter. But it isn't bad to be what I am. In childhood, the willow boughs gobbled my crude home-made streamers, or occasionally a fish did . . . , and broke off. I'd huff out of the woods, the biting insects strafing me, my brow a mess of sweat and cobweb. So life has indeed kept turning brighter since.

She has fallen asleep in the other seat, and she's better than I deserve, by far. Her hair trails out the window, and the moon capers on it.

I am unusually cool when the tire goes flat—unpack our fishing gear from the trunk with deliberation, trouble to read instructions on the jack, make the change. After Avila, there's another river to the north, and we've reserved a beat. There will be trout in my world forever.

I further astonish myself on hearing the crinkly sound under the Peugeot's back wheel. By God, I *am* being rational: I realize that if I hadn't run over my flyrod, I'd have driven away, abandoning it where I put it while removing the spare from the car's trunk. You only take one honeymoon, I tell myself (wrongly, but I won't know that for years): I'll just buy some cheap rod in Avila, whose soft lights now rise in columns, much as Crado's did.

And do. For this, clearly, is Crado. I have driven in a great circle.

How can it be that—having consistently kept those mountains (surely the Sierras) off to my right—I have arrived where I started, at the very place where I threw an eyeless mayfly imitation into the brush three hours ago? I've mean-while crushed my Leonard eight-footer with a car, whose steering wheel I now twist, with a strength that age will mercifully sap, till it breaks in my hand.

★ ★ ★

Hard hands in a soft moon. I can see them even now, a quarter-century later. They had yet to learn the full story, yet to learn gentleness. I would have to stroke my children's heads. I would have to draw a fish back and forth in cur-rent till it regathered vigor and swam off into memory, in which realm I might better comprehend the meaning of calm.

Sydney Lea is author of eleven books, including the outdoor meditations *Hunting the Whole Way Home* and *A Little Wildness*, and his work has appeared in some fifty anthologies. He founded and for thirteen years edited *New England Review*. He is best known as a poet, and was a finalist for the 2001 Pulitzer Prize in that genre. His latest volume is *Ghost Pain*. "One of the things I have most loved about being a 'creative' writer, and particularly a poet," he writes, "is that I've never known just when I was working and when not. My outdoor pur-suits—fly fishing all over the nation at or near the top of the list—have turned out, as I'd not known at the time, to be valuable 'research.' Every fly angler, poet or not, knows what I'm talking about: the world, physical and otherwise, coming right up close for long periods of time."

Keeping Busy
When not on the
Casting Deck

LEFTY KREH

It's more fun and certainly you'll catch more fish if you and your companion in a flats boat work as a team. While one stands on the platform, ready to throw at the next fish, his companion should be just as busy, maybe more so, than the person in the ready-to-fish position.

A major problem for the person on the bow is that the line remains free of tangles and obstructions. Wind blows the line around. It can slide unknowingly underfoot, or it can catch on a rod holder or a piece of gear in the boat, spoiling a cast. Because the fly fisherman is concentrating on seeing the fish and then making a good presentation, he is often unaware that disaster lurks nearby.

Sitting in the boat, the companion can observe what is happening to the line. He constantly makes sure all line is tangle-free. When the angler is false casting prior to throwing to a fish, his friend can alert him that his foot is on the line. If the caster or the boat changes position this can affect how the line is lying on the deck. His teammate constantly monitors the line to make sure it is okay to cast.

The companion can have ready additional flies and leader material. If the angler breaks off his fish either on a hook-up or during the fight, the companion has a leader tippet and fly ready. It is much quicker for him to repair the leader and attach the fly than the man standing on the bow.

Quite often one pattern isn't drawing strikes and a change in flies is needed. The friend can have several flies ready. He can quickly snip off one fly and tie on another. I make it a practice that anytime I miss on two hookups, I check the hook point for sharpness. If the man sitting behind the caster has a file ready, he can check the point and hone it in seconds.

If a fish is hooked and the companion sees that a knot is developing in the line, there is often time for him to remove the knot before the escaping fish pulls the line through the guides. I know of several times when my friend saved a fish by such quick action.

If a fish is hooked and there is some rough water, the friend can often step to the platform and help stabilize the fisherman as he fights his quarry.

Each time you reach a new fishing location line has to be pulled from the reel. This can be time consuming for the angler. But, if the companion will pull the line hand-over-hand from the reel, the chore can be accomplished in seconds. Sometimes the fly line has coils in it that can spoil the cast. Again, the companion can stretch the line to remove them.

Many fish are difficult to see on a flat. A snook hiding among the mangrove roots can be near impossible to spot. Despite its size, a permit can often be difficult to see—even for the guide on the poling platform. There are many indicators that help locate a fish on the flats. It can be a silvery flash in the water. A small shower of minnows indicates something chasing them. A subtle mud puff could tip off the anglers to a feeding bonefish. A tail that appears above the surface for only a moment can lead to a catch. A bird flying low over the flats will often briefly frighten a permit, bonefish, red fish, or tarpon. The guide and the angler are looking for all of these indicators. But, so can the companion. Many times it is the person that is not fishing that first locates a fish.

The guide usually stands on the poling platform, which is elevated above the deck. When the angler hooks a fish and brings it to the boat, the guide must stow the pole and climb off the platform to land the fish. All of this takes time and the boat either has to be staked out or anchored or is not under control during this time. Instead, the guide can maintain the boat if the companion will land the fish for his friend.

And, once the fish has been landed, the angler often wants a photograph of it. Many guides, especially outside the United States, know little or nothing about handling a camera or taking a good photo. This is where a friend can really help out.

Several years ago I realized something that took a long time to understand. I began to carry a fly swatter on flats boats. In Florida and the tropics there are biting flies that really hurt. These stinging bloodsuckers have caused many fish to escape, as the angler is distracted trying to kill the pests. Some of these flies are tough. I have knocked them unconscious with my hat, only to see them revive later and fly away. No so with a fly swatter. The companion can carry a fly swatter at the ready. Not long ago Mike O'Brien, a fishing buddy, and I killed so many flies with my swatter that we actually wore it out. I piled a big number of their carcasses on the deck, laid the ruined swatter beside it and took a picture of what I called a "fly cemetery." The companion not only can keep these pesky critters from bothering either him or the fisherman, but it sure helps to pass the time when not fishing. And, I might add, there is a certain satisfaction in killing them.

I have seen many pairs of fly fishermen in a flats boat. One stands on the platform, ready to fish. The other person simply sits back and relaxes.

But the person who becomes a team player will get more fun out of the day, and both of them will probably catch more fish.

Lefty Kreh, in an active fifty-year career, has written for most outdoor magazines in the United States and for many abroad. He has written twenty-eight books. He received Lifetime Achievement Awards from both the American Sportfishing Association and the North American Fly Tackle Trade Association. He is a Hall of Fame honoree by four fishing groups, including the International Game Fishing Association. He was a senior advisor for several terms for Trout Unlimited and Federation of Fly Fishers. Lefty has fished most of the world's waters, all over the Americas and in Europe, Iceland, Australia, and New Guinea. He has taught photography to the National Wildlife Society and was L.L. Bean's photo consultant for years. Lefty is most proud that he has been married for almost sixty years to his best friend, Evelyn, who made it possible for him to pursue his career.

2000 Words of Heartfelt Advice

VERLYN KLINKENBORG

One spring morning many years ago, I woke up urgently needing to fish with a fly rod. I'd never been fly fishing, and I hadn't fished at all since I was 12, a boy with a bait rod in a boat. All I remembered about fishing was that sunfish have spines and bullheads have barbels and that it's better to eat lunch as soon as you pull away from the dock, before the sandwiches start to smell like bait. That wasn't much to go on. I called my dad, a longtime fly fisherman. He gave me some good advice. "Start fishing," he said. But I lived in Manhattan. I had little money and no car. All I had was an appetite for an unfamiliar sport, an appetite aroused by the sudden dreamlike memory of sitting on shore when I was very young, watching my dad cast a wet fly in the White River near Meeker, Colorado.

As it happened, I learned to fly fish much as my dad had: I figured it out for myself. But there was a difference. He learned on the high mountain lakes and streams of Colorado. I built a fly rod—it was cheap and I wanted to build one anyway—and took it up to the roof of the building I lived in, which was narrow but nearly a hundred feet long. There in the swirling wind four stories above Third Avenue, I taught myself to cast, using a kiddie pool as my target. I practiced almost every evening for an entire summer. It would have been a ridiculous thing to do, if it hadn't been so effective.

The hardest part about being a beginner in any sport is knowing nothing. The problem isn't just what to learn, it's how to learn, a problem that's even worse in a sport like fly fishing, where a lot of emphasis is laid on tradition and on the supposedly scientific rigor of its best-known modern practitioners. In fact, fly fishing is often presented as a form of connoisseurship, which can be—and is often meant to be—very intimidating. But to some people, the apparent elitism of the sport is part of its attraction. So here's a rule of thumb. If you come across anglers, or angling writers, who make it sound as though the art of the dry fly gets passed down from firstborn to firstborn, ignore them. No one ever inherited a prose style or a casting stroke.

Fly fishing is basically a simple sport, no matter what you hear to the contrary. Casting is easy, not half as hard as learning to swing a golf club or rope a calf. Compared to spin-fishing and bait-casting gear, the equipment is mechanically simple. Fly fishing becomes elitist only if you want to own or lease private water, and in this country that's strictly a matter of cash, not breeding. The thing to remember is this: People spend enormous amounts of money for access to easy fishing. Really hard fishing is usually free. And no matter how far you progress in the sport or how exalted your ambitions become, there's no pleasure in angling as pure as the emotion you feel when you catch your first fish with a fly rod. That moment will echo down your sporting life, whether you find yourself casting for bluegills in a farm pond or for permit on Ascension Bay.

It's natural to want to sign up for fly-fishing school right away, and there are good reasons for doing so. The level of instruction and camaraderie at fishing schools can be very high, even though the enormous network of fly-fishing courses these days resembles a giant intake valve sucking beginners and their cash into the sport. I say, teach yourself instead. You'll be giving the tackle companies enough of your money anyway. Professional instruction can save you some time, but you learn nothing from the mistakes you don't make. Fly fishing isn't a product you consume while worrying about the shortness of time. It's a pursuit that gets interwoven with time itself. Teaching yourself, you learn about the techniques of fly fishing, of course, but, more importantly, you also get a chance to rediscover how you learn. That will be important on the stream. To paraphrase Heraclitus, you can never fish in the same river twice. Conditions are always different, minute by minute, cast by cast, and the ability to adjust to changing conditions—to instruct yourself quickly—is a good measure of an angler's success. If that sounds like mere philosophizing, wait till you find yourself at the onset of a Baetis hatch on the Bighorn River in early May.

Learning isn't just a matter of absorbing information. It's the act of winnowing information. I think the best, though not the fastest way to learn to fly fish is to read widely in the literature of the sport, which is a long-lasting pleasure in itself. Subscribe to the magazines; buy or borrow the books. (Watch the videos too.) Read everything and believe nothing until you've tried it out. Then keep what you can use and throw out the rest. Experience teaches you to read skeptically, and reading makes you a better judge of experience. Practicing on my rooftop long ago, I tried to copy the dissimilar casting styles of Joan Wulff, Lefty Kreh, and Charles Ritz. I also tried to ape every diagram in every fly-casting article I saw. Ultimately the dynamics of the cast itself—how a double haul felt when I did it right—taught me what I needed to know, but by trying out so many different casting styles I discovered that there is no single right way to cast. There is, instead, the broad range of what works.

Over the years, I've spent almost as much time watching anglers as I have fishing. It's a habit I picked up as a beginner, partly because I was lucky enough to be fishing with friends who were, and still are, vastly more skillful than I am. They never gave me advice, and I never asked for it, and yet their example meant everything to me. But in a way I've learned almost as much from watching men and women who were struggling with the sport. In their clumsiness, I could see my own, and I began to correct it little by little. I saw anglers for whom the loss of a fly or a tippet provoked a crisis, because it meant they had to tie an improved clinch knot or, worse, a blood knot. I saw anglers standing in water they should have been casting to, anglers casting to utterly barren stretches of river, anglers lashing the pool behind them with every backcast, anglers hopelessly entangled in the slack they had stripped from their reel, anglers whose rudeness had earned them the contempt of everyone around them.

And what I learned was that there's no substitute for practice or awareness or economy of motion or courtesy. Those are the fundamentals of fly fishing. These days, for instance, it's a fairly common habit to buy prefabricated leaders, knotted or knotless. When I began fly fishing I decided I wanted to tie my own leaders, following the same logic that led me to build my first fly rod and tie my own flies. I bought Art Lee's *Fishing the Dry Fly on Rivers and Streams* and made up a couple of dozen leaders according to his formulas. (Tying leaders in the evening allowed me to pretend that I was fishing.) When I began, a blood knot was merely an aspiration, something I hoped one day to achieve. When I was done tying leaders several nights later, it was an instinct. Now I buy knotless leaders, but I still have a bombproof blood knot. The peculiar thing about learning to fly fish is this: every shortcut you take when you're a beginner ultimately diminishes your feel for the complexity, the subtlety of fly fishing. That's why, if at all possible, you should also learn to tie your own flies. The joy of catching a trout on a fly rod is compounded many times when you do it with a fly of your own making.

When I think back over my fly fishing education—thus far, that is—the single most instructive moment was an evening in June more than a decade ago. I had driven to the Catskills to interview a famous angler, and he invited me to go fishing with him. We drove along the Beaverkill, pausing here and there to look at the stream, and then we parked, geared up, and walked down to the river. I was tense with impatience, with nervousness. I wanted to wade right in and begin to pretend fishing, because, of course, what I really wanted to do was to watch this man fish. Instead, we sat down on a big rock near the high water mark. He didn't say much. He smoked a cigarette all the way down, and then he lit another one. He watched the water, and he tried to help me look where he was looking, although he couldn't actually make me see what he was seeing.

The current ran heavy along the far bank, and the river thinned out over a flat that ended on the near shore, so that most of that broad, beautiful river was in fact very shallow. Well upstream, at a picturesque distance, a couple of anglers were drifting dry flies along the edge of the deep current, a place that looked naturally inviting—to humans, at least. But that wasn't where this man was looking. His gaze ended at a line of rocks in water only a few inches deep, just a dozen yards upstream from us. I can't explain to you how long it seemed before I saw what he was looking at, but when I finally saw it I felt very stupid. It was the tail of a large brown trout, the tail an almost iridescent brown, glowing as it wriggled, half out of water. The fish was nymphing, nosing around in the sediment beneath the rocks. After offering me the chance, the man stood up, paid out line, made a single cast, and caught the fish, which he released.

It wasn't the cast, the catch, or the release that mattered to me, though they were elegant and unhurriedly efficient. It was the lesson about observation. Like most beginners, I had spent so much time thinking about gear and technique that I neglected the most important thing of all: the fact that my real subject was the river. I had watched the water every time I went fishing, watched it as I waded out to what I thought would be a good starting point, watched it as I made my backcast, as my fly drifted downstream. But I had never taken the time to sit down and absorb the river, to realize that what I should really be watching was the way the river differed from itself instant by instant. I had never realized that those differences—in light, in current, in sound—would show me trout, if only I could be patient enough to look for them. It was time to begin fishing in something besides my preconceptions.

That's a hard shift for most of us to make. It's easy enough to emphasize the rituals of fly fishing, its daily and seasonal rhythms, the languorous, almost supplicating beat of a long casting stroke. These are some of the things that make fly fishing a lifelong sport, a sport of ever-deepening complexity. But those rituals and rhythms inevitably belong to the everyday world we inhabit, and they overlay, on the stream, a world we perceive only in flashes, when, for a moment, we're able to concentrate on the swiftness, the abruptness, the almost unimaginable profusion of what nature has laid before us. It is to lengthen those moments of concentration that one goes fly fishing, and a lifetime is barely long enough to learn what they contain.

Verlyn Klinkenborg was born in Colorado in 1952 and raised in Iowa and California. He graduated from Pomona College and received a Ph.D. in English Literature from Princeton University. He is the author of *Making Hay* (1986), *The Last Fine Time* (1991), *The Rural Life* (2003), and *Timothy: Or, Notes of an Abject Reptile* (2006). His work has appeared in many magazines. He has taught literature and creative writing at Fordham University and Harvard University and will be the visiting writer in residence at Pomona College in 2007. He lives in rural New York State with his wife, Lindy Smith, and is a member of the editorial board of *The New York Times*.

Head-Spinning

ED GRAY

Dry fly, wet fly. Who cares? Throw 'em some salami if it works.

Salami? This could be good. I stopped to listen; they didn't notice me.

"Look. The trout wants to eat a real bug, right?"

"Right."

"And if you put that actual bug on your hook, that's bait, right?"

"Right."

"So anything else, that ain't the real bug, that's a fake, right?"

"Right."

"So what's a fake?"

"What's a fake?"

"Yeah. What's a fake?"

"Well, you just said . . ."

"An artificial."

"An . . . Yeah, okay."

"An artificial. Am I right?"

"Yeah. Right."

This was good. Two guys I didn't know, sitting at the lunch counter on a grey Tuesday in March. "Just coffee," I said. I could wait this one out. Socrates went on.

" 'Artificial Lures Only.' Give me a break."

" 'Artificial Flies Only' is going to be the rule."

"Yeah, I know. Sheee . . ."

"And catch-and-release, too."

A mumble from Socrates.

I knew what they were talking about: the new "quality-fishing" stretch on the Nipumet River. All the local bait fisherman and plug casters were opposed, of course; I had a few reservations myself.

Socrates was back on the podium:

"If we're gonna put 'em all back, who cares what we use to catch 'em?"

"Well . . ."

"'Long as we don't hurt 'em."

"Yeah . . ."

"I mean, why not feed 'em some real food while we're playin' around with 'em?"

"Well, yeah, but . . ."

"Ahh, come on. You mean you think we're doing a trout a big favor by letting him munch on old feathers stored in moth balls?"

"Now wait . . ."

"Dipped in head cement? You ever sniff that stuff?"

"Yeah. I mean, no. But it's dried . . ."

"And then we what? Save the marshmallows for ourselves?"

Who was this guy? I ordered a doughnut; wondered if they had a flagon of hemlock in the back room, waiting.

"Okay, then," he went on. "Let me ask you this: A deer-hair mouse okay on that water?"

"Yeah, sure."

"That's an artificial fly, right?"

"Yeah. You know that. It's a classic."

"A classic. Yeah. Okay, okay then. Then do you have to use deer hair?"

"No. Of course not. That's just the name. You can use caribou or moose, I suppose. Deer hair works best, I think . . ."

"Can you use mouse hair?"

"Mouse hair?"

"Yeah."

"Well, it wouldn't float. It's not hollow."

"But you can use it."

"I guess so. Sure."

"Okay, how about I use a whole mouse?"

"No way. That's not a fly. That's bait."

"Oh. So the whole mouse is out, but the hair is okay."

"Yeah."

I felt like a kid in the movies, wanting to yell out, Look out — Here it comes! Socrates sat up straight on the stool:

"Okay, okay. I get a hook, spin on some mouse hair. It's okay, right?"

"Yep."

"And I tie in a little hackle, maybe some chenille, a strip of rabbit fur?"

"Might be lousy fly."

"But legal."

"Yeah."

"How about if I take out the rabbit fur, put in some mouse fur?"

"Yeah . . ."

"How about I take out the hackle and the chenille and put in a lot of mouse fur?"

" . . ."

"How about I wrap a whole mouse fur around the hook? How about a stuffed mouse? How about a whole mouse without the formaldehyde?"

"Whoa. That just became bait."

"Bait."

I started to get up.

"Man, there are some weird guys making up these rules . . ."

Outside the sleet had started, but I felt warm and refreshed. The coffee had been good. I like a place that serves it with real cream.

Ed Gray's books include *Gray's Journal* (Volumes I and II), *Flashes in the River*, *Shadows on the Flats*, and *The Lake of the Beginning*. With his wife Rebecca he founded *Gray's Sporting Journal* in 1975 and was its editor for sixteen years. He has been a contributing editor to *Esquire Sportsman* and *Sports Afield* and writes books, essays, and magazine articles from his home in New Hampshire. He describes both the magazine he founded and all of his own fishing writing as "why-to," not "how-to."

Fishing the Run

JOHN GRAVES

I'd made the mistake, the evening before, of mentioning to my younger daughter that I'd heard the crappie and sand bass were running in the Brazos. Therefore that Saturday morning, a clear and soft and lovely one of the sort our Texas Februaries sometimes offer in promise of coming spring, filled with the tentative piping of wrens and redbirds, I managed to get in only about an hour and a half's work in my office at the rear of the barn before she showed up there, a certain mulish set to her jaw and eyelids indicating she had a goal in mind and expected some opposition.

I said I need to stay a while longer at the typewriter and afterward had to go patch a piece of net-wire boundary fence in the southeast pasture, shredded by a neighbor's horned bull while wrangling through it with my own Angus herd sire. She reminded me that the winter before we had missed the best crappie day in local memory because I'd had something else to do, one some-what greedy fellow whom we knew having brought home eighty-three in a tow sack. She was fifteen and it struck me sometimes, though not to the point of neurosis, that maybe she deserved to have been born to a younger, less preoc-cupied father. In answer to what she said I raised some other negative points but without any great conviction, for I was arguing less against her than against a very strong part of myself that wanted very badly to go fishing too.

The trouble was that those two or three weeks of later winter when the crappie and the sandies move up the Brazos out of the Whitney reservoir, in preparation for spawning, can provide some of the most pleasant angling of the year in our region on the fringes of dry West Texas, where creeks and rivers flow tricklingly if at all during the warmer parts of a normal year. Even when low, of course, the good ones have holes and pools with fair numbers of black bass and bream and catfish, and I've been fishing them all my life with enjoyment. But it's not the same flavor of enjoyment that a hard-flowing stream can give, and those of us who have acquired—usually elsewhere—a penchant for live waters indulge it, if we've got the time and money, on trips to the mountain states, and look forward with special feeling to those times when our local waters choose to tumble and roll and our fish change their ways in accordance.

The Brazos in this section, my own personal river of rivers if only because I've known it and used it for so long, is a sleepy catfishing stream most of the time, a place to go at night with friends and sit beneath great oaks and pecans, talking and drinking beer or coffee and watching a fire burn low while barred owls and hoot owls brag across the bottomlands, getting up occasionally to go out with a flashlight and check the baited throwlines and trotlines that have been set. Its winter run of sand bass and crappie is dependable only when there's been plenty of rain and the upstream the impoundments at Granbury and Possum Kingdom are releasing a good flow of water to make riffles and rapids run full and strong, an avenue up which the fish swim in their hundreds of thousands. To catch them in drouthy winters you have to drive down to Whitney's headwaters above the Kimball Bend, where the Chisholm Trail used to cross the river and the ruins of stone factory buildings recall old Jacob De Cordova's misplaced dream of water-powered empire, back in the 1860s. But that is lake fishing, best done from a boat and short on the concentrated excitement that a strong current full of avid live things can give.

Generally you fish the river run blind, choosing a likely spot where fast water spews into a slow pool, casting across the flow and letting it sweep your lure or fly in a long arc downstream to slack water near shore, working it in with what you hope are enticing twitches and jerks and pauses, then casting again. It is the venerable pattern still most often used with Atlantic salmon and the West Coast's steelheads, though our local quarry is far less impressive than those patrician species, since a pound-and-a-half crappie is a good one and the sandies— more properly known as white bass—only occasionally exceed a couple of pounds or so.

There are plenty of them when a good run is on, though, and unless you overmatch them with heavy stiff tackle they can put up a reasonable fight in the strong water. For that matter there's always an outside chance of hooking a big striped bass, a marine cousin of the sandy introduced to the salty Brazos reservoirs in recent years and reaching fifteen or eighteen pounds or more. To have a horse like that on a light rig is quite an emotional experience, at least if you're of the tribe that derives emotion from angling, but the end result is not ordinarily triumphant. The annoyed striper hauls tail swiftly and irresistibly downriver while you hang onto your doubled, bucking rod and listen to the squall of your little reel yielding line, and when all the line has run out it breaks, at the end if you're lucky, at the reel if you're not.

★ ★ ★

I've never been very happy fishing in crowds, and after word of a run of fish has seeped around our county the accessible areas along the river can be pretty heavily populated, especially on weekends in good weather and even more especially at the exact riverbank locations most worth trying. So that morning when without much resistance I had let Younger Daughter argue me down, I got the canoe out, hosed off its accumulation of old mud-dauber nests and barn dust, and lashed it atop the cattle frame on the pickup. If needed, it would let us cross over to an opposite, unpeopled shore or drop downriver to some other good place with no one at all in sight.

After that had been done and after we had rooted about the house and outbuildings in search of the nooks where bits of requisite tackle had hidden themselves during a winter's disuse, the morning was gone and so was the promise of spring. A plains norther had blown in, in northers' sudden fashion, and the pretty day had turned raw. By the time we'd wolfed down lunch and driven out to the Brazos, heavy clouds were scudding southeastward overhead and there was a thin misty spit of rain. This unpleasantness did have at least one bright side, though. When we'd paid our dollar entrance fee to a farmer and had parked on high ground above the river, we looked down at a gravel beach beside some rapids and the head of a deep long pool, a prime spot, and saw only one stocky figure there, casting toward the carved gray limestone cliffs that formed the other bank. There would be no point in using the canoe unless more people showed up, and that seemed unlikely with the grimness of the sky and the cold and probing wind, which was shoving upriver in such gusts that, with a twinge of the usual shame, I decided to use a spinning rig.

Like many others who've known stream trout at some time bait nearly in their lives, I derive about twice as much irrational satisfaction from taking fish on fly tackle as I do from alternative methods. I even keep a few streamers intended for the crappie and white bass run, some of them bead-headed and most a bit gaudy in aspect. One that has served well on occasion, to the point of disgruntling nearby plug and minnow hurlers, is a personal pattern called the Old English Sheep Dog which has a tinsel chenille body, a sparse crimson throat hackle, and a wing formed of long white neck hairs the from the amiable friend for whom the concoction is named, who placidly snores and snuffles close by my chair on fly-tying evenings in winter and brooks without demur an occasional snip of the scissors in his coat. Hooks in sizes four and six seem usually to be about right, and I suppose a sinking or sink-tip line would be best for presentation if you keep a full array of such items with you, which I usually don't. . . .

But such is the corruption engendered by dwelling in an area full of wormstick wielders and trotline types, where fly-fishing bass and search is still widely viewed as effete and there are no salmonids to give it full meaning, that increasingly these days I find myself switching to other tackle when conditions seem to say to. And I knew now that trying to roll a six-weight tapered line across that angry air would lead to one sorry tangle after another.

We put our gear together and walked down to the beach, where the lone fisherman looked around and greeted us affably enough, though without slowing or speeding his careful retrieve of a lure. A full-fleshed, big-headed, rather short man with a rosy Pickwickian face, in his middle or late sixties perhaps, he was clearly enough no local. Instead of the stained and rumpled workaday attire that most of us hereabouts favor for such outings he had on good chest waders, a tan fishing vest whose multiple pouch pockets bulged discreetly here and there, and a neat little tweed porkpie hat that ought to have seemed ridiculous above that large pink face but managed somehow to look just right, jaunty and self-sufficient and good-humored. He was using a dainty graphite rod and a diminutive free-spool casting reel, the sort of equipment you get because you know what you want and are willing to pay for it, and when he cast again, sending a tiny white-feathered spinner bait nearly to the cliff across the way with only a flirt of the rod, I saw that he used them well.

Raising my voice against the rapids' hiss and chatter I asked him if the fish were hitting.

"Not bad," he answered, still fishing. "It was slow this morning when the weather was nice, but this front coming through got things to popping a little. Barometric change, I guess."

Not the barometer but the wind had me wishing I'd mustered the sense to change to heavier clothing when the soft morning had disappeared. It muffled the pool's water darkly, working against the surface current. Younger Daughter, I recalled, had cagily put on a down jacket, and when I looked around for her she was already thirty yards down the beach and casting with absorption, for she was and is disinclined toward talk when water needs to be worked. My Pickwickian friend being evidently of the same persuasion, I intended to pester him no further, though I did wonder whether he'd been catching a preponderance of crappie or of sand bass and searched about with my eyes for a live bag or stringer, but saw none. When I glanced up again he had paused in his casting and was watching me with a wry half-guilty expression much like one I myself employ when country neighbors have caught me in some alien aberration such as fly-fishing or speaking with appreciation about the howls of coyotes.

"I hardly ever keep any," he said. "I just like fishing for them."

I said I usually put the sandies back too, but not crappie, whose delicate white flesh my clan prizes above that of all other local species for the table and, if there are many, for tucking away in freezer packets against a time of shortage. He observed that he'd caught no crappie at all. "Ah," I said, a bilked gourmet. Then, liking the man and feeling I ought to, I asked if our fishing there would bother him.

"No, hell, no," said Mr. Pickwick. "There's lots of room, and anyhow I'm moving on up the river. Don't like to fish in one spot too long. I'm an itchy sort."

That being more or less what I might have said too had I been enjoying myself there alone when other people barged in, I felt a prick of conscience as I watched him work his way alongside the main rapids, standing in water up to

210

his rubber-clad calves near the shore, casting and retrieving a few times from each spot before sloshing a bit farther upstream. It was rough loud water of a type in which I have seldom had much luck on that river. But then I saw him shoot his spinner-bug out across the wind and drop it with precision into a small slick just below a boulder, where a good thrashing sand bass promptly grabbed it, and watched him let the current and the rod's lithe spring wear the fish down before he brought it to slack shallow shore water, reaching down to twist the hook deftly from its jaw so that it could drift away. That was damned sure not blind fishing. He knew what he was doing, and I quit worrying about our intrusion on the beach.

By that time Younger Daughter, unruffled by such niceties, had caught and released a small sandy or two herself at the head of the pool, and as I walked down to join her she beached another and held it up with a smile to shame my indolence before dropping it back in the water. I'd been fishing for more than three times as many years as she had been on earth, but she often caught more than I because she stayed with the job, whereas I have a longstanding tendency to stare at birds in willow trees, or study currents and rocks, or chew platitudes with other anglers randomly encountered.

"You better get cracking," she said. "That puts me three up."

I looked at the sky, which was uglier than it had been. "What *you'd* better do," I told her, "is find the right bait and bag a few more crappie for supper pretty fast. This weather is getting ready to go to pieces."

"Any weather's good when you're catching fish," she said, quoting a dictum I'd once voiced to her while clad in something more warmly waterproof than my present cotton flannel shirt and poplin golfer's jacket. Nevertheless she was right, so I tied on a light marabou horsehead jig with a spinner—a white one, in part because that was the hue jaunty old Mr. Pickwick had been using with such skill, but mainly because most of the time with sand bass, in Henry Fordish parlance, any color's fine as long as it's white. Except that some days they like a preponderance of yellow, and once I saw a fellow winch them in numerously with a saltwater rod and reel and a huge plug that from a distance looked to be lingerie pink. . . .

I started casting far enough up the beach from Younger Daughter that our lines would not get crossed. The northwest wind shoved hard and cold and the thin rain seemed to be flicking more steadily against my numbing cheeks and hands. But then the horsehead jig found its way into some sort of magical pocket along the line where the rapids' forceful long tongue rubbed against eddy water drifting up from the pool. Stout sand bass were holding there, eager and aggressive, and without exactly forgetting the weather I was able for a long while to ignore it. I caught three fish in three casts, lost the feel of the pocket's whereabouts for a time before locating it again and catching two more, then moved on to look for another such place and found it, and afterward found some others still. I gave the fish back to the river, or gave it back to them: shapely, forktailed, bright-silver creatures with thin dark parallel striping along their sides, gaping rhythmically from the struggle's exhaustion as they eased away backward from my hand in the slow shallows.

I didn't wish they were crappie, to be stowed in the mesh live bag and carried off home as food. If it wasn't a crappie day, it wasn't, and if satisfactory preparation of the sandies' rather coarse flesh involves some kitchen mystery from which our family's cooks have been excluded, the fact remains that they're quite a bit more pleasant to catch than crappie—stronger and quicker and more desperately resistant to being led shoreward on a threadlike line or a leader. In my own form of piscatorial snobbery, I've never much liked the sort of fishing often done for them on reservoirs, where motorboaters race converging on a surfaced feeding school to cast furiously toward its center for a few minutes until it disappears, then wait around for another roaring, roostertailed race when that school or another surfaces somewhere else. But my basic snobbery—or trouble, or whatever you want to call it—is not much liking reservoir fishing itself, except sometimes with a canoe in covish waters at dawn, when all good roostertailers and waterskiers and other motorized hypermanics are virtuously still abed, storing up energy for another day of loud wavemaking pleasure.

In truth, until a few years ago I more or less despised the sand bass as an alien introduced species fit only for such mechanized pursuit in such artificial waters. But in a live stream on light tackle they subvert that sort of purism, snapping up flies or jigs or live minnows with abandon and battling all the way. It isn't a scholarly sort of angling. Taking them has in it little or none of the taut careful fascination, the studious delicacy of lure and presentation, that go with

212

stalking individual good trout, or even sometimes black bass and bream, but it's clean fine fishing for all that.

Checking my watch, I found with the common angler's surprise that nearly three hours had gone a-glimmering since our arrival at the beach, for it was after four. Younger Daughter and I had hardly spoken during that time, drifting closer together or farther apart while we followed our separate hunches as to where fish might be lying. At this point, though, I heard her yell where she stood a hundred yards or so downshore, and when I looked toward her through the rain—real rain now, if light, that gave her figure in its green jacket a pointillist haziness—I saw she was leaning backward with her rod's doubled-down tip aimed toward something far out in the deep pool, something that was pulling hard.

If she had a mature striper on her frail outfit there wasn't much prayer that she'd bring him in. But I wanted to be present a bit more for the tussle that would take place before she lost him, and I hurried toward her shouting disjointed, unnecessary advice. She was handling the fish well, giving him line when he demanded it and taking some back when he sulked in the depths, by pumping slowly upward with the rod and reeling in fast as she lowered it again. She lost all that gained line and more when he made an upriver dash, and he'd nearly reached the main rapids before we decided that he might not stop there and set off at a jogtrot to catch up, Younger Daughter reeling hard all the way to take in slack. But the run against the current tired him, and in a few minutes she brought him to the beach at about the point where we'd met Mr. Pickwick. It was a sand bass rather than a striper, but a very good one for the river. I had no scale along, but estimated the fish would go three and a half pounds easily, maybe nearly four.

"I'm going to keep him," she said. "We can boil him and freeze him in batches for Kitty, the way Mother did one time. Kitty liked it."

"All right," I said, knowing she meant she felt a need to show the rest of the family what she'd caught, but didn't want to waste it. The wind, I noticed, had abated somewhat but the cold rain made up for the lack.

"Listen," I said. "I'm pretty wet and my teeth are starting to chatter. Aren't you about ready to quit?"

A hint of mulishness ridged up along her jawline. "You could go sit in the truck with the heater and play the radio," she said.

I gave vent to a low opinion of that particular idea.

"There's his hat," she said. "The man's."

Sure enough there it came, the tweed porkpie, shooting down the rapids upside down and half submerged like a leaky, small, crewless boat, and no longer looking very jaunty. It must have blown off our friend's head somewhere upstream. Riding the fast tongue of current to where the pool grew deep, it slowed, and I went down and cast at it with a treble-hooked floating plug till I snagged it and reeled it in.

"I guess we can drive up and down and find his car, if we don't see him." I said. "It's a pretty nice hat."

She said in strange reply, "Oh!"

The reason turned out to be that Mr. Pickwick was cruising downriver along the same swift route his hat had taken but quite a bit more soggily, since his heavy chest waders swamped full of water were pulling him toward the bottom as he came. He was in the lower, deepening part of the rapids above us, floating backward in the current—or rather not floating, for as I watched I saw him vanish beneath surging water for five or six long seconds, surfacing again as his large pink bald head and his shoulders and rowing arms broke into sight and he took deep gasps of air, maintaining himself symmetrically fore-and-aft in the river's heavy shove. He stayed up only a few moments before being pulled under again, then reappeared and sucked in more great draughts of air. It had a rhythmic pattern, I could see. He was bending his legs as he sank and kicking hard upward when he touched bottom, and by staying aligned in the current he was keeping it from seizing and tumbling him. He was in control, for the moment at any rate, and I felt the same admiration for him that I'd felt earlier while watching him fish.

I felt also a flash of odd but quite potent reluctance to meddle in the least with his competent, private, downriver progress, or even for that matter to let him know we were witnesses to his plight. Except that, of course, very shortly he was going to be navigating in twelve or fifteen feet of slowing water at the head of the pool, with the waders still dragging him down, and it seemed improbable that any pattern he might work out at that extremely private point was going to do him much good.

Because of the queer reluctance I put an absurd question to the back of his pink pate when it next rose into view. I shouted above the hoarse voice of the water, "Are you all right?"

Still concentrating on his fore-and-aftness and sucking hard for air, he gave no sign of having heard before he once more sounded, but on his next upward heave he gulped in a breath and rolled his head aside to glare at me over his shoulder, out of one long blue bloodshot eye. Shaping the word with care, he yelled from the depths of his throat, "NO!"

And went promptly under again.

Trying to gauge water speed and depth and distances, I ran a few steps down the beach and charged in, waving Younger Daughter back when she made a move to follow. I'm not a powerful swimmer even when stripped down, and I knew I'd have to grab him with my boots planted on the bottom if I could. Nor will I deny feeling a touch of panic when I got to the edge of the gentle eddy water, up to my nipples and spookily lightfooted with my body's buoyancy, and was brushed by the edge of the rapids' violent tongue and sensed the gravel riverbed's sudden downward slant. No heroics were required, though—fortunately, for they'd likely have drowned us both, with the help of those dead-weight waders. Mr. Pickwick made one of his mighty, hippo-like surfacings not eight feet upriver from me and only an arm's length outward in the bad tongue-water, and as he sailed logily past I snatched a hold on the collar of his many-pocketed vest and let the current swing him round till he too was in the slack eddy, much as one fishes a lure or a fly in such places. Then I towed him in.

Ashore, he sat crumpled on a big rock and stared wide-eyed at his feet and drank up air in huge, sobbing, grateful gasps. All his pinkness had gone gray-blue, no jauntiness was in sight, and he even seemed less full-fleshed now, shrunken, his wet fringe of gray hair plastered vertically down beside gray ears. Younger Daughter hovered near him and made the subdued cooing sounds she uses with puppies and baby goats, but I stared at the stone cliff across the Brazos through the haze of thin rain, waiting with more than a tinge of embarrassment for his breathing to grow less labored. I had only a snap notion of what this man was like, but it told me he didn't deserve being watched while he was helpless. Maybe no one does.

He said at last, "I never had that happen before."

I said, "It's a pretty tough river when it's up."

"They all are," he answered shortly and breathed a little more, still staring down.

He said, "It was my knees. I was crossing at the head of this chute, coming back downriver. They just buckled in the current and whoosh, by God, there we went."

"We've got your hat," Younger Daughter told him as though she hoped that might set things right.

"Thank you, sweet lady," he said, and smiled as best he could.

"That was some beautiful tackle you lost," I said. "At least I guess it's lost."

"It's lost, all right," said Mr. Pickwick. "Goodbye to it. It doesn't amount to much when you think what I . . ."

But that was a direction I somehow didn't want the talk to take, nor did I think he wanted it to go there either. I was godawfully cold in my soaked, clinging, skimpy clothes and knew he must be even colder, exhausted as he was. I said I wished I had a drink to offer him. He said he appreciated the thought but he could and would offer me one if we could get to his car a quarter-mile down the shore, and I sent Younger Daughter trotting off with his keys to drive it back to where we were. The whiskey was nice sour-mash stuff, though corrosive Skid Row swill would have tasted fine just then. We peeled him out of the deadly waders and got him into some insulated coveralls that were in his car, and after a little he began to pinken up again, but still with the crumpled shrunken look.

He and I talked for a bit, sipping the good whiskey from plastic cups. He was a retired grain dealer from Kentucky, and what he did mainly now was fish. He and his wife had a travel trailer in which they usually wintered on the Texas coast near Padre Island, where he worked the redfish and speckled trout of the bays with popping gear or sometimes a fly rod when the wind and water were right. Then in February they would start a slow zigzag journey north to bring them home for spring. He'd even fished steelhead in British Columbia—the prettiest of all, he said, the high green wooded mountains dropping steeply to fjords and the cold strong rivers flowing in from their narrow valleys. . . .

When we parted he came as close as he could to saying the thing that neither he nor I wanted him to have to say. He said, "I want . . . Damn, I never

216

had that happen to me before." And stopped. Then he said, "Jesus, I'm glad you were there."

"You'd have been all right," I said. "You were doing fine." But he shook his strangely shrunken pink head without smiling, and when I turned away he clapped my shoulder and briefly gripped it.

In the pickup as we drove toward home, Younger Daughter was very quiet for a while. I was thinking about the terrible swiftness with which old age could descend, for that was what we'd been watching even if I'd tried not to know it. I felt intensely the strength of my own solid body, warmed now by the whiskey and by a fine blast from the pickup's heater fan. If on the whole I hadn't treated it as carefully as I might have over the years, this body, and if in consequence it was a little battered and overweight and had had a few things wrong with it from time to time, it had nonetheless served me and served me well, and was still doing so. It housed whatever brains and abilities I could claim to have and carried out their dictates, and it functioned for the physical things I liked to do, fishing and hunting and country work and the rest. It had been and was a very satisfactory body.

But it was only ten or twelve years younger than the old grain dealer's, at most, and I had to wonder now what sort of sickness or accident or other disruption of function—what buckling of knee, what tremor of hand, what milkiness of vision, what fragility of bone, what thinness of artery wall—would be needed, when the time came, to push me over into knowledge that I myself was old. Having to admit it, that was the thing. . . .

Then, with the astonishment the young bring to a recognition that tired, solemn, ancient phrases have meaning, my daughter uttered what I hadn't wanted to hear the old man say. She said, "You saved his life! "

"Maybe so," I said. "We just happened to be on hand."

She was silent for a time longer, staring out the window at the rain that fell on passing fields and woods. Finally she said, "That's a good fish I caught."

"Damn right it is," I said.

John Graves is most interested in man's relationship with the land—and water. From his farm in Texas, he has explored that theme in many articles and in the books *Goodbye to a River, Hard Scrabble: Observations on a Patch of Land*, and *From a Limestone Ledge: Ruminations on a Country Life in Texas*. His writing incorporates fiction, folklore, autobiography, and philosophy and observation. He writes, "Land and what people have done to it and what it's done to them aren't things you can understand fully, but you come a little closer with time, and you know more than ever that they matter greatly." His papers are in the Southwestern Writers Collection at Southwest Texas State University.

The Shanty

JERRY GIBBS

The ice was dead gray. It stretched as far as you could see looking north up the big, ragged lake. Snow that had once brightened the surface had melted into hills of slush or two-inch-deep sheets of water that the wind riffled passing through. Beneath the water the ice showed bleakly. It was still safe, still over a foot thick, far from the blackness that would herald its final rottenness.

At the access parking lot stood remnants of a once-bustling ice-fishing village, shanties that had been hastily pulled during the thaws to prevent them being locked in when the weather turned again. The few ice houses still on the lake were owned by hard-core regulars who would fish them daily or nightly keeping watch on the weather.

It was the worst time of year in the North Country. Roads crumbled or turned to mud. Shrinking snow revealed mounds of preserved winter litter. Trees stood exhausted and bare. The crows had returned, though, and their sharp rasping knifed across the woodland valleys. You could say it was spring, the way it is spring in the North.

The two men and the big black Labrador retriever were 50 yards out heading south on the ice toward a long point guarding the entrance to a bay. The dog ran ahead, quartering, returning to check. Its owner, Bud Tuttle, pulled the sled that carried most of their equipment. The dog was very happy.

"Ought to harness your energy, foolish dog," Tuttle told the Lab. "This sled is getting waterlogged and heavy."

"Let me haul it for awhile," the other man said. He was a little shorter, but broader than Bud. His name was Earl Waite. The two were old friends who had not seen one another for some time.

"Nah," Bud told him. "I only let friends haul coming back—when I'm beat from digging holes."

"Right," Earl laughed.

Far off the point were several ice fishermen. Some had set out tip-ups but most worked short jigging rods or sticks for yellow perch.

"Don't know why they keep fishing out that far," Bud Tuttle said. "Those schools of yellows are moving in here by now. Those fish want deeper water they can find it off the point. Then it shallows fast soon as you get to the bay mouth. Course there's a better chance at a passing trout or salmon outside, but I pick up trout right at the drop, too."

Around the point, not far from it, stood a fragile shanty of wood framing and black roofing paper. "Look at that shack," Bud continued. "That's old René Tatro's. He's in there most all the time day or night. Anybody catches fish through a hole in the ice, it's him."

They sloshed a little way on without talking, then Earl said, "I haven't had a good perch feed in so long, almost forgot how they taste."

"Should get them," Bud said.

Earl took the auger and started the first hole. Bud set a jig rod and a Styrofoam cup of live maggot bait near the drilling, then dragged the sled through the slush-water angling toward the point. The dog splashed ahead like a spring colt. The first hole done, Earl walked over and the two men grabbed the auger together, alternating grips along the handle to cut the second hole fast. Then Earl returned to the first hole. He freed the hookless attractor spoon and ice flies secured to the jig rod guides and baited the fly hooks. He sent the silver spoon followed by the flies on droppers above it down the hole, found bottom and cranked up a few turns.

"Work from the bottom up, you never know where you'll hit them," Bud called over. "I'll be in a little deeper water here."

"You using the same rig?"

"I put on one of those Rapala jigs—you know, the things that swim around in little circles. Never can tell when a stray trout or pike might eat. I got the flies on above it."

It was quiet across the lake, then came the floating strains of a song sung in a dry, cracking voice.

"Who's singing?" Earl called over.

"That'll be old René in his shack," Bud laughed. "All the time he spends in there, guess he gets lonely. Keeps a bottle a rum for company. If he gets really tuned we'll have some music."

The first holes produced nothing and the two moved just off the point, drilling at new spots, Earl farther out, Bud closer in. Strains of a song in Quebec French came across to them from the shanty.

"He hasn't got started," Bud said. "You'll see. He switches back to English sometimes."

The dog appeared around the corner of the musical shanty, snuffling its edges.

"Ace, get over here," Bud yelled. The dog came up panting, nuzzled Tuttle's leg. "Good boy." He rubbed the dog's ears. "You leave the old man's shack alone, hear." Then he straightened. "Old Tatro's got a smelt system in there. Got a whole long trench he keeps open; a bunch of fishing lines spaced along it on a rack. Lines come off little wood spools, go through open brackets. Fish hits, he just plucks the line off, hand-over-hands it in unless it's a big one. They use the same thing up to the St. Lawrence fishing Tommy cod. Slick as owl dung in the rain. He won't get smelt now, though. Perch are just fine with him, too."

"Sounds like a production line," Earl said.

"He catches em, old geezer. I worry one day he'll slip through that trench after enough a that rum."

Earl counted off line in two-foot pulls. "It's deep," he said to himself. He cranked up until he figured he was at 15 feet. Overhead, streaks of thin clouds backed by a high, gray dome gave the sky the look of cool, polished tombstone. Far to the north the lake was empty. It seemed a very lonely place and Earl was glad he had company.

After a time, his second hole producing nothing, Earl started in. Bud had done no better. With Ace leading they headed around the point to the bay side closer to the old man's shanty. The black and gray shack sagged toward the left. "He builds it up new every year," Bud said. "It's not the strongest thing."

They drilled new holes inside the drop edge where the bottom rose from 40 to 18 feet. They drilled closer together, more for company than any insight into fish location.

René's shanty had been quiet for some time. Suddenly the old man's disembodied voice boomed across the ice. He sang in English this time, high in his nose in grand country fashion. First something about Texas ladies, then he segued into ". . . 90 miles an hour down a dead-end road . . . you gotta be bad to have a good time. . . ." It was all delightfully incongruous for the time and place. Then Earl felt a peck and he struck with the jig rod.

He used the tip of the rod and his non-rod hand in a kind of alternating cat's cradle to pick up line and bring the fish in. He dropped the monofilament on the ice, the perch following.

"Nice," he said, "nice perch."

The fish was fat, gleaming brassy-gold, its black vertical bars vivid. It splayed its sharp-pointed gill covers, arched its spiny dorsal. Earl brought it to the bucket on the sled.

Hearing excitement Ace trotted back from one of his circuits, coming up just as a fish hit Bud's rig. "Just a couple feet off bottom," he said happily.

"That's where mine hit."

The dog danced, lunged for Bud's fish. "Ace, back!" Tuttle ordered. The dog backed reluctantly, wanting the fish. "You'll get fin-pricked," Bud grumbled affectionately, "not to mention slobbering dinner."

They took two more fish each but it was not fast and they spread out, drilling new holes, looking for the main school. They tried shallower, drilling a hole line, then moved out on the drop again and here they hit the school.

The fish were so tightly concentrated that holes a couple of yards apart meant the difference between an occasional fish or rapid action. They ended with four holes drilled in a cluster, alternating between them as one cooled and another became productive.

In his shack old René started in again singing ". . . we got winners we got losers, we got bikers we got truckers . . . an' the girls next door dress up like movie stars . . . I love this bar, I love this bar. . . ."

"He's getting there," Bud laughed.

"So are we," Earl said sticking another fish.

"Let's string out these holes and connect them," Bud said. "Make a trench like old René's so we can keep moving right on top of the fish."

They augered new holes, connected the old ones. Then Bud grabbed the long steel ice spud from his sled and widened the slot. The opening was a long, rough rectangle.

Ace stayed with them now, feinting at each new fish, whining happily. Over in his shack René had launched into a sad-sweet ballad in Quebec French. Two crows circled overhead eyeballing for scrap bait. Just then Bud struck but this time his little jigging rod bowed over, line tearing from the reel with a soft zipping sound. "No perch!" he yelled.

Quickly Earl reeled in, ran over. The fish finished its first run and Bud was getting line back now, reeling smoothly. Then the fish went again. It was a shorter run but deeper, and when the fish was turned it came only a little way before going a third time, this run toward the point and just beneath the ice. Bud thrust his rod half down into the trench. "He's awfully close to the top. He'll cut me off on the ice edge if I let him."

Ace danced close, tail wagging, excited as the men.

"I got him coming," Bud said. He reeled faster now, gaining line. Then they saw the fish.

"Trout! Nice rainbow," Earl said. He raced for the sled. "You got a net?"

"Ah, no," Bud said worriedly. The fish was at the surface. It thrashed, showering Bud on his knees, reaching for it. Then it ran again forcing him to punch the rod into the trench.

"I have heavy line," Bud said. "If I can get him to hold on top a second I can scoop him with one hand, just swing him over."

The fish came. It lay on the surface, Bud holding it with raised rod, reaching under its belly with his other hand, scooping it, the fish arcing brightly through the air to the ice, gleaming, bold magenta stripe on its side. It arched its body, hard muscles lifting it from the ice. Earl grabbed it but instantly it slipped away. The fish spun on the ice, flopped, and Ace was on it but not fast enough. The rainbow's last effort took it from between the dog's feet back into the trench, the Lab after it, hitting the frigid water, diving.

"Ace!" Bud bellowed. He pounded with his boot heel on the ice. Earl jabbed his own jig rod under, searching. Bud ran to the sled, came back with the ice sieve, dropped to his belly. His arm up to the shoulder in the water, Bud swung the sieve in wide circles under water searching frantically for the dog.

"Ace, Ace!" he called. "Oh the damned, stupid . . ." He rolled over on the ice, his hand gone angry red. "I can't hold onto this scoop."

"Here give it to me." Earl grabbed the sieve. He was down now scooping at the other end of the wide trench.

A scream sliced the air. They saw René's shanty rock once before one black paper wall exploded, flimsy framing splintering, spewing the old man in green suspenders and baggy wool trousers. His white hair flared in ragged streamers, his eyes rolled madly, and from his sunken cavern-dark mouth came a wavering, tortured wail. René Tatro hit the ice running. He slipped to all fours, regained his feet, staggering for shore, not seeing the anglers, not seeing anything now but the safety of shore.

"La bête . . . sauvage!" he screamed, "the beast, the beast!"

He reached the shore, crashed into the woods. The two anglers were running now, heading for the destroyed shanty, reaching it, staring in. Inside was a shambles. Tackle was strewn everywhere. A half-filled can of corn had scattered kernels like confetti. Bits of lunch joined the yellow niblets. An empty rum bottle lay on its side. And in the middle of it all was Ace, tail beating as he wolfed down everything edible.

"Ace you fool!" Bud told the dog. "Come here." The dog even gave up eating to come. Bud grabbed the Lab around the shoulders and Ace shook his hindquarters showering both men.

"Can't believe this," Earl said.

"Oh yeah, it's real. Look at that setup. Ace must have boiled right up the middle of René's ice trench looking like the devil himself."

They both began laughing. They sat in the debris and could not stop laughing.

"That poor geezer. If he didn't think it was old Ned he likely thought it was the lake monster we're supposed to have," Bud said wiping tears from his eyes.

"Oh, I remember that—like the one in Loch Ness," Earl said.

"Ace you are a monster all right. Nothing's hurt with the fishing setup anyway," Bud pointed. "But the shack's sure finished."

"I'm shutting down this stove," Earl said. Ace squirmed to get back at the food.

"No more, you. You've done enough for the day," Bud told the dog. "I'm gonna call poor René. He won't believe me. Maybe I shouldn't tell him the truth. I bet he goes on the wagon for a while. Got to fix his shack for him. I wonder if I can ever get him back on the ice again."

"We better get out of here before we freeze," Earl said. "I'm starting to feel it."

"Same here. I think my arm's frozen," Bud said.

They staggered to the sled, started back fast toward the access, looking at one another, beginning to laugh again so hard that walking became difficult. The dog ran in front pleased with it all.

Finally Earl said, "You know, along with everything we have enough fish for supper."

"Good thing," Bud told him. "Nobody'll believe the rest."

Overhead along the shoreline two crows headed north into the silence of spring.

Jerry Gibbs was Fishing Editor for *Outdoor Life* for thirty-three years. He is the author of technical fishing books as well as the award-winning collection of short stories, *Steel Barbs, Wild Waters*. Gibbs has fished across the U.S. and Canada, Europe, the Caribbean, Central and South America, Russia, New Zealand, and Australia, and has no plans for stopping. His work received the 2006 F.C. Johnson Journalism Award, which included a $5,000 gift to the FishAmerica Foundation. He comments on his fishing life, "After twenty-odd years, it was easy to justify a move from the Vermont-Quebec border to the Maine coast in the name of reducing the commute to salt water. The tactical challenge now is scheming ways of heading yet farther south when the stripers and baby bluefin tuna do."

A Fly Box

JOHN ENGELS

In those days when even the beaches
of Green Bay were clean enough
for swimming, the marshes
had muskrat houses and dogfish minnows
and snipe and nesting mallards,
and the wild blue iris that we called
sweet flag—in those days

we fished Queen of the Waters, Ginger Quill,
Coachman, Grizzly King, Brown
Hackle, Gray Hackle,
White Miller, maybe

a Parmacheene Belle from time
to time, Cowdung or Beaverkill,
but I favored
the Professor for tail fly, Silver Sedge
or Pink Lady for the dropper,
though nowadays

such dressings won't do,
the trout are all entomologists,
they don't find the idea

of a hatch of Professors
or Queen of the Waters especially
credible, and so

if you want a dressing
that seems to appeal to the large
modern trout, here's one, copied

from the Peshtigo's
Hexagenia limbata: wing—dark

brown hair, bucktail, raccoon or mink, upright
and divided. *Tail*—hair fibers, as above.
Body—yellowish spun fur, ribbed
with bold spirals of brown. Rib the body
with a brown hackle stem. *Hackle*—furnace, all this

on a 6 or 8 XL Orvis Supreme. With this dressing
I've had much luck across the years, even when
it went by the name
of *Dark Michigan Mayfly*.

Then, of course, there's the Red Quill,
Ephemerella subvaria, a great standby
throughout the early spring,
and at other times as well, and good
for several other flies common
in Vermont, one of them
an *Epeorus* of dark
complexion. *Leptophlebia*

cupida, this
is the Whirling Dun, although
you are likely to find it burdened

by almost any name, depending
on what fly the angler thinks
he's imitating. We have an outdoors writer
on the *Post* who called it last spring
"The Barrington" because
that happened to be the fly he was using
during the hatch, and he caught
a few fish, and so he wrote

"*The sky was full of Barringtons.*" A difficult fly
to dress, for the wing
has lost its richness of slate,
and while almost transparent has
something of a brownish—bluish shade
lent it by the veins. As for the March Brown—
no comment needed. He won't often

be required, but when he is
you'll be sick if you haven't
a supply. *Stenonema vicarium,*

an admirable fly. If *Stenonema*
were an angler, he would be
wise, witty, clear-spoken, graceful, never

ponderous or opaque, never, or at least
not often, given
to ripe philosophizing,
forever observant, colorful, full of abhorrence
for the quaint and admiration
for the truly strong of character
and personality. Most authors say
you can substitute the March Brown for
the Gray Fox, when the gray *Stenonema*

is hatching, and *vice versa*, and no doubt
they are right, but I
have never tried it, and why should I, because
it's a great entertainment
to dress them both, no better waste
of time I can think of, and besides

if one is going in for imitation,
why do it half way? So I say
make up a dozen of the Gray Fox, and you'll be delighted
when you see the natural, abundant in Vermont,
Stenonema ithaca by name, dressed

in grayish mode, legs
handsomely banded dark
and light, very lively, quick

and independent of disposition,
with a personality that seems
developed, at least compared
with other mayflies. The Light Cahill is another fly

it's a pleasure to make, and lovely
to use when the eyes
are not as sharp as they used
to be, and even when they are, because
no matter, you can always see it.
And to it I owe

one three-pounder at the head
of Healy's Rapids, and the memory
of one of the same size lost
when the hook bent, and many smaller.
Black Gnat, Equinox Gnat

or Mosquito, these I employ
on the upper meadows of the Clyde, though seldom
on the Connecticut, where they have not
proved useful. The big idea
is to keep them small, no more
than two-thirds the size

the hook will accommodate, and even then
they'll look hopelessly too large. As for
the Blue Dun, an important fly

for the smaller hatches, I don't care
if you dress it as dark blue or iron blue,
but in either case keep it small. Sometimes

in the rain the trout will be slashing away
at the hatch of this fly,
and the gnats will be attacking
the little sails as they come down
the current, and you'll be able

to see the natural better
than the artificial, though if
you're wearing glasses,
you'll be hopelessly
up against it, because
in such weather the lens

fogs over the no doubt
already fogging eye, and I've seen
more than one angler gone thus blind
say the hell with it, clip off

his fly, sit down
discouraged on a rock,
and fish breaking all over the pools!

John Engels is a poet and a professor of English at St. Michael's College in Vermont. He has for more than 65 years tied trout and salmon flies, and fished on the waters of Indiana, Wisconsin, Michigan, Georgia, Alabama, Virginia, West Virginia, Quebec, and Vermont. He sees a parallel between the quest of the poet and the angler, with the important difference that the poet is always fishing blind over big waters with general patterns instead of casting to the "curl occasioned by the rise" with a close imitation. He has held Guggenheim, Fulbright, Rockefeller, and National Endowment for the Arts fellowships, and many other awards. His poems have appeared in *The Nation*, *The New Yorker*, *Harper's*, and elsewhere. His latest book is *Recounting the Seasons: Poems 1958–2005*. "A Fly Box" is from his collection *Big Water*.

Life, Death, and Tuna

DAVID DiBENEDETTO

My older brother, Steve, and I have been fishing partners since we were old enough to strike out in our family's 14-foot aluminum jonboat. Back then in Savannah, Georgia, redfish and seatrout topped our list of targeted species. When we both ended up in New York City, we found a used 21-foot boat to pursue our passion in Montauk, New York. Late in 2003, we stepped up to a 26-foot center console for one reason—to carry us to the tuna grounds. As a former first mate on a charter boat, I had landed a variety of tuna, but Steve had yet to nail a bluefin. He had seized upon the fish and wouldn't rest until he had landed one. We hit one snag.

On December 25, 2003, Steve became ill with meningitis, an infection that inflames the lining of the brain. A few days later, he was a coin toss away from death. With the help of a nine-day stint in the intensive care unit, a half-dozen antibiotics and some plain good luck, he beat the illness. Recovery would take months. At the beginning, just standing up was a monumental chore.

On the 13th floor of St. Vincent's Hospital, which offered a view of ice floes bumping down the Hudson River, we talked about tuna to pass the time during those seemingly endless days. We debated the best lures for bluefin and yellowfin, devised trolling spreads and talked about likely spots we would hit come summer—the Mud Hole, Jenny's Horn, the Ranger Wreck.

Spring arrived. So did the striped bass. The blue sharks and makos weren't far behind. We caught them all. Then one day in late July, we had a tuna window.

The wind, having blown for two weeks, laid down. The weatherman was calling for northwest winds at ten knots. Seas two to three feet. It was time.

We left the dock before sunrise, putting the cursor of the GPS on a spot along the 40-fathom line 29 miles southeast of Montauk Point. Twenty-eight miles out I saw a fish breach out of the corner of my eye. We slowed the boat. Maybe it had been a free-jumping mako or a tuna crashing bait. We decided to drop the lines.

The blue jethead lure had been in the water for no more than a minute before the rod jerked to life, and we landed a small bluefin. We hooted and hollered, slapped high fives and released it. Moments later the cedar plug just off the stern vanished in a boil. We were tight to another tuna and would be all day.

As afternoon approached, we released our last fish and cut the engines. The ocean was just starting to ruffle under an afternoon sea breeze, and there wasn't another boat in sight. Hard to imagine those January days that had almost snatched my brother, my fishing partner. There was no need to acknowledge it. We knew now that, as our old man likes to say, the jackals are always waiting. And fishing was more important than ever.

David DiBenedetto is the editor of *Garden and Gun* magazine and, before that, was the editor of *SaltWater Sportsman* magazine. He is the author of *On the Run: An Angler's Journey Down the Striper Coast*. He grew up in Savannah, Georgia, on the Wilmington River. Much of his youth was spent in a boat in pursuit of seatrout, reds, sharks, and pelagic species. A version of this piece first appeared in *SaltWater Sportsman* in 2005.

Excerpt from
An Outdoor Journal

JIMMY CARTER

A few miles north of the Okefenokee was the small village of Hortense, not far from where the Little Satilla River joins the Big Satilla. This was one of my father's favorite fishing spots; he tried to go there every year with some of his associates in the farming, peanut, and fertilizer business. On two occasions he took me with him, when I was about ten or twelve years old.

We stayed in a big and somewhat dilapidated wood-frame house, on a small farm near the banks of the Little Satilla. The house had been built to accommodate at least three generations of a family, but now there were just a man named Joe Strickland, his wife, Shug, and two daughters, one a pretty girl in her teens named Jessie. Joe was the guide for our group of about six people. The women cooked our meals and plowed mules in the small fields during the day while we were fishing. It was the first time I had seen women plowing, which I found quite surprising, but they all seemed to take it as a matter of course.

The Little Satilla is a serpentine stream in the flattest part of Georgia's coastal plain, weaving back and forth from one bend to another. A number of oxbow lakes had been left behind when the river changed its course. We fished in the area of what was called Ludie's Lake. On the outside of almost every bend of the stream there was a deep hole, often cut into a steep bank, and on the opposite side of the river was usually a sand bar. There were not as many bushes and snags in the water as we had around Plains, and the bottom was sandy and firm.

I had never done this kind of fishing before. We spent our time in the stream, wading halfway across it to fish in the deep water under the overhanging banks, using the longest cane poles we could handle. I wore cutoff overall pants with no shirt, and tied my fish stringer to one of the belt loops. Joe and I were the only ones barefoot; all the other men had on old tennis shoes or brogans to protect their tender feet. We fished with large pond worms and caught mostly "copperheads," which were very large bluegill bream whose heads, when mature, assumed a bronze color, perhaps from the tannin stain in the water.

The group of us would string out along the river, my daddy and I usually fishing within sight of each other. We always had a fairly good idea of what luck each fisherman was having. For some reason I have never understood, the men would shout "Billy McKay!" when they had on a nice fish. The words would roll through the woods as all of us smiled; the enthusiasm of the voices was contagious. Each night after supper I went to bed early, but the men stayed up to play poker and to have a few drinks. Sometimes they made enough noise to wake me up, but I didn't mind. It seemed to make me more a member of the party if they weren't trying to stay quiet just for me. Most often I was tired enough to go right back to sleep.

While we were in the river Joe moved quietly from one of us to another, just to make sure we were properly spaced and to give advice about the water and some of the bypasses we had to take around obstacles. He tried—successfully—to build up a reputation as something of a character and always gave the group something to talk about during the months between our visits to Hortense.

Once we were walking single file along a path toward the river and Joe called, "Watch out for the barbed wire!"

One of the men said, "Joe, you didn't look down. How do you know wire's there?"

Joe said, "My feet will flatten briers or thorns, but I can feel barbed wire when I step on it."

Another time, when we had to cross the river, Joe walked down the bank, entered the water with his pole and lunch over his head, and moved smoothly across toward the other side with the water never higher than his armpits. The next man, whom I called Mr. Charlie, was the oldest in the group, and he stepped off in the water and immediately went down out of sight. He came up sputtering, and shouted, "Joe, how deep is it here?"

Joe replied, "Oh, I reckon it's about fifteen foot." Joe could tread water like a duck, and just wanted to demonstrate his prowess so that none of us would forget.

Then came my most memorable day. Late one afternoon, after a good day of fishing, Daddy called me over and asked me to keep his string of fish while he went up the river to talk to one of his friends. I tied it on with mine on the downstream side of me while I kept fishing, enjoying the steady pull of the current on our day's catch. It wasn't long before I watched my cork begin to move slowly and steadily up under a snag and knew I had hooked a big one. After a few minutes I had a large copperhead bream in my hands, but as I struggled with it and wondered how I was going to hold the fish while untying the stringer, a cold chill went down my spine. I realized that the tugging of the current on the stringers was gone, as were all our fish! My belt loop had broken.

I threw my pole up on the nearest sand bar and began to dive madly into the river below where I had been standing.

Then I heard Daddy's voice calling my nickname, "Hot," he said, "what's wrong?"

"I've lost the fish, Daddy."

"All of them? Mine too?"

"Yes, sir." I began to cry, and the tears and water ran down my face together each time I came up for breath.

Daddy was rarely patient with foolishness or mistakes. But after a long silence, he said, "Let them go." I stumbled out on the bank, and he put his arms around me.

It seems foolish now, but at that time it was a great tragedy for me. We stood there for a while, and he said, "There are a lot more fish in the river. We'll get them tomorrow." He knew how I felt and was especially nice to me for the next couple of days. I worshipped him.

At Joe's home we ate fish and whatever was in season. Both times I went, our breakfasts consisted of biscuits, grits, green beans, and fried fish. It was the first time I had eaten green beans early in the morning, but soon it seemed like a normal thing to do. With plenty of butter and sugar-cane syrup to go with the piles of hot biscuits, we never got up from the table hungry.

When I left Joe's place to come home, his daughter Jessie told me that she had brought me a going-away present. She then handed me a baby alligator about a foot long, whom I immediately named Mickey Mouse. When I returned to our house I installed him inside a large truck tire, partially buried in the ground and covered with boards. For a number of weeks I fed him earthworms, crickets, wasp larvae, and anything else he would eat. My friends were quite envious of my new pet. Unfortunately, the cats and dogs around the farm were also interested. One morning I went out to feed Mickey and found the boards pushed aside and the little alligator missing. Daddy was very considerate and said he was sure the 'gator had escaped into the nearest swamp. I was not quite naive enough to believe him, but from then on I stayed on the lookout for my 'gator whenever I was fishing or exploring along the neighborhood creeks.

Almost fifty years later, after I left the White House, I stopped by Hortense, Georgia, to try to find the place we used to visit. I couldn't remember the roads or even Joe's last name when I inquired of some folks in the service station. I did recall the pretty daughter, but one of the men told me: "We had a lot of pretty daughters around here." At least I remembered the bare feet, barbed wire, good catches, lost fish, Mickey Mouse, and green beans for breakfast. When I described some of these things to the postmistress, she said, "You must mean Joe Strickland. Miss Jessie still lives at the same place, but in a new house." I followed her directions and found the cottage in what had been the large yard of the old house, just a few steps from the Little Satilla River.

Miss Jessie responded to our knock on her door, saying, "Won't y'all come in!" even before she knew who we were. We had a good time reminiscing about old times. Both her parents had died long ago, and she was intrigued that I remembered so much about them. She said she remembered my visits: "I told a lot of people while you were in the White House that the President had fished with my daddy."

To which I replied, "When I was in the White House, I told several people the same thing about yours. Many of the most highly publicized events of my presidency are not nearly as memorable or significant in my life as fishing with my daddy and yours when I was a boy. Certainly, almost none of them was as enjoyable!"

Jimmy Carter was the 39th president of the United States, 1977–1981. Through The Carter Center, founded in 1982 with his wife Rosalynn Carter, he has mediated conflict, promoted peace and human rights, and helped eradicate disease all over the world. He received the Nobel Peace Prize in 2002. Carter has written more than twenty books, many about political and social issues. His book *An Outdoor Journal* reflects his lifelong appreciation of nature.

Excerpt from
Sowbelly

MONTE BURKE

George Perry lived in a more innocent time, before our age of technology and stringent rules and media consciousness made records the objects of ravenous desire. His fish remains an anomaly in our modern era, which is remarkable for its unsentimental attack on records of all kinds. Whether it's from improved fitness, advanced technology, illegal supplements—or some potent combination of the three—the significant feats of the past continue to fall. Roger Bannister's 3:59-minute-mile mark has been lowered by 16 seconds since 1954. Bob Beamon's historic long jump stood for twenty-three years until Mike Powell bettered it by two inches in 1991. In baseball, Lou Gehrig's consecutive game streak set in 1939 was broken 56 years later by Cal Ripken, Jr., and Roger Maris's 1961 single-season home-run record has been twice topped, first by Mark McGwire in 1998, then again three years later by Barry Bonds. Even important fishing records, like those for brown trout (1992) and Pacific Blue Marlin (1993), to name just two species, have fallen. Part of the hubris of our age is the belief that we can always do things better than we once did. But Perry's record, almost three-quarters of a century later, remains unbroken.

In order to qualify for an all-tackle (using any pound test line) world-record catch today, fishermen must go through a somewhat tedious process. The IGFA requires the following: that the fish is weighed on an IGFA-certified scale in front of witnesses who must be shown the actual tackle used to catch the fish; that the fish is 2 ounces heavier than the previous record; and that the angler mail in a photograph showing the fish, the tackle, the scale, and the angler with the fish. For the more important records, like the largemouth bass, the IGFA reserves the right to administer a polygraph exam. The certification process is not fail-safe, which has compelled more than a few to try to cheat it. But in general, it weeds out the imposters. In January 2004, a controversial pending world-record bass caught by a woman named Leaha Trew was thrown out for not meeting the standards.

The irony, of course, is that Perry's fish would have never qualified today. Neither a photograph nor a mount of his fish exists. No one knows for sure the make of the rod and reel he used to catch it. And no one ever subjected him to a polygraph test. Perry did nothing more than weigh the fish on a postal scale in front of a few witnesses and send the measurements in to a *Field & Stream* magazine fishing contest.

Then he took the bass home and ate it.

His nonchalance was completely understandable: In 1932, the record was no big deal. His bass wasn't officially recognized as the world record until two years later, and only became the IGFA's Standard when *Field & Stream's* records were transferred to that organization in the 1940s. The conspiracy theorists have always debated the authenticity of Perry's catch, a din that only grew louder when he died in a plane crash in 1974, taking all of the secrets of the world's most hallowed fishing record with him to the grave.

But since 1932, the importance of the record has grown immensely, corresponding with the incredible rise in popularity in the United States of the large-mouth bass, which has unequivocally become America's fish. How and where to catch the next world record has been a perennial favorite story of the nation's outdoor periodicals like *Field & Stream, Bassmaster, Outdoor Life*, and *Sports Afield* since the 1970s. And the heightening fixation on the record has had a strange effect on a handful of bass fishermen: It has turned them into record chasers, individuals who play out their passion in relative obscurity, known primarily only to others who are in pursuit of the same scaly grail, on the lunatic fringe of the $12-billion bass industry.

The true record chasers have no rabid fans cheering them on, no million-dollar national tournament tours to compete in, no television shows to host, no lucrative sponsorship deals to sign. And as four notable modern anglers—Bob Crupi, Mike Long, Jed Dickerson, and Porter Hall—know all too well, unless you break the 22-pound, 4-ounce mark, you earn no riches. And even that money exists more in the theoretical realm than the actual one. The outdoor press often repeats that the angler who breaks the record will reap at least $1 million in endorsement money, but not if that angler happens to be using the wrong rod or reel, or the tackle companies deem him not marketable. Every so often, a magazine will put up prize money, but it's usually closer to $10,000 than $1 million. The Big Bass Record Club was offering $8 million to any member of its organization who caught the biggest bass in the world, but it folded in 2003 due to a lack of new members and the untenable burden of heavy insurance premiums.

That's not to say that fame and money can't be made in bass fishing. Denny Brauer, a tournament angler from Missouri, appeared on a Wheaties box in 1998 and has made almost $2 million in career tour earnings and another $1 million in endorsements. Together the CITGO Bassmaster and the Wal-Mart FLW tours have minted a dozen millionaires, and enabled another five hundred or so anglers to make bass fishing a full-time career. And then there are television personalities like Roland Martin, who can be found five days a week on the Outdoor Life Network kissing bass before he drops them back into the water, his hair bleached blond from the hours in the sun and his shirt festooned with as many sponsorship patches as a NASCAR driver's Nomex suit. Even a hybrid of the two types of bass shows has been broadcast. In 2004, a bass tournament angler was featured on the reality show *The Bachelor*. Plenty of individuals have become famous and made very comfortable livelihoods from simply catching bass. But no one has ever made a living from pursuing the world record (though some, as you'll see, have spent a fortune in doing so). And what's ironic to record chasers is this: Most of the fish these famous bassers catch are . . . well . . . small.

There's a reason for that. Truly huge bass are extremely rare. Let's say, for argument's sake, that the 11 million frequent bass anglers in the United States each catch five bass a year (a gross undercalculation that doesn't take into account bass anglers in other nations or the millions of bass caught by the 33 million other freshwater anglers in the United States). Most of these bass will weigh between 2 and 3 pounds. In 2003, there was one bass caught in the world that was officially 20 pounds or more, one of only twelve such fish on record since 1923. That means, at the very best, your annual chance of catching a 20-

pounder in the United States alone is 1 in 55 million. That's what statisticians call an outlier. You are far more likely to be struck by lightning or become a U.S. Senator than catch a 20-pound bass. There just aren't that many around.

But fishermen in general rely on an almost theological faith—"Faith that the water that you are fishing has got fish in it, and that you are going to catch one of them," as the novelist and noted fishing bum William Humphrey once wrote. Fishing is the sport of optimists. Every cast into the unknown water world is merely an expression of that optimism, and thus no guarantee of some connection with another living being. The world-record chasers have taken this faith a step even further. They are perhaps the fishing world's biggest optimists in pursuit of a bass that, statistically speaking, may not even exist. Each of these anglers believes somewhere deep down that catching the world's biggest large-mouth bass will get him or her something—personally, financially . . . each has his or her own reason.

And to get there, they've each turned this pursuit into an obsession. Susan Orlean wrote in *The Orchid Thief* that once people become adults, they view obsessions about seemingly inconsequential things—like flowers or big bass—as a bit naive. But very rarely in this world does someone achieve the absolute pin-nacle of his or her profession without some sort of obsession. For these record chasers, that fixation has manifested itself in various ways. Some things have been irretrievably lost: Edenic innocence and purity and even the enjoyment of a sport that most fell in love with as children. But others have been gained: notoriety among peers, a profound faith in the unknowable and, perhaps most significantly, a sense of purpose in an otherwise chaotic world.

But here's one thing that gnaws at the gut of each and every one of these record chasers: Anyone could break it. Whereas you or I will never top the single-season home-run record in baseball, we could land the next world-record bass. An eight-year-old on his or her first fishing trip is just as likely to pull off the feat as someone who has spent a lifetime on the chase.

And yet this dedicated collection of individuals persists—casting, retrieving, and hoping for that one fish.

The question is, Why?

I was a religion major in college, and one of the things I studied is a school of thought in theology that interprets certain parts of the Bible—especially in the Old Testament—not as literal stories, but as myth-histories, or in academic speak, stories that are "profoundly true." That is, there might not have been an evil talking snake in a garden, or a parting of an entire sea, or a tower that reached up into the heavens, but the details in those cases aren't the point. Instead, these stories are meant to impart some knowledge: of the divine, of some explanation for His will and design, and of some lessons for man.

The George Perry story is, in many ways, the Genesis chapter of the world-record bass chase. I started to think that maybe the George Perry story—true or not—could be interpreted the same way. Maybe it's a lesson from the bass gods that the world record is meant to come from the masses, given to someone of their choosing, perhaps again by a poor farmer whose main purpose for fishing is food. Perhaps the lesson, too, is that lusting after the record for the record's sake is a perversion, a false god. A modernday bass theologian might say that the sport has become idolatrous, full of heathens, and, that record chasers should be instead working on their boats, on the lookout for a big flood.

If indeed the George Perry story is meant to be a myth-history, a story that functions as a canonical lesson with a moral that's meant to be heeded by the masses, there are some folks out there who just aren't listening.

Monte Burke, a staff writer at *Forbes*, has written for *The New York Times*, *Field & Stream*, *Outside*, and *Gray's Sporting Journal*. He is the author of *Sowbelly: The Obsessive Quest for the World Record Largemouth Bass* and the co-editor of *Leaper: The Wonderful World of Atlantic Salmon Fishing*. He lives in Brooklyn with his wife and daughter on the banks of the East River. "I love fishing," he adds.

Martha's Vineyard Island, Mass.

NELSON BRYANT

Scores of fireflies flashed about us as—fly rods in hand—my son Jeff and I walked down the path through the woods to Lambert's Cove Beach in West Tisbury an hour after sunset in early July in quest of striped bass.

Our five previous attempts, in late May and late June, to catch stripers that could legally be kept had been unsuccessful—in Massachusetts an angler is allowed two of them a day, minimum length 28 inches—although we had hooked and released more than a dozen bass less than 20 inches long at the Dogfish Bar area of the Vineyard's Lobsterville Beach in Aquinnah.

I was at the family camp in Maine the first two weeks of June and during that time the bass fishing at Dogfish Bar had improved then slowed down.

The last phrase requires some clarification: When I returned from Maine, Dogfish Bar wasn't producing at the hours Jeff and I usually choose to fly fish the beach—from sundown until 11 P.M. on evenings when the tides are rising and falling with vigor—but some big bass were being caught by others at midnight and later.

Kib Bramhall, a close friend who pursues stripers relentlessly, had told me that Lambert's Cove was yielding good fish and as Jeff and I walked south along the beach I was beset by nostalgia. This was where nearly 60 years ago after returning home from World War II I had first caught striped bass with a fly rod. The beach has remained virtually unchanged although the lights of new houses were shining from the high ground inland and more than a score of fly fishermen were scurrying up and down the strand. During the fall of 1946 when I made perhaps 20 night sorties to the Lambert's Cove-Paul's Point area, I had never encountered another human being, let alone a fly fisherman.

A stiff southwest breeze had roughened the water but when my son and I reached the James Pond opening we could see small bass surface feeding as they chased sand eels. We soon caught and released six of them and then retraced our steps a few hundred yards to see if bigger fish had moved against the shore in that area. Several more bass of about 24 inches were landed and released and then in less than an hour we had three fish over 30 inches long on the beach. All had taken a floating sand eel fly of my own design.

We returned to Lambert's Cove the following evening. There was no wind, no fog, no cloud cover and a strong falling tide. Vineyard Sound was smooth and shimmering. We could see lights on the mainland and the Elizabeth Islands across the Sound and we could also see bass breaking everywhere out in front of us. Hundreds of sand eels, most about two inches long, had been stranded on the beach, driven there by the marauding bass, and we waded through dense schools of them as we entered the water and began casting.

Jeff immediately began getting strikes and hooking and releasing bass up to two feet long, while I, only 30 yards to his right, had only one hit in the first half hour. This was puzzling because we were using seemingly identical flies—my aforementioned sand eel imitations—and retrieving them similarly.

"Let's swap flies and see what happens," Jeff said.

We swapped. I went back to my spot and got hits on my first three casts. I then hooked a 31-inch bass, which I kept. During that time, Jeff had no action.

We examined our flies with the aid of flashlights and could discern no difference in them. Both were about three inches long with hollow tubular bodies of medium-diameter, gold body braid, a bit of blue-dyed calf's tail on the aft end and No. 2 short-shanked stainless steel hook at the forward end. Red tying thread had been used and a tubular piece of dense plastic foam had been inserted in each to provide floatation. I extract these pieces from three-inch-thick disks cut from a lobster pot buoy, using a drill press and a plug cutter fashioned from a short length of copper tubing. We dangled the flies in the water to see if they floated similarly. One of them rested level on the surface. The other—the one that was catching fish—hung head down with the tip of its tail barely awash. When retrieved slowly in short jerks it apparently had an up and down jigging motion that bass found attractive.

Using it and a conventional blue and white bucktail streamer fly we caught many more small bass and two more keepers.

The following day after filleting, vacuum packaging and freezing the bass, I fashioned eight replicas, save for adding a No. 4 hook at the tail end, of the rewarding sand eel fly, that—because it stands on its head in the water—I dubbed the Acrobat. Jeff and I took the Acrobats to Dogfish Bar that evening. We departed less than three hours after we arrived, Jeff in front of me dragging our three keepers, one nearly three feet long, along the beach and through the dunes past ghostly white blooms of Rosa rugosa.

Nelson Bryant, carpenter, cabinetmaker, logger, dock builder, twice-wounded WWII paratrooper, and managing editor of the *Claremont N.H. Daily Eagle* for fifteen years, wrote a hunting and fishing column for *The New York Times* from 1967 to 2006. He has contributed to *Outdoor Life, Field & Stream, The Atlantic Monthly,* and *Beloit Poetry Journal.* His published books include *Outdoors and Fresh Air* and *Bright Water.* He lives on Martha's Vineyard Island where he was raised as a child. Although he has often released fish—they might have offered no gustatory delight, tarpon being an example, or they might have been threatened with extinction, such as the wild brook trout, in recent years fully protected, of Maine's Rapid River—that could have been legally killed, he would rather bring the wheel full circle, give thanks to the species and to the gods of the chase, and dine on his quarry. To put it another way, he does not regard a splendid game fish as a toy for mankind.

Take Me Fishing

JOHN BRYAN

It's nearing the end of the summer of 2006. Robert Turner stands hunch-shouldered as he elbow-leans over the pier's railing. He holds a well-fished rod.

The story of this day is in his eyes. They're downcast.

The observant vacationer—if there were indeed even one left on the boards of this longest ocean pier in the entire state—would observe "downcast" as simply the eye posture Robert uses to watch his flounder line.

Robert's eyes do watch the line, but the story in today's eyes isn't flounder.

Today Robert Turner is the last angler on the pier. The last angler ever on this pier. Fifty years ago he first fished here; it has been his fishing home ever since. His eyes—always bright and blue—are today also distant and melancholy.

"Take me fishing" should have been Robert's first words. He can't remember not loving to fish, and he can't remember his father not taking him. "That's the one thing Daddy loved more than anything—fishing. And I've been fishing ever since I could carry a fishing pole."

A military brat born at Fort Bragg and introduced to fishing in Michigan, Robert first walked onto this longest pier in North Carolina when he was eight. "We lived near Fayetteville, and Daddy met the owner of the pier—Mr. Radcliff—when his company was installing some ironwork on our house. He invited Daddy to come over and fish on the pier. So we did—Mama, Daddy and me. They were really biting, and I've been coming here ever since."

Robert suddenly lifts the rod tip and then lets it back down. "Uh oh, you might get to see one." For five minutes he steers the weighted mullet minnow among the pilings and then reels it in. "See those teeth marks? Flounder'll some-times do that before they eat it. I should have let him take it longer. Killed my minnow, see?" He nets a new minnow from the bucket, inserts the #6 treble hook, and lowers it into the Atlantic. "This is my favorite size minnow—about four inches." He leans and casts his eyes down and again weaves the line among the pilings.

"Once I caught a six-pounder on an eight-inch minnow," he says with raised eyebrows. "A friend had the minnow and said it was too big to catch a flounder. I told him I'd try it and pretty soon that big one took it."

Robert used to fish for spot and whiting and anything else that would bite. Now he's after trout and flounder. In an average year he'll catch 100 or more flounder from this pier. Last year he learned how to catch king mackerel and caught six—including a 39-pounder. "Some people pier-fish for kings for years and never catch even one."

This August day is calm and the water is clear and Robert's eyes continue to search the pilings as his flounder line moves among them. His is the only line left for this pier's fish to see.

The pier closed earlier this year. Family-owned, the pier was finally sold and the new owners razed the tackle shop and the restaurant and the motel and then subdivided and began selling what has become red-hot beach property. They hired Robert—retired from 31 years with Kelly Springfield Tire Company—to be the pier's security guard. He catches an occasional trespassing surfer or tourist on the pier, but hasn't yet seen an angler. Robert is encouraged to fish as much as he wants. But this is a new look for the pier—only one angler.

"When the spot were running this pier used to be elbow to elbow," Robert smiles. "My Mama was five-one and they'd be standing behind her two-deep casting over her head." He lifts his eyes and looks the length of the pier both ways. "Actually Mama was the one who showed me how to throw that Penn 9.

"Daddy had a Plymouth station wagon and we'd come down on Saturday and fish all night and do some sleeping in the wagon. When we'd get here Daddy and Mr. Radcliff would sit and drink beer while Mama and Mr. Radcliff's wife and I fished. Then they'd come running when the fish started biting.

"My grandmother loved fishing too and once in the late 1960s she stayed here for a month in one of the cinderblock duplexes and I stayed with her.

"I've got friends that fish the other piers, and they're good, but this pier here—it's home." Robert's eyes focus into a glassy distance. "I don't know where my new home's going to be."

Today is not just August, it's an August Saturday—an August Saturday morning. One group of Saturday-to-Saturday vacationers is departing and another is on the way. Thus Robert's presence is framed by deserted beaches.

And the breeze—admittedly a gentle breeze—is out of the north. Reputed to put the fish down, this northerly breeze has done just that. The entire Atlantic panorama—horizon to horizon—is void of arching porpoises, void of exploding blues and Spanish, even void of splattering mullet minnows. The beaches, the ocean, the pier—blank except for this last angler.

Robert Turner's blue eyes—always a fresh, youthful blue—brighten. "When I'm out here I'm not worried about nothing—not a thing to worry about. Just fishing." His forearms guide the minnow below. His elbows pivot on the pier's railing. "If people could fish and clear their mind they wouldn't need a psychiatrist . . . I don't believe."

Robert knows 80 percent of the anglers on all three of this island's piers. He is regularly asked for advice. He likes meeting people and claims he has never met a stranger. And he is indeed skilled. Last year he caught fish that put his photo in the newspaper and on the Web every week. The year before he caught flounder and black drum that won the pier competitions: rods and reels, t-shirts, money.

His best day on this pier? The one day in his 50 years on this pier that he would most like to relive?

"My first time out here. I believe that would be it." He shows his biggest grin of the morning. "I had that little Zebco 202 and the fish were biting so good that Daddy didn't have time to teach me how to use a baitcaster. So he bought me a 33 at the pier's tackle shop. Those 202s weren't much more than a toy. I later graduated to a Penn 9 that I've used ever since."

Why did his Daddy enjoy taking him fishing? "Because I'd pay attention to what he said. I took to fishing right off. I learned my knots and learned how to throw a line."

Robert's wife loves to fish but has a bad back and can no longer stand on the pier. Their two children grew up in the tradition. "The whole family would come. We used to come and stay at the motel at the pier for four weeks a year." What about his 13-year-old granddaughter? "She loves it!"

Robert's father's nickname was Slingturn. He was from Cumberland Mills and they gave him that name watching him catch so many fish. He'd sling one in and turn and catch another. Friends shortened it to Sling and called him that the rest of his life.

Robert's mother was just as avid. He once saw her fish on this pier for 18 hours straight. Robert would sleep in a sleeping bag next to her.

Take Me Fishing is the family mantra.

Robert removes the minnow and puts on a live shrimp. He gets a bite and the shrimp is gone. "Black drum," he says. "They'll do that." He feeds the drum three more shrimp. "One more and I'll stop. When they're in a school—like the other day when I caught eight—they compete to get the shrimp. But when it's just a single—like now—they're picky.

"Flounder are different. Flounder's one of the dumbest fish in the world. You can break a hook off in his mouth and an hour later you can catch him—with that same hook in his mouth. Or you can lift him out of the water and an hour later he'll be back in the same hole."

Robert's 50 years on this pier are surely a time warp. That first day is yesterday-fresh—the day he charged onto this pier with his 202 and a whole ocean to embrace. This longest of piers would never end.

The sale of the pier was not only a surprise, it was a shock. The pier was in good shape, was popular, was a community focus, was home to Robert.

"I'd rather be right here than on a boat. Right here. I'd much rather be right here."

He lifts a small pompano that has grabbed the live shrimp. His only fish this warm August morning. He smiles and tosses it back. "I've been out here and it's been so cold there've been icicles hanging on your beard and mustache . . . raining."

How good is the fishing on this pier? "When spot runs would come through they'd catch them three at a time. But the commercial netters have really killed fishing on this part of the coast. Down here the shrimp boats can come as close as they want—right alongside the pier. Other states have a three-mile limit."

But he still loves it here. He's seen big sharks—80-pounders—landed on this pier. "Black tip. Good eating." And a couple of years ago a friend of his even caught a tarpon here. "Seems like he weighed 85 pounds."

The boss arrives. The pier's owner. Robert greets him with a twinkle: "I'm going to need a raise by next week. Look here," he sticks out his left foot, "I tore my flip-flop."

Four more persons arrive: mean-looking, tanned, muscled. They're the ones who will tear down this pier. They have a mile-long tape measure which they carve down the middle of the pier like a scalpel. The owner says their dirty deed will take seven or eight weeks.

Robert packs his fishing gear onto his cart and rolls it reverently alongside the yellow tape.

Where can Robert be found next year? On the other pier three miles down the beach? "I don't know. I may be right here just fishing in the surf."

He pauses in serious thought. Pensive. Then he lifts his head, eyes upcast: "I want to win the lottery. So I can buy it. And that way it'll stay."

John Bryan has written for publications including *Sports Illustrated*, *Field & Stream*, and *Delta Sky*. His paintings and writings have appeared together in *Gray's Sporting Journal*, *Fly Fisherman*, and others. His books include *The James River in Richmond*, for which he received the James River Association's "Guardian of the River" award. He and his wife, artist Janet Gilmore-Bryan, live in Richmond, Virginia.

The Man Who Lived Two Lives in One—Zane Grey

ROBERT H. BOYLE

There never has been anyone quite like Zane Grey. Famed as the author of *Riders of the Purple Sage* and fifty-seven other Westerns tinged with purple prose, Grey ranks as the greatest bestselling novelist of his time. For years the total sales of his books fell behind only the Holy Bible and McGuffey Readers. At his death in 1939 his novels had sold more than 15 million copies in the United States alone, and 30 years later they were still selling at the rate of 750,000 to a million books a year. Magazines paid Grey as much as $85,000 for the serial rights to a single work, and Hollywood transferred epic after epic to the silver screen. Gary Cooper, Cary Grant, Warner Baxter, Warner Oland, Richard Arlen, Richard Dix, Randolph Scott, Wallace Beery, Roscoe Karns, Harry Carey, William Powell, Jack Holt, Jack LaRue, Billie Dove, Lili Damita, Fay Wray, Jean Arthur and Buster Crabbe are among the stars who got their start in Zane Grey movies.

On film or in print Grey's Westerns enthralled the public. The books were stilted, awkward and stuffed with painful dialogue ("If you think I'm wonderful and if I think you're wonderful—it's all really very wonderful, isn't it?"), but they throbbed with the narrative drive of a true storyteller and the fervor of a moralist who made certain that virtue triumphed over evil on the range. "Never lay down your pen, Zane Grey," John Wanamaker, the white-haired merchant prince, once advised, putting a friendly hand on the novelist's shoulder. "I have given away thousands of your books and have sold hundreds of thousands. You

are distinctively and genuinely American. You have borrowed none of the deca-
dence of foreign writers. . . . The good you are doing is incalculable."

Grey received acclaim and money (and some critical brickbats) for his writings, but in another field his distinction was almost beyond compare—he was
one of the finest fishermen the world has ever known.

In the words of Ed Zern, who edited the anthology *Zane Grey's Adventures
in Fishing*, "It is reasonable to assume that no one will ever challenge his right to
be known as the greatest fisherman America has ever produced." It has been said
that the dream of many American males is to have $1 million and go fishing.
"Well," writes Zern, "Zane Grey had $1 million, and he really went fishing."

Grey is the classic case of the compulsive angler. He was truly obsessed by
fish. "Not many anglers, perhaps, care for the beauty of a fish," Grey wrote in
Tales of Fishes, one of his eight books on angling, "but I do." He would rhap-
sodize on the beauty of a huge tuna that "blazed like the sword of Achilles" or
marvel over the shimmering colors of a dolphin, only to feel a pang because the
dolphin was dying and he was "the cause of the death of so beautiful a thing."
The leaping of fish absolutely fascinated him, and even fish fins and fishtails had
what he called, with a flourish, "a compelling power to thrill and excite me."

From black bass to blue marlin, Grey pursued fish the world over with
unmatched avidity. He explored and established new fishing grounds and techniques in Florida, California, Nova Scotia, New Zealand and Australia. He took
great delight in fishing where no one had ever fished before, and his sense of
anticipation was so keen that even arranging tackle for a trip gave him exquisite pleasure. He was the first man to catch a fish weighing more than 1,000
pounds on rod and reel. In his day he held most world records: 582-pound
broadbill swordfish; 171-pound Pacific sailfish; 758-pound bluefin tuna; 318-
pound yellowfin tuna; 1,040-pound striped marlin; 1,036-pound tiger shark;
618-pound silver marlin; 111-pound yellowtail; and a 63-pound dolphin. The
record for the yellowtail and the yellowfin tuna have not been beaten since the
International Game Fish Association began keeping records in 1938. Grey was
held in such high regard that the Pacific sailfish was named for him, *Istiophorn
greyi*. Hardy's in England manufactured a Zane Grey reel, while in the United
States there was a Zane Grey bass bug, a Zane Grey steelhead fly and a Zane
Grey teaser.

Grey had his bad days fishing—he once passed 88 days without a strike—but he remained enthusiastic. "The enchantment never palls," he wrote. "Years on end I have been trying to tell why, but that has been futile. Fishing is like Jason's quest for the Golden Fleece. . . . something evermore is about to happen." When something did, Grey wrote about it exuberantly. If he made an unusual catch he would wire *The New York Times*. There were some critics who thought him guilty of exaggeration. A friend, Robert H. Davis, the editor of *Munsey's Magazine*, wrote Grey, "If you went out with a mosquito net to catch a mess of minnows your story would read like Roman gladiators seining the Tigris for whales." Davis added, "You say, 'the hard diving fight of a tuna liberates the brute instinct in a man.' Well, Zane, it also liberates the qualities of a liar!" Grey cheerfully reported these comments himself in *Tales of Fishes*. Such criticisms did not bother him. But he was vexed and angered when his sportsmanship was called into question, as it was on a couple of occasions.

Zane Grey's passion for fishing, which, by his own admission, grew stronger through the years, started in his childhood. "Ever since I was a little tad I have loved to chase things in the water," he wrote. He was born in Zanesville, Ohio, on January 31, 1872. His Christian name was actually Pearl, and the family name was spelled Gray. After college he dropped Pearl in favor of his middle name of Zane, and he changed spelling of Gray to Grey. He also shaved three years off his age, according to Norris F. Schneider, the foremost authority on Grey, and on his death obituaries reported he had been born in 1875.

Grey came from pioneer stock. His great grandfather, Colonel Ebenezer Zane, settled what is now Wheeling, West Virginia in 1770 and moved into Ohio after the Revolution. Zanesville is named for him. Grey's father, Dr. Lewis Gray, was a farmer and a preacher who eventually became a dentist with a practice in the Terrace section of Zanesville.

The oldest of five children, young Pearl was so mischievous that he was known as "the terror of the Terrace." On one occasion he destroyed a bed of imported tulips planted in front of the Zanesville Historical and Art Institute. The name Pearl, especially in conjunction with the name Gray, apparently bothered him considerably. The only time he ever liked it was during his adolescent years, when he strove to dramatize himself by dressing in pearl-gray suits.

He was six when he saw his first fish. "Looking down from my high perch into the clear pool directly under me, I saw something that transfixed me with a strange rapture. Against the sunlit amber depths of the little pool shone a wondrous fish creature that came to the surface and snapped at a bug. It flashed silver and rose." The experience stayed with him. In school and church Pearl Gray was a dreamer. "I dreamed, mostly of fields, hills and streams. . . . As I grew older, and learned the joys of angling, I used to run away on Sunday afternoons. Many a time have I come home late, wet and weary after a thrilling time along the river or stream, to meet with severe punishment from my outraged father. But it never cured me. I always went fishing on Sunday. It seemed the luckiest day." Dr. Gray told Pearl the only good fishermen who had ever lived were Christ's disciples, but the boy paid no heed; and he became the admirer of a local bum named Muddy Mizer who was always fishing on the Muskingum River.

Besides fishing, Pearl's other love was baseball, a sport at which he and his brother Romer, called R.C., excelled. Pearl was a pitcher, and he and R.C. played semipro ball around Ohio. Dr. Gray wanted Pearl to become a dentist, and he had him start by polishing sets of false teeth on a lathe. His pitching arm stood him in good stead. When the family moved to Columbus, Pearl unofficially went into practice on his own, pulling teeth in Frazeysburg until the Ohio Dental Association compelled him to stop. He continued playing baseball, and after one game a scout from the University of Pennsylvania offered him a scholarship. His father allowed him to accept it on the condition that he major in dentistry.

At Penn, Grey was at first highly unpopular. Ignorant of student traditions, he accidentally entered the upper class section of a lecture hall one day and triggered a riot in which his clothes were torn off and the room wrecked. After another contretemps he was chased by sophomores into a stairwell, where he managed to hold them off by hurling potatoes. His name and his refusal to go along with the crowd, to smoke, to drink or to gamble, made him the butt of jokes, and he escaped by spending most of his time reading in the library and playing baseball. He proved to be so good a ballplayer that, as he wrote later, "The bitter loneliness of my college days seemed to change. Wilborn, captain of the track team, took me up; Danny Coogan, the great varsity catcher, made me a member of Sigma Nu; A1 Bull, the center on the famous football team that beat Yale and Princeton and Harvard, took me as a roommate."

Grey played left field for Penn. His one lapse came in a game against Harvard, when he accidentally stepped into a hole and a fly ball hit him on the head, allowing the winning run to score. Ordinarily his fielding was excellent. He once made a catch that helped Penn beat the Giants at the Polo Grounds. In his senior year he came to bat in the ninth inning against the University of Virginia with Penn trailing by a run. There were two out and a man on second. A verbose professor shouted, "Grey, the honor of the University of Pennsylvania rests with you!" Grey homered to win the game.

Grey was graduated with a diploma in dentistry in 1896. He opened an office in Manhattan on the West Side, and there he languished. He did not like the city, and he got away whenever possible. He played baseball for the Orange Athletic Club in New Jersey, and he became the youngest member of the Camp Fire Club. There a fellow member suggested that Grey write a story about his bass fishing on the Delaware. He did, and the story—his first effort—was published in *Recreation* in May 1902. The appearance of the article gave him direction, and he began writing an historical novel about his ancestor, Betty Zane, who carried gunpowder to her brother, Colonel Zane, during the siege of Fort Henry in the Revolution. All winter Grey labored over the book in a dingy flat. Upon completing it he drew the cover and inside illustrations. No publisher would accept *Betty Zane*, and, after a wealthy patient offered to back it, Grey had it printed privately. Sales were nil, but in a visit to Zanesville in 1904, Grey grandly announced that he had given up dentistry to devote himself "exclusively to literature."

In 1905 Grey married Lina Roth of New York, whom he had met a few years earlier while he was canoeing down the Delaware in one of his escapes from dentistry. She had faith in her husband and a bit of money to boot, and he gave up his practice to write while living in a house overlooking the Delaware in Lackawaxen, Pennsylvania. There he wrote, hunted, fished and savored "the happiness that dwells in wilderness alone." R.C., by now a professional ballplayer, chipped in with an occasional dollar, and Zane later repaid him by making him his official secretary and constant fishing companion.

Grey followed up *Betty Zane* by writing a couple of other books about the Ohio frontier, *The Spirit of the Border* and *The Last Trail*, which the A. L. Burt Company eventually published. They were flops. But Grey hung on, and in 1907 he went west with one Buffalo Jones, visiting the wilder parts of Utah and Arizona. Jones had a ranch on the rim of the Grand Canyon, where he was hybridizing black Galloway cattle with buffalo and calling the offspring cattalo. In his spare time he liked to lasso mountain lions. Grey loved it all, and, upon returning to the East, he wrote a book about Jones, *The Last of the Plainsmen*, which he took to Harper, a firm that had rebuffed him previously. Eagerly he awaited word and, hearing none, he visited the publishing house, where an editor coldly informed him, "I don't see anything in this to convince me that you can write either narrative or fiction." It was the bleakest moment in Grey's life. He was 36 years old, he had abandoned dentistry, his wife was pregnant with their first child and he had failed again. "When I staggered down the old stairway and out into Pearl Street I could not see," he later recalled. "I had to hold on to an iron post at the corner, and there I hung fighting such misery as I had never known. Something came to me there. They had all missed it. They did not know . . . and I went back to Lackawaxen to the smile and encourage-ment that never failed me."

He promptly wrote his first Western novel, *The Heritage of the Desert*. Harper yielded and published it in 1910—the year of the birth of his first son, Romer—and Grey thought he was at last on his way. Quickly he wrote *Riders of the Purple Sage*, but Harper rejected it as too "bulgy." Grey asked a vice-president of the firm to read the manuscript. He liked the novel, and so did his wife, who stayed up until three in the morning to finish it. The book was published, and Grey was permanently established. In fifteen years *Riders of the Purple Sage* sold two million copies. Grey also turned out half a dozen juveniles, many of them dealing with his baseball experiences. In *The Young Pitcher* he wrote of the potato episode at Penn and drew himself as Ken Ward, the hero. His brother, R.C., also called Reddy, was Reddy Ray, spark plug of the team. In *The Shortstop*, Grey named the hero after Chase Alloway, a professional player he had known in Ohio. (In the Western *The Lone Star Ranger* Grey named one of the villains Chess Alloway.)

Although comfortably off, Grey continued to write feverishly. He could not abide waste of time. As a writer and as an angler Grey was a finisher, and he fol-lowed both callings to the hilt. "It is so easy to start anything, a fishing jaunt or a career," he wrote, "but it is an entirely different matter to finish. The men who fail to finish in any walk of life, men who have had every opportunity . . . can be numbered by the millions." At top speed, Grey found he could write 100,000 words a month. He would pen himself up in his study, where he would sit in a Morris chair, writing in longhand on a lapboard, furiously chewing the top of a soft No. 1 pencil when a sentence failed him. He compiled notebooks of vivid phrases and expressions, and he often thumbed a worn copy of a book, *Materials and Methods of Fiction*, by Clayton Milton. Grey's son Romer said, "That was father's bible. It had a greater influence on his writing than any other work." Grey wrote only one draft of a book; he left the finishing of the manuscript to his wife. When not writing he fished. He knew a long stretch of the Delaware by memory. "I own nearly a thousand acres of land on it," he wrote. "I have fished it for ten years. I know every rapid, every eddy, almost, I might say, every stone from Callicoon to Port Jervis. This fifty-mile stretch of fast water I con-sider the finest bass ground I have ever fished." In July, when the river was low, he would scout the water for big bass by going upstream and drifting face down on a raft. "I see the bottom everywhere, except in rough water. I see the rocks, the shelves, the caverns. I see where the big bass live. And I remember." When the time came to fish, Grey became part of the landscape; he trod the slippery stones "as if I were a stalking Indian. I knew that a glimpse of me, or a faint jar vibrating under the water, or an unnatural ripple on its surface, would be fatal to my enterprise." Not every visiting angler exalted the fishing; some referred to Lackawaxen Creek as the Lackanothing or Lackarotten.

With money coming in, Grey and R.C. began fishing in Florida. They went after bonefish, snook and tarpon. Grey was among the first to go after sailfish, and he did so well that other fishermen flocked to the Gulf Stream. He was intrigued by wahoo, then seldom caught, reasoning that they could be taken because "all fish have to eat." He caught wahoo, and he helped put the Keys on the map. Wherever he went, he fished. On a trip to Mexico to gather material for a novel, his train chanced to pass by a jungle river, the Santa Rosa. Immediately Grey wondered, "Where did that river go? How many waterfalls and rapids hastened its journey to the Gulf? What teeming life inhabited its rich banks? How wild was the prospect! It haunted me!" In time he made the trip in a flat-bottom boat. On a trip to Yucatán, he happened to hear of "the wild and lonely Alacranes Reef where lighthouse keepers went insane from solitude, and where wonderful fishes inhabited the lagoons. That was enough for me. Forthwith I meant to go to Alacranes." Forthwith he did. There he met a little Englishman, Lord L., and "it was from him I got my type for Castleton, the Englishman, in *The Light of the Western Stars*. I have been told that never was there an Englishman on earth like the one I portrayed in my novel. But my critics never fished with Lord L."

Grey never lost any time. On a fishing trip he was up before everyone at four in the morning, transcribing the adventures of the previous day. If fishing was slack, he worked on a book until breakfast. He wrote much of *The Drift Fence* and *Robbers' Roost* at sea, and he piled up such a backlog of books that *Boulder Dam*, which he wrote while off on a trip in the 1930s, was not published by Harper until 1963.

In 1914 Grey started going west to Catalina each summer, where he tried swordfishing. In his first year he spent over three weeks at sea, trolling a total of 1,500 miles. Grey saw nineteen swordfish but did not get one strike. Instead of becoming discouraged, he was pleased. "By this time," he wrote, "I had realized something of the difficult nature of the game, and I had begun to have an inkling of what sport it might be." On the twenty-fifth day Grey sighted a swordfish, which he hooked. But the fish broke away, and Grey was sick at heart. The following summer found him back in Catalina. "I was crazy on swordfish," he admitted. To get his arms, hands and back into fighting trim, he rowed a boat for weeks on end. His patience and training were rewarded—he set a record by catching four swordfish in one day.

Between gathering material for novels and advising on movies and fishing, Grey began to visit Southern California so frequently that he moved his family to Los Angeles in 1918. Two years later he bought the small estate in Altadena that now serves as the headquarters of Zane Grey, Inc. Once established on the West Coast, Grey took up steelhead fishing in Oregon, and on a trip down the Rogue River he ran into a prospector who offered to sell his shack and land. Grey bought the place at Winkle Bar as offhandedly as he would buy a dozen new rods. He also owned some land and a small hunting lodge in Arizona. He shuttled from one place to another, writing, fishing, hunting, and gathering material. "[The year] 1923 was typical of what I do in the way of work and play," he replied to an admirer who had asked what a typical year was like.

"The pleasant paradox, however, is that my play turns out to be valuable work. January and February I spent at Long Key, Florida, where I wrote, read, fished and wandered along the beach. The spring I spent with my family in Altadena, California, where I wrote and studied, and played with my family. Tennis is my favorite game. During this season I motored with Mrs. Grey down to San Diego and across the mountains to El Centro and Yuma, through the wonderful desert land of Southern California. June found me at Avalon, Catalina Island, a place I have found as inspiring as Long Key, and infinitely different. Here I finished a novel, and then began my sword-fishing on the Pacific. My brother, R.C., and I roamed the sea searching for giant swordfish. Sometimes we ran a hundred miles in a day. The sea presents a marvelous contrast to the desert. It inspires, teaches, subdues, uplifts, appalls and remakes me. There I learned more of nature than on land. Birds and fishes, strange sea creatures, are always in evidence. In September I took Mr. [Jesse] Lasky and his [Paramount] staff to Arizona to pick out locations for the motion picture, *The Vanishing American*. Upon the return I parted with the Lasky outfit at the foot of Navajo Mountains. . . . I, with my guide Wetherill, with selected cowboys and horses, tried for the third time to reach Wild Horse Mesa. In October I went to my hunting lodge in the Tonto Basin, where the magnificent forests of green pine and silver spruce and golden aspen soothed my eyes after the long weeks on sea and desert. Here I hunted and rode the lonely leaf-covered trails, lay for hours on the Rim, listening to the bay of hounds, and spent many a pleasant evening round the camp-fire, listening to my men, the gaunt long-legged and lead-faced backwoodsmen of the Tonto Basin. November and December found me back again at Altadena, hard as nails, brown as an Indian, happy to be home with my family, keen for my study with its books and pictures, and for the long spell of writing calling me to its fulfillment."

Gray always had some new adventure going. A Norwegian named Sievert Nielsen, a sailor turned prospector, read Grey's novel *Desert Gold* and wrote to him under the misapprehension that the story of the treasure in the farfetched plot was true. Grey was so charmed with the letter that he invited Nielsen to see him. They became friends and hiked across Death Valley for the thrill of it.

Grey's success at landing big fish prompted a correspondence with Captain Laurie Mitchell of Liverpool, Nova Scotia. Mitchell, who was to become one of Grey's fishing companions, was enthusiastic about giant bluefin tuna off Nova Scotia. He himself had landed only one—it happened to be a world-record 710 pounds—and had lost between fifty and sixty of the big fish. Other anglers had caught perhaps a total of ten. The fish were simply too tough for ordinary tackle. This was just the sort of challenge that appealed to Grey, who promptly began laying plans to fish in Nova Scotia. He reasoned that his swordfish tackle would be adequate for the tuna, provided that the boat from which he was fishing was fast and maneuverable. He had two light skiffs built in Nova Scotia, and from Florida he ordered a special launch, twenty-five feet long and equipped with two engines capable of doing eighteen miles an hour. The launch was so designed that at full speed it could turn on its own length. Grey installed Catalina fighting chairs in each boat.

Within a couple of weeks Grey proved his strategy to be right. He hooked three tuna and landed two, one of which was a world-record 758 pounds and the largest fish of any species ever caught on rod and reel.

Before leaving Nova Scotia, Grey fulfilled a boyhood dream of buying "a beautiful white ship with sails like wings to sail into tropic seas." The three-masted schooner, which he called *Fisherman*, held the record for the run from Halifax to New York City. Grey scrupulously made certain she never had been used as a rumrunner; ever the teetotaler, he would not have a bootlegger's boat as a gift. He had *Fisherman* outfitted with all the tackle that "money could buy and ingenuity devise," and, with R.C. and Romer, he set sail for Galápagos, Cocos Island, the Gulf of Panama and the Pacific coast of Mexico. On this trip he caught a 135-pound Pacific sailfish, the first known to science, but otherwise fishing conditions were not good because of an abundance of sharks.

Broadbill swordfish remained Grey's great love. In 1926 at Catalina, he and his brother caught a total of 10, including Zane's world-record 582-pounder. In that same year R.C. caught five marlin, all weighing more than 300 pounds. No other angler had then caught more than one 300-pound fish, and the 354-pounder taken by R.C. was a world record. It was a great year for the brothers, and, as Grey wrote, "Not the least pleasure in our success was to run back to Avalon with the red flag flying at the masthead, to blow a clarion blast from the boat's whistle, and to see the pier filled with excited spectators. Sometimes thousands of visitors massed at the end of the pier to see the swordfish weighed and photographed. On these occasions R.C. and I would have to stand the battery of hundreds of cameras and shake hands until we broke away from the pier."

Not everyone cheered Grey. He and R.C. broke early with members of the Catalina Tuna Club over Grey's choice of tackle. Although a light-tackle man in freshwater, Grey used very heavy tackle for big game fish. He argued that fish that broke off light tackle either became prey to sharks or died.

Grey accepted the invitation of the New Zealand government to investigate the big-game fishing possibilities in that country. Captain Mitchell and R.C. went with him. They revolutionized local practices; instead of fishing with bait deep down, they took fish by trolling. Grey caught a world-record 450-pound striped marlin and a record 111-pound yellowtail, while Captain Mitchell set a record with a 976-pound black marlin. Grey's greatest pleasure, however, was finding copies of Westerns in even the remotest homes he visited. "This was surely the sweetest and most moving of all the experiences I had; and it faced me again with the appalling responsibility of a novelist who in these modern days of materialism dares to foster idealism and love of nature, chivalry in men and chastity in women."

Back home, Grey had difficulties in Arizona. In 1930 the state passed game laws and established seasons, and Grey, accustomed to hunting bears whenever the mood was on him, was angered. He felt that he was entitled to hunt year round, because he had put Arizona on the map. When a warden refused to issue him a resident license Grey was "grossly insulted," and he gave up his lodge in the Tonto Basin. "In twelve years my whole bag of game has been five bears, three bucks and a few turkeys," he said. "I have written fifteen novels with Arizona background. Personally it cost me $30,000 to get material for one book *To the Last Man*. My many trips all over the state have cost me $100,000. So in every way I have not been exactly an undesirable visitor." He was so indignant he said he would never return and, as a parting shot, he said that the game commission and the Forest Service had sold out to "the commercial interest." As a case in point, he cited the north rim of the Grand Canyon as nothing more than a "tin-can gasoline joint." Grey felt strongly about the Grand Canyon, so much so that he could not bring himself to write about it. It was simply too marvelous to describe.

Fishing in the Pacific lured him more and more. He revisited New Zealand and Tahiti, where he caught his record 1,040-pound marlin. The fish was mutilated by sharks; had it not been, it would have weighed 200 pounds more. When the Australian government asked him to explore big-game fishing there, Grey went to Australia and landed his record tiger shark off Sydney Heads. Always the unknown beckoned. He spent $40,000 for a steel-hulled schooner originally built for the Kaiser, and another $270,000 went into refurbishing the ship, which he named *Fisherman II*. His dream of dreams was to fish the waters of Christmas Island off Madagascar, where there were reports of sailfish twenty-two feet long. Equipped with six launches, *Fisherman II* embarked for Christmas Island on a round-the-world cruise. The ship was 195 feet long, but she had a narrow twenty-eight-foot beam and she rolled, even in a calm sea. Even Grey got sick. "We had so much trouble it was unbelievable," said his young son, Loren. "We got as far as Totoya in the Fijis. The captain was ill. The chief engineer had appendicitis. We were there for over a month or more with costly repairs. Father finally called the trip off because of a pressing business matter with his publisher." Eventually Grey gave up on the ship, and she ended her days as a cannery tender for a West Coast tuna fleet.

While steelhead fishing in Oregon in 1937 Grey suffered a stroke. Romer and a guide carried him to a car and got him home, where he recuperated. Within a year he seemed recovered. He went to Australia to fish and then back to Altadena to write, before going on to Oregon for steelhead. There he insisted that Loren and three friends fish "not only all day, but every day in the week," said Loren, who became a professor of education at San Fernando Valley State College. "We finally had a big fight with him and said we wanted to go home. If he wouldn't let us go home, would he at least let us go into town on weekends and live it up a little bit? He finally gave in, so we'd fish just five days a week."

Determined to make a complete recovery, Grey worked out with a rod in a fighting chair set on the porch of the west wing of his house. Every day Grey would battle imaginary fish, pumping the rod perhaps 200 times before calling it quits. He was getting ready for the next expedition. It never came. On October 23, 1939 Zane Grey died. His workouts in the fighting chair apparently had been too much for him. He once wrote, in his younger days, "There is only one thing wrong with a fishing day—its staggering brevity. If a man spent all his days fishing, life would seem to be a swift dream." For Zane Grey, compulsive angler, the swift dream was over.

Robert H. Boyle and his wife Kathryn have a farm in Cooperstown, New York. A former senior writer now a special contributor to *Sports Illustrated*, he is the author of a number of books, among them *The Hudson River, A Natural and Unnatural History*, now undergoing revision, and *Dapping*, his latest. The founder of Riverkeeper and the Hudson River Foundation for Science and Environmental Research, he was named one of the 100 Champions of Conservation for the 20th Century by *Audubon* magazine. He writes, "I owe whatever I have done for this world to the fact that I am a fisherman, who, out of necessity, became deeply involved in the workings and protection of nature."

Nothing Fishy About Trout

DAVE BARRY

There comes a time when a man must go into the wilderness and face one of Mankind's oldest, and most feared, enemies: trout.

For me, that time came recently In Idaho, where I go every summer. Many people think Idaho is nothing but potato farms, but nothing could be further from the truth: There are also beet farms.

No, seriously, Idaho is a beautiful state that offers—to quote Emerson—"nature out the bazooty." This includes many rivers and streams that allegedly teem with trout. I say "allegedly" because until recently I never saw an actual trout, teeming or otherwise. People were always pointing at the water and saying, "Look! Trout!' But I saw nothing. I wondered if these people were like that creepy little boy in the movie *The Sixth Sense* who had the supernatural ability to see trout.

Anyway, on this Idaho trip my friend Ron Ungerman—and "Ungerman" is NOT a funny name, so let's not draw undue attention to it—persuaded me to go trout fishing. We purchased fishing licenses and hired a guide named Susanne, who is German but promised us that she would not be too strict.

Susanne had me and Ron Ungerman (Ha ha!) put on rubber waders, which serve two important purposes: (1) they cause your legs to sweat; and (2) they make you look like Nerd Boy from the Planet Dork. Then we hiked through roughly 83 miles of aromatic muck to a spot on the Wood River that literally throbbed with trout. I, of course, did not see them, but I did see a lot of blooping on the water surface, which Susanne assured us was caused by trout.

But there was a problem. To catch trout, you have to engage in "fly casting," a kind of fishing that is very challenging, and here I am using "challenging" in the sense of "idiotic." When I was a boy, I fished with a worm on a hook, and it always worked, and I will tell you why: Fish are not rocket scientists. They see a worm, and in their tiny brains they think, "Huh! This is something I have never seen before underwater! I had better eat it!"

But with "fly casting," you wade into the river and attempt to place a "fly"—a furry little hook thingy weighing slightly less than a hydrogen atom—on top of the water right where the trout are blooping. You do this by waving your fishing rod back and forth, using the following rhythm, as explained to us (I am not making this up) by Susanne: "CO-ca CO-la, CO-ca CO-la." On your third CO-la, you point your arm forward, and the "fly," in a perfect imitation of nature, lands on your head. Or sometimes it forms itself into a snarl that cannot be untangled without the aid of a chainsaw AND a flamethrower.

At least that's what kept happening to me and my friend Ron Ungerman. (Yes! "Ungerman!") We stood there for hours, waving our rods and going "CO-ca CO-la," but most of the time we were not getting our flies anywhere near the blooping. The trout were laughing so hard at us that they considered evolving legs so they could crawl onto land and catch their breath.

But Susanne was a good teacher, and very patient, and finally, just when I thought I would never ever catch a trout, it happened: I got a citation for not having my fishing license with me. Really. I left the license back in the car. The Idaho Fish and Game official who cited me was very polite, and so was I, because he was wearing a sidearm. I considered asking him if I could borrow it to shoot a trout, but there's probably some rule against THAT, too.

As the day wore on, our efforts—"CO-ca CO-la; CO-ca CO-la"—took on an air of desperation, because it was becoming clear that Susanne, a true professional, was NOT going to let us leave until we caught a blooping fish. So you can imagine how blooping happy we were when Ron (Ungerman) finally managed to haul in a trout. It was not a large trout. It was the length of a standard Cheeto. But it WAS a trout, dammit, and it meant we could stop.

Later, Ron and I agreed that it had been a lot of fun and we would definitely never do it again. So, to any trout reading this column I say: You are safe from us. And to the Idaho Fish and Game Department, I say: You'll never take me alive.

Dave Barry has been a humor columnist for twenty-five years, his work appearing in more than 500 newspapers in the United States and abroad. In 1988 he won the Pulitzer Prize for Commentary. Many people are still trying to figure out how this happened. Dave has also written twenty-five books, two of them the basis for the CBS TV sitcom *Dave's World*.

Excerpt from
Crazy for Rivers

BILL BARICH

I really hated fishing by the time I turned sixteen. I rebelled against the entire concept of a family vacation and whined and protested until my parents agreed to let me stay home alone. (Not incidentally, that was the summer I lost my virginity to a lusty cheerleader in my very own upstairs bedroom, treating her to an ice-cream pop from a circling Good Humor truck immediately afterward because I had no idea what else to do.) I thought that sitting in a boat in the middle of nowhere was the dumbest activity known to mankind and swore I would never fish again—and I might have kept my promise, too, if my brother hadn't intervened by accident, thirteen years later.

I had taken Horace Greeley's advice by then and migrated west to seek my fortune, although not to *work* for it. I was living in San Francisco, in a spacious Haight-Ashbury Victorian that we renters failed to dust even once during our tenancy. My hair, suffice it to say, was not in a Hollywood crew cut anymore, and I'd mastered the fine art of slacking. As for David, he had what we referred to as a "straight" job (book salesman in Manhattan), but he'd managed to finagle a transfer to California so he could savor the hippie glories I'd described to him. On a whim, he brought some of my father's old tackle with him, and we passed a comical evening sorting through it, laughing as we dredged up the names of the long-forgotten lures—Hawaiian Wigglers in lurid purple skirts, an evil black Sonic, a wacky Crazy Crawler, and a single Lazy Ike, yellow with bright-red polka dots.

We stored the tackle in the basement, where it languished. It might have stayed there forever, or at least until our landlord evicted us, if I hadn't fallen for a new girlfriend and invited her on a romantic trip to the Sierra Nevada. Not that I'd ever been to the Sierra Nevada myself, but that hardly matters when you're wild about someone. I studied the maps and made the plans and knew in my heart that we would be all right wherever we landed, as long as the place had a bed. After packing the car and loading the cooler, I went downstairs at the last minute and grabbed one of the vintage spin rods and a reel, South Bend and Zebco respectively, although I wasn't truly conscious of why I might be doing it and moved about as a person does in a daze or a dream.

We wound up in a rustic cabin on Stuart Fork of the Trinity River, in the shadow of the Trinity Alps. The cabin resembled a packing crate inside and had an icebox instead of a fridge, but it fronted on the river and was blessed with an open-air porch, where we slept on a lumpy mattress and gazed up at the brilliant stars and moonlit peaks and felt that we must be the most fortunate couple on earth. We went hiking, played games of cribbage, and cooked steaks over the coals, and yet not once did it occur to me that I was reliving the family vacation. I was still very young then and blind to so many things, and I didn't realize how a past experience can touch us deeply, can shatter us or set us free, even though we've never reckoned with its power. But I know it now. The past is never wholly gone.　　　•

Those days in the mountains were glorious days. It was late in September, but the afternoons were still blazing hot, and we liked nothing better than a nap on the porch after lunch, with the sun falling all around us and the air rich with the scent of sun-warmed pines. One afternoon, I woke before my girlfriend and stood looking at the river, so low and clear I could count the pebbles of the streambed. Trout in there? I doubted it, but I rigged up the rod for fun, rolled up my jeans, and waded barefoot into the water. I could see the sun glinting off the spoon I'd bought at the resort's store and could hear some Steller's jays bickering in the tall trees, and I drifted so far away from Stuart Fork that when a fish hit my lure, it had the effect of yanking me out of the clouds and back into my body.

High up leaped a silvery little rainbow, as hooked in the moment as I was.

Bill Barich's books include *A Fine Place to Daydream: Racehorses, Romance, and the Irish, Crazy For Rivers, Laughing in the Hills,* and the novel *Carson Valley.* His writing on fishing has appeared in *The New Yorker* and other publications.

Permissions Acknowledgments

Dave Barry, "Nothing Fishy About Trout." This column reprinted with permission from *The Miami Herald*, September 19, 2004.

Robert H. Boyle, "The Man Who Lived Two Lives in One—Zane Grey." Originally published in *Sports Illustrated*, April 29, 1968.

Jimmy Carter, "Excerpt from *An Outdoor Journal*." This excerpt is reprinted with permission from University of Arkansas Press.

Ted Leeson, "Red, White, and Bluegill." July 2004, "Red, White and Bluegill" Copyright Time 4 Media, Inc. Reprinted with permission from *Field & Stream* Magazine. All rights reserved. Reproduction in any medium is strictly prohibited without permission from Time 4 Media, Inc.

Steven J. Meyers, "Winter Fishing—Looking Over My Shoulder." This essay previously appeared in a slightly different form in *Inside Outside Southwest Magazine*.

Seth Norman, "A River of Child." Reprinted from *Meanderings of a Flyfisherman*, www.lyonspress.com.

Steve Raymond, "Like Father, Like Son." From *The Year of the Angler* and *The Year of the Trout*, Copyright 1995 by Steve Raymond, used by permission of The Lyons Press, www.lyonspress.com.

Louis Rubin, Jr., ""Excerpt from *An Even-Tempered Angler*." Some of the material included herein first appeared, in a somewhat different form, in *The Chapel Hill Newspaper*. I should like to express my gratitude to the other editor and publisher of that newspaper, Orville Campbell. The description of flounder fishing is taken, in excerpted form, from an article, "Tales of an Elusive Flounder," first published in *Southern Living Magazine* (March 1983). For permission to reprint I am indebted to *Southern Living Magazine* and to John Logue, creative director.

Ted Williams, "Environmentalists vs. Native Trout: Sometimes the Good Guys Are Part of the Problem." Reprinted with author's permission from *Fly Rod & Reel*, April 2004.